Peggy and I

Peggy and I in Budapest, 1933

PEGGY AND I

A Life Too Busy

For a Dull Moment

BY WILLIAM A. M. BURDEN

WITH A FOREWORD BY

GENERAL MAXWELL D. TAYLOR

NEW YORK 1982

The author wishes to thank the following for permission to reprint material: Carl Solberg for quotations from his authoritative *Conquest of the Skies* published by Little, Brown & Company; the late Rabbi Joshua Loth Liebman for his eloquent paragraph in *Peace of Mind* published by Simon and Schuster, Inc.; Hamilton Fish Armstrong for his description of roller-skating in New York in *Those Days*, published by Harper & Row; James A. Michener for the evocative paragraph in his autobiography, *The Fires of Spring*, published by Random House; and Bascom N. Timmons for his admirable characterization of *Jesse H. Jones, The Man and the Statesman*, published by Holt, Rinehart & Winston. And thanks to Ellen Garwood, the daughter of Mr. and Mrs. Will Clayton, for permission to use the picture of her parents, reproduced in *Will Clayton: Economic Statesman*, copyrighted in 1952 by the Condé Nast Publications Inc.

TO PEGGY

Contents

Foreword

ALTHOUGH a friend of thirty years or more, I have learned much about William A. M. Burden II from *Peggy and I*. Prior thereto I had become reasonably well acquainted with a few of the variegated interests and activities described in his book. His service in Washington during and immediately after World War II was a matter of general knowledge although I knew little of the details. I was best acquainted with his twenty-year tenure in Washington as Chairman of the Board of the Institute for Defense Analyses and his contribution to the quality of the output of this "think tank" serving the Secretary of Defense and the Joint Chiefs of Staff.

In lesser matters, I had become well aware of his penchant for fast driving, made so by the scare of my first ride with him at the wheel of an automobile. It had taken but one invitation to lunch to recognize in him the perfect gourmet who respected and enforced the highest standards of gastronomy.

But there is so much about the man I did not know—his boyhood for instance. Bill grew up, the reader will learn, as a fatherless scion of great wealth carefully reared by a widowed mother at a time in history when American life did not yet revolve around the income tax and the inheritance tax was practically nonexistent. But if Bill and his brother Shirley knew few unsatisfied desires in their youth, theirs was a relatively secluded life. Bill's close friends were few, usually fellow students in the private schools he attended in New York in preparation for entrance into Harvard. In this environment without the guidance of a father, Bill developed little interest in sports, girls or possible future professions. He had no immediate goal beyond Harvard where he would follow in the footsteps of his father and grandfather.

He did, however, exhibit two traits that to a degree foreshadowed his future: a love of good books largely instilled by his mother and an early fascination for toys representing various forms of mechanical locomotion—automobiles, ships and airplanes.

When he entered Harvard, Bill was probably one of the most shy, most innocent and most carefully reared Freshmen entering in the class of 1927. This new world contained drastic changes for him, the most important being daily association with young men of his own age who, though usually like him from wealthy families, had vastly different interests and standards of conduct. Academically, he quickly showed himself a serious student, eventually to receive a B.A. cum laude upon graduation. Although his studies, largely in the humanities, deepened his love of literature and his appreciation of the fine arts, beyond one short course in meteorology, they contributed little to his scientific knowledge. Somewhat in compensation for this void, he found time to frequent automobile salesrooms in Boston and New York which exhibited the latest models of foreign cars and to debate their relative merits with the salesmen. In any case he left Harvard academically ill-prepared for the career which awaited him, one that would be steeped in the developing technology of the automobile, the airplane, and the airship—eventually also the space rocket. But upon graduation he did not know where he was heading.

Not long after graduation, however, a sequence of events took place which brought an end to his aimlessness and set his life on a new course from which he seldom varied in the future. Returning from a round-the-world trip with a Harvard classmate, by chance he met a young lady, Peggy Partridge, in London who promptly enthralled him. I shall leave it to Bill to describe in his own words the ensuing courtship which ended in their marriage in 1931 and the formation of the inseparable team of "Peggy and I." Upon reading Bill's account of these times I suspect that others will share my impatience for his shameful procrastination in making a proposal which, to all interested bystanders, was both desirable and inevitable, and long overdue.

His marriage marked a critical turning point in Bill's career. With encouragement from Peggy, he proceeded to jettison his family tradition that its male members should enjoy their wealth quietly with little serious effort to develop a career in business, politics or government. Instead, he set out aggressively first to establish a Wall Street reputation as an authority on stocks and investments in the expanding aviation industry. In doing so, he made the acquaintance of most of the pioneers in flight and the founders of the aviation industry. Also he collected a library of some 10,000 books on various aspects of aviation, the largest extant at the time.

His knowledge in the aviation field brought him his first job in government at the start of World War II. At the request of Nelson Rockefeller, then the Coordinator of Inter-American Affairs, in the summer of 1941 he undertook a mission to Brazil for the purpose of obtaining the eviction of German and Italian airlines from South America. Their offense was to have used their planes for locating and reporting Allied shipping in the Atlantic to German submarines. Despite the reluctance of

South American governments, the State Department and U.S. oil companies, Bill and his colleagues achieved their purpose by year's end.

This mission was followed by more than a decade of government service. First he worked for Jesse Jones and Will Clayton in the Department of Commerce where, before leaving in 1947, he became Assistant Secretary of Commerce for Air. After a short return to civilian life during which he launched the highly successful William A. M. Burden and Company, a partnership designed to manage the family's investments, he returned to Washington in 1950. This time he joined forces with Tom Finletter, the Secretary of the Air Force, in the capacity of Special Assistant for Research and Development. This was a critical period for the Air Force when the advent of nuclear weapons and long-range missiles was changing the aspect of future warfare. Bill was well equipped to help.

His government service reached its apogee during his two years, 1959–61, as Ambassador to Belgium. He had long hoped to be Ambassador to France but his own modesty and a hesitancy to push his case in the White House united to deprive him of the appointment. Despite this disappointment the Burdens found Brussels a most congenial post, the more so since their fluent French facilitated close relationships with the leaders of the government and society. It added to their pleasure that most of their new friends attached the same importance to good food and vintage wines as did the Burdens. In this ambience, Peggy's role as a charming hostess was a potent factor in the success of his mission. In a quite different way, so was his sympathetic understanding of the problems of the Belgian government engrossed at the time in the tortuous process of giving independence to the Belgian Congo. Burden concluded from his experience as Ambassador that "gaining the trust of the insiders is the touchstone of diplomacy." I would say that this

formula explains much of his success in many of his other un-
dertakings.

It would be misleading if I stopped with this list of a few high
spots in Bill's business and government activities. Concurrently
he was serving a host of civic and cultural causes which demand
at least brief recognition.

From early in this period to the present, Burden's contribu-
tions of funds and personal services to Harvard have been mani-
fold, culminating in 1971 in the family's presentation of Burden
Hall to the University, erected in honor of his father and his
deceased son William. He has been most responsive over these
years also to the needs of Columbia University which he has
served as a trustee. In the case of M.I.T., he has donated funds
to establish there a professorship in astrophysics.

Bill and Peggy are long-time patrons of the arts, particularly
of modern art. Evidence of his dedication thereto is his thirteen
years of service as President of the Museum of Modern Art, in
the course of which he arranged for the Museum to hold an
exhibition in Paris of American-owned paintings by French
artists from David to Toulouse-Lautrec. It lasted ten and a half
weeks and was admired by some 200,000 visitors.

During his wartime residence in Washington, Bill had paid
little attention to the Smithsonian Institution. But chosen a
Regent in 1962, he became and remains a stalwart supporter,
particularly of the Air and Space Museum. It was he who persuaded President Nixon to make available the funds necessary
to build the Museum in time to open for the Bicentennial. Once
open, Bill gave it his vast collection of books on aviation and his
balloon memorabilia—furniture, porcelains, prints and books,
all in some way commemorating the balloon. Of more practical
value perhaps has been his long service in handling the investment funds of the entire Institution.

Despite Bill's many achievements of which the foregoing are

but illustrative, I would suspect that he himself regards his marriage with Peggy as his crowning success. The reader will find many passages in "Reverie," the final chapter, which bear on his home life with Peggy, their four sons and his mother. But these are subjects far too intimate for alien comment.

So without more ado, I yield this book to the reader, already made impatient no doubt by this overlong but still inadequate introduction, that he may read for himself the entire absorbing record of shared achievements that *Peggy and I* has compiled.

MAXWELL D. TAYLOR

Acknowledgements

THIS MEMOIR was written by hand over a period of ten years, then transcribed and checked by my invaluable assistant, Mrs. Charles Wesley Metcalf, to whom I shall be ever grateful.

In 1980, Edward Weeks, editor emeritus of *The Atlantic*, helped me organize and amplify the material. In the preparation he has had the constant advice and interpretation of Peggy, of my brother Shirley, who has contributed his recollections of several episodes, and the editorial assistance of Mrs. Metcalf. I am indebted to Miss Mildred Pou who was responsible for collecting the illustrations.

I wish to thank General Elwood Quesada for his vivid account of the testing of the Hydrogen Bomb at Eniwetok, Dr. James R. Killian, Jr., for checking my account of the Institute for Defense Analyses of which I was chairman for two decades, and John Ponturo for his stimulating résumé of the Institute's proceedings. My dear friend, Garrison Norton, helped me recall our work together on Research and Development when we were assistants to the Secretary of the Air Force, Thomas K. Finletter. Another good friend, Cecil Lyon, permitted me to quote from his diary describing Peggy's and my visit to Peking. Mr. George Hildebrand was my consultant in the automotive field.

I had lively conversations with Mr. Joseph Donon as he described the cuisine at "Florham" over which he presided for more than forty years. Mr. James Rarity, one of my Grandmother's footmen, recalled the "upstairs-downstairs" duties at "Florham." Finally I thank Lt. Colonel Vincent P. Ford (Ret.), Mr. Ernest K. Gann, Miss Ann Rose Oetiker, Miss Heidi Zbinden, Mr. Carter Burden, Mr. Ruric Jordan and Mr. Alec Ulmann for their various assistance.

WILLIAM A. M. BURDEN

Peggy and I

CHAPTER I

New York Boyhood

BROTHERS who are close in age can become intensely competitive or inseparable. I was born on April 6, 1906, and my brother Shirley three years later; we were different in many ways but life drew us together and our affection for each other deepened as we matured. Our father, William Armistead Moale Burden, a famous Harvard athlete, captain of the football team and First Marshal of the Class of 1900, died of Hodgkin's disease in the fifth year of marriage, leaving me only the faintest remembrance of him and we were brought up in a rich, sheltered environment by our mother, Florence Vanderbilt Twombly, who devoted her life to doing what she thought was best for us.

I have only a dim recollection of my father but I remember, as clearly as Henry Adams recalled the bright band of sunlight on the kitchen floor in which he sat as a child, how I enjoyed the warm comfort of my varnished English baby carriage, how jealous I was when Shirley arrived and demanded attention, and how energetically he managed to annoy me by the time I was six and he three. He was boisterous while I was quiet and though we had separate rooms that did not keep him away from my things. Our Irish nurse Nan O'Malley always seemed to be somewhere else when I needed her help.

The elder whom we held in awe was our maternal grandmother, Florence Adele Vanderbilt Twombly, the granddaughter of "the Commodore," then a widow as her husband,
Hamilton McK. Twombly, died four years after I was born.
On our visits, every spring and fall, to "Florham," her palatial
country estate in New Jersey, and in summer to "Vinland,"
her stylish "cottage" in Newport we respected (and sometimes
rebelled against) her ceremonial way of living. She seemed so
distant and unaffectionate, so unlike her strenuous younger
daughter, Aunt Ruth, or her elder daughter, our quiet, loving
mother, whom we called "Moms."

An early memory is of being taken for drives in Grandma's
brougham drawn by a pair of high-stepping horses. The big
carriage was painted maroon and was upholstered with whip-
cord which I recall because it had such a clean smell. The
door would be opened for us by a footman in livery wearing a
high hat with a cockade. On the box would sit Grandma's
German coachman, Hoffman, very stiff, and at Moms' approach he would touch the brim of his high hat with his long-
handled whip. At a later date, after father's death, Grandma
would send her big new electric brougham to take Moms
shopping. It was the same color, ran absolutely silently and
was operated by a chauffeur, in livery, perched high on the
box and steering by a lever which controlled the rear wheels.

We lived at 5 East 73d Street, the house which my parents
had rented after their marriage; it was built of white limestone
and its most impressive feature was the two green marble
columns flanking the front door which to my childish mind
gave it a certain distinction not found in the regular "brown-
stones" in the neighborhood. Actually it was a modest, narrow
dwelling, one room wide and two rooms to a floor; at the
outset my father had the idea that they could live on what he

earned. When his health began to fail an electric elevator was installed, with a diamond grilled gate; it was controlled by a push button and if it stuck between floors much shouting ensued until a mechanic arrived to release us. Much more regal on the same side of our street was Joseph Pulitzer's mansion with its soundproof room where the brilliant, blind editor controlled his newspapers.

For my first twelve years mother's town house was the center of Shirley's and my world, and we shared the gloom or happiness of its different rooms. The second floor front was "the drawing room," always cold, seldom used, the furniture stiff and formal. In one corner stood a surly black Steinway grand piano and on its top a metronome beneath whose ticking I struggled to acquire the rudiments of music from an unimaginative teacher, Miss Weiss. It must have been obvious after a few lessons that I had no ear, no aptitude, but she postponed this admission as long as possible since her livelihood depended on giving lessons. My drudgery went on for years, culminating each spring in a ghastly recital for the parents at which—early in the program—I plowed through such rudimentary compositions as "The Happy Farmer" while my nimbler colleagues showed off with a "Barcarole" or the short pieces which Bach had written for the small hands of his (talented) children. Mother loved music and she was encouraged when Shirley showed progress. Eventually she agreed to end my fruitless lessons and I can feel to this day my joy when they stopped.

From the drawing room one entered the dining room, usually in shadow, panelled in dark mahogany, short of sunlight, even at noon, as the light had to pass through sealed, stained-glass windows, giving on a court enclosed by high buildings. This was an important room as good food and good eating were a cardinal requirement in the Burden family—though not for the young. It was the room I associated with father, for the most magnificent feature was a circular (expanded by leaves) mahogany table with the symbol of the A.D. Club at Harvard, a rampant bull, carved in its center. This was a wedding present from father's ushers, his classmates in the Club. What I believe was an inheritance was the large grandfather's clock which solemnly struck the quarter and half hours, as well as showing the phases of the moon. To me it was a mechanical wonder and I listened for its cheerful booming. There was also a built-in sideboard of mahogany with a large mirror above, as bleak in appearance as the meals Shirley and I were served: breakfast was an unvaried succession of hot cereal and boiled eggs and for lunch weak chicken broth, followed by boiled chicken. We suspected there was something wrong about this but did not realize that it was because of mother's deep-rooted fear of disease. Then at some miraculous moment the restriction was lifted. Mother had found a Swedish cook and we had for a change a delicious variety of "good plain Swedish food." Mother was very fond of coffee and she imported beans in 25-pound bags from Brazil, had it ground in the kitchen and brewed in a percolater at the breakfast table. We were not allowed to have any but that exotic smell gave me a notion of a foreign world.

On the third floor at the front of the house was the library where we enjoyed ourselves in the late afternoons and after supper. Mother was fascinated by the English novelists of the mid-nineteenth century (no history, no biography, but novels including translations of Victor Hugo, Dumas and Jules Verne), and these she read aloud to us, almost every evening, as she was always in. She read well, clearly and with enthusiasm, and I hung on her every word. The reading did not have much effect on Shirley, partly because he was younger and partly because his strong desire for independence made (and still makes) him want to be different from me, so he resisted the idea of liking what I liked just because *I* liked it.

At the very beginning Moms read us fairy tales and Thornton Burgess, followed by G. A. Henty. But we moved up to the great Victorians at a very young age. Dickens with his humor, his excitement and his odd or lovable characters—he could make people come to life in an instant—was our favorite. We laughed aloud over *Pickwick Papers*, and the spookiness of *A Christmas Carol*, on Christmas Eve we listened to with fascination. *A Tale of Two Cities* was the first story I heard about France, and it made a deep impression.

Mother chose what she wanted from the tall, glass-fronted mahogany bookcases which were filled with standard sets, all bound in handsome Levant leather, Dickens in red, Thackeray in green, Robert Louis Stevenson in black, Bulwer-Lytton in blue, Edgar Allen Poe and Mark Twain in rose. These, we were told, were Daddy's books—though he had not put his name in them—and she told us that they often read aloud to each other. I noticed how carefully she handled each book, using the silver paper cutter so as not to tear the page, and the bookmark which kept our place.

Thackeray with his long descriptions of English society was over my head and dry compared with Dickens. What we liked was the adventure of *The Three Musketeers* by Dumas and Stevenson's *Treasure Island*, although the sinister Long John Silver really scared us. And Mark Twain's humor was so amusing that mother would reread some of our favorite episodes. *The Adventures of Tom Sawyer*, *The Adventures of Huckleberry Finn*, *A Connecticut Yankee in King Arthur's Court* (which aroused my interest in mechanics), and *The Innocents Abroad* were all read to me, and later I finished most of his works on my own, getting a taste for erotica in his short stories.

The great tales of Edgar Allen Poe, "The Gold Bug" and "The Pit and the Pendulum" and "The Maelstrom" had an eerie fascination. I liked being mystified by Conan Doyle's Sherlock Holmes, and the excitement of Jules Verne, with his foretaste of science in *From the Earth to the Moon* and *The Tour of the World in Eighty Days*, but now I am beginning to confuse what was read to me and what I read to myself. My hero was that twentieth-century pioneer, Tom Swift: there were some forty books about him, *Tom Swift and His Flying Boat*, *Tom Swift and his Airship*—and I read them all.

Shirley would listen but with no such absorption because he was afflicted with a then-undiagnosed reading difficulty, probably a symptom of "dyslexia," and reading is an ordeal he has never mastered. When he began to fidget, our attention would shift to the upright mahogany phonograph, with the records stored beneath, which stood by the door. It was a windup model and our favorite records were by Harry Lauder or a funny monologue like "Cohen on the Telephone," and for mother the Red Seal records of Caruso. On the library table stood a small bronze, "The Bronco Buster" by Frederic Remington which father had loved. For the three of us the library was a magic room and by the soft glow of the Tiffany lamp it became the focus of our family life and of my intellectual awakening.

My bedroom was on the fourth floor at the front of the house, flooded with sunlight and decorated with wallpaper depicting John Gilpin's ride. I wanted nothing better than to be left there alone with my books and my toys. Here, until Shirley was old enough to intrude, I spent hours even days in bed, not because I was thought to be an invalid—my subsequent life has proved that not to be the case—but because

Portrait of Mother

Father in football uniform

Mother at time of engagement

In my perambulator, Moms in background

Nan, our Irish nurse, was convinced that I was so delicate that I needed special care. I think she got that notion from Moms.

My mother had an almost morbid apprehension of illness and death for reasons I could not comprehend. My parents' first child, a daughter, lived only one month. By the time I was born father was unwell and then came the diagnosis of Hodgkin's disease. Moms was anxiously taking care of him, when her only brother Hamilton, whom she adored, was drowned while serving as a counselor at the Groton Summer Camp on Squam Lake. We were too young to relate all this grief to her apprehension which transformed every sniffle into pneumonia and every stomach upset into something worse. When these normal afflictions occurred I was put to bed on a diet of milk toast and the everlasting chicken soup, spending hours between the cool linen sheets with ample time for my beloved reading.

Mother's bedroom was in back of the library and to enter it one passed through her boudoir, with closets, mirrored doors and her dressing table. This was known as "between the rooms" and it was off-bounds in December, for our Christmas presents were stored there until the great day.

We rarely ventured into Moms's room, and then on tiptoe for we sensed that she shielded her privacy. We could not have imagined how many miserable nights this gallant and still young woman (she was only twenty-eight when father died) must have tossed in her bed, longing for the man whom she had loved. We could not know that she had determined never to marry again. "No, I have had the best, and I never want anything else!" as she told her sister Ruth. We lived with a luxury I took for granted, served by a large staff including a butler and chauffeur. Mother spent little on herself, but she splurged on us at Christmas.

This was the high point of the year which we had been look-

ing forward to for weeks. The magic began Christmas Eve
when Nan and Moms trimmed the tree in the library and the
mounds of beautifully wrapped presents were placed at the
base. We believed in the real Santa Claus, not to be confused
with the old men with red noses who in their costumes were
ringing bells along Fifth Avenue; we solemnly hung our empty
stockings over the fireplace, confident that they would be
filled before dawn. Then Moms read aloud Dickens's *Christmas
Carol*. It is hard to believe that we were moved by the troubles
of Bob Crachit and the stinginess of Scrooge with all those
mysterious gifts only twelve feet away, but we were. And that
was one night we eagerly went to bed.

Early, very early, on Christmas morning, in pajamas and
wrappers, we raced downstairs to explore the bulging stockings
—proof positive that Santa had indeed been down *our* chimney.
Then a hurried dressing and breakfast before we tackled the
large presents. While we tore into them Moms carefully made a
list of which relatives had given what. That done, all the servants, headed by Nan and Gurton, the butler, were called in to
receive their Christmas checks. There was never time enough
to sample our toys before we were trooped off dutifully to St.
Thomas Church to the service with the beautiful choir and a
rousing sermon by Dr. Stires, who was impressive in the pulpit,
and behind him the chancel banked with red and white poinsettias.

Back at 5 East 73rd Street our uncles, Ike Burden and David Dows, with their wives, would arrive late for Christmas
"lunch" (never called dinner in our family). Very festive in
their morning coats and striped trousers and somewhat red
faced from the extra cocktails taken on the way, the uncles
having suspected rightly that they'd get none with us. Mother
did not drink and disapproved of serving alcohol in any form,
but did provide a glass of excellent claret on Christmas.

Christmas lunch, prepared by our Swedish cook, was copious, excellent and traditional: oyster stew, turkey with chestnut stuffing, sweet potatoes with toasted marshmallows on top, creamed onions, (Why traditional? Were they the only vegetables the Puritan fathers could get in winter?), mince pie, pumpkin pie, plum pudding afire with real brandy—denied of course to Shirley and me.

Lunch over, the uncles went to work trying to put together the more complicated mechanical gifts which were too old for us. I remember the trouble they had with a small motion picture projector (8 mm). Threading that simple machine seemed enormously difficult for these grown men who were somewhat befuddled by alcohol, overfed and desperately anxious to get home. The picture they were struggling with finally appeared upside down on the screen, and the session ended with some of the film torn and everyone thoroughly frustrated. They departed, and we were left to sort out, lackadaisically, our more manageable gifts.

In retrospect, the toys of 1912–1914 were much more fun than the plastic things of today. They were usually of metal, with sharp edges, but to us those windup or self-propelled boats and trains were miniatures of the real thing. The best were German made, and how temptingly they were displayed in Schwarz's high-ceilinged store at Fifth Avenue and 31st Street, the most glamorous toy store in America. It was a long drive from our home and the special trips we made before birthdays and Christmas were exciting, and told mother what we craved.

Lead soldiers were not for me; I wanted things to move like my light monoplane, the motor being a strong elastic, which one would wind up by twisting the propellor. Our playroom on the fifth floor gave us plenty of space to lay out the $1\frac{3}{4}$-inch gauge track for our swift, brightly painted model trains.

The engines were powered by electricity and to watch them, one's head at floor level, as they raced through tunnels and past the stations, was thrilling.

The largest of my boats were models, which I made believe were in dry dock as they could not float. I had a two-foot long destroyer with four stacks, and the flagship of the White Fleet, the battleship *New York* with basket masts, two-gun turrets and searchlights. My diving submarine was all right in water but needed more depth than our bathtub. Nan cautioned mother not to buy one of the steam-driven torpedo boats as we'd be blinded if it should explode. Germany was then involved in an enormous naval program to overtake England and Mr. Schwarz, patriotically, followed the lead of his fatherland.

Building blocks were all right for beginners but when I advanced to prefabricated metal, the Mecano set made in England and the Erector, an American invention, I figured out how to put things together. The sets came in increasing size, and I being a perfectionist and Moms indulgent, I had the largest of both.

Each set had a catalogue, illustrating the projects, the cars, bridges and cranes that could be put together if one followed the directions and with the Erector came a little battery-powered electric motor. I remember the great pride with which I exhibited to Uncle David Dows—one of the few men who early entered my life and then only at Christmas—an electric powered crane which I had built from an Erector set and which both lifted and swiveled. He was suitably impressed. But not Shirley. Probably because he could not read the directions he took a grudge against them and if I wasn't looking or had left the room over they'd go, sometimes deliberately pulled apart. I am even-tempered but there were times when

I hit out and Nan would have to separate us. I didn't rough him up often and he never held it against me. He just liked to get my goat.

Actually he began teasing me before he learned to walk. Nan or mother would take his hands, hoist him up and urge him forward, but no go, he'd relapse on his bottom and smile. One day, according to Nan, when we were together on the floor of the playroom I was absorbed with a stuffed rabbit, my special pet, when something distracted my attention. I left the room and that was enough for Shirley. He got up off the floor, scuttled over to the sacred rabbit, seized it, and tottered toward the door, Nan after him.

*   *   *

Moms wore mourning all during our childhood, black with a veil in winter, unadorned white in summer. One rarely thinks of one's mother as beautiful; ours used no cosmetics or perfume and her charm seemed perfectly natural. Shirley and I, as she occasionally remarked, were "all she had"—or seemingly wanted—and she took us everywhere.

New York was then a much more open and picturesque city than it is today. Boarding a Fifth Avenue bus was tricky for a boy; one climbed the swaying, circular stairway to the open seats on top and scrambled to one up front, to lord it over the pedestrians. When the conductor came you pressed a dime into the metal contraption like a pistol, which held the fares. I remember the horse-drawn trolley cars which ran cross-town, and best of all, the ferry rides on the Hudson to the railroad terminals in Jersey City. The wind smelt of the sea, and on the long ride from the 34th Street dock it was fascinating to watch the river traffic of barges and small craft and to hear the deep-throated blasts as the tugs slowly warped a

Cunard liner into her dock. The docks were well filled with freighters, too, and we could tell their countries from their flags.

Moms and I went to the Aquarium far down at the Battery, the lowest tip of Manhattan, where one looked across at the Statue of Liberty before going in to gaze at the fish and the sea lions. We went to the Hippodrome where everyone laughed at Marcelline, the famous clown, and where beautiful girls marched down into the vast tank of water below the stage—and never bobbed up again. We visited the waxworks in the Eden Musée and saw the marvelous "mechanical" chess player. And on the way uptown she pointed out the house on lower Fifth Avenue where Mark Twain had lived. Regularly on Sunday, rain or shine, we sat beside her in the family pew at St. Thomas's, where she and Daddy had been married.

The year after father died, 1910, Grandma Twombly, out of sympathy, made her a large gift. I had not the slightest idea of the value of money at the time, but I was told, later, that it amounted to a million and a half dollars.

That year mother purchased a new Renault (her first, a town car, was a wedding present), now we had a forty HP open touring car, and a French chauffeur named Lucien. She herself had no wish to drive; she told us that when they were first married and were spending the summer in Newport, Daddy had taught her to "operate" his Winston Six with the result that she steered the car into a ditch and it overturned. She never took the wheel again but I should add that when being driven, she liked to go as fast as the law allowed, or faster.

Her love of speed was acquired in competition. She and her younger sister Ruth were both expert horsewomen and won blue ribbons and championship cups at the Morristown Horse Show and at Madison Square, Ruth driving a four-in-hand, and mother the more difficult tandem.

As time passed Moms cheered up. She was a keen bridge player, and enjoyed playing in the afternoons with friends like Pauline Robinson, Mrs. Potter and Mrs. Iselin. There would be laughter when vivacious Aunt Ruth dropped in to gossip and again when that very tall Bostonian, Peter Higginson, who had been father's roommate and captain of the Harvard crew, came uptown to call. Mother's eyes would glisten as they reminisced about Cambridge. And from the persistence of his visits I suppose that Bill Post was one of her suitors who was slow to take "No" for an answer. On his return from a trip around the world, he brought everyone beautiful presents, for us boys a miniature Japanese village with people and tiny blue ponds. But neither Shirley nor I liked him.

I don't know how many snowy Christmases we had in my early youth but it seems as if there were more than today and that the snow stayed on the ground longer. Those white streets were a delight. There would be wonderful sledding in Central Park and a surprising number of sleighs with jingling bells would appear on Fifth Avenue, the most elegant ones built by Brewster with the riders protected by mink, or buffalo robes.

When the snow was really deep the sleighs used to race from the Plaza Hotel to the famous Claremont Inn Restaurant near Grant's Tomb on Riverside Drive. I remember one thrilling day when Aunt Ruth took Shirley and me with her in her sleigh over this traditional run but in a race she always drove alone.

There was also a little ceremony at Christmastime when the wealthy members of society being driven down Fifth Avenue in their carriages would pause at busy intersections to give the policeman on duty his "Christmas" envelope, insuring that he would be looking "the other way" should a traffic violation occur. This tipping "in the spirit of Christmas" continued through the 1920s as motor cars replaced the carriages.

The model automobiles one bought at Schwarz's in my youth were beautiful replicas of the real cars—all of foreign make like our Renault. I was not sorry to see the horse go: the riding lessons I was obliged to take in the Riding Academy were unpleasant—the horse knew the moment I was in the saddle that I was scared of him. In my dream world there were cars but no horses, and as a boy, in the words of Bob Lovett, I began my "lifelong love affair with the internal combustion engine." Beginning when I was twelve I have owned fifty-three automobiles, small and large; the 1920s were the Golden Age for motors, and I thank my stars that I lived at a time when the finest in the world were being built.

*   *   *

Our family's wealth was built up by my two brilliant fore-bears, great-great-grandfather "Commodore" Vanderbilt and great-grandfather Henry Burden, the inventor. But Shirley and I were diverted from any ancestor worship by mother. Every time a Vanderbilt descendant did anything—getting married, or divorced, or dying—anything that got into the newspapers—the "Commodore," as he was always referred to, was once again proclaimed, and mother who was a very modest woman shied away from the notoriety. It was not until I was in college that I began to appreciate his remarkable enterprise: in boyhood about the only thing I knew was that at his death the "Commodore" was the wealthiest man in America, and I probably got this from Nan.

Great-grandfather Burden meant more to me because I had

some visible evidence of what he accomplished. He was a Scottish inventor of such promise that an American consul urged him to go to America and armed him with letters of introduction. Burden settled in Troy, New York, then one of the wealthiest towns in America. With iron from the Catskills he built a popular iron plow, invented an automatic puddler, and a miraculous machine that turned out horseshoes, at the rate of three thousand an hour, for the Union Army and as many as the Confederates could pay for, shipped through Canada. To power his ironworks he constructed the largest waterwheel in the world—and Shirley and I marveled at it when Moms with her sense of duty took us on a visit to Troy.

We three stayed with the inventor's daughter, my great-aunt, a remarkable old lady well over ninety, Margaret Proudfit. Mrs. Proudfit was living in great-grandfather Burden's very large family estate called "Woodside." As was common among industrialists of the period he had built his home on a beautiful property overlooking the Burden Iron Works.

At the time of our visit Mrs. Proudfit and her nurse were the only occupants of the large house. Although her mind remained extremely clear she was obviously reaching the end of the road physically. At meals her vivid description of her brilliant father, Henry Burden, and his achievements was sometimes interrupted by gastric distress.

I liked everything I was told about that great man. In 1833 for his pleasure (not only pleasure—to test his theories of ship design) he built a two-hulled boat with a single paddle-wheel mounted in the middle. The boat was three hundred feet long and of unique design, clearly a predecessor to the Western type catamaran built in the 1870s. His incompetent captain wrecked the boat in the Hudson. Henry Burden predicted that ocean liners of the future would be long and slender, not tubby.

The three of us were taken on a tour of the Burden Iron Works which was still operating at a high level, producing horseshoes and other iron products. While we were obviously too young to appreciate many of the fine points of iron manufacture we were much impressed with the size and efficiency of the factory. Horseshoes were still being turned out red hot at a tremendous rate by each machine, but it did not occur to us or the workers that the automobile industry was in increasing competition with horse-drawn vehicles. Here it was just business as usual. As we completed our tour of the plant Shirley and I were presented with a miniature gold horseshoe to wear on our watchchains.

As we grew older (and our table manners improved) we were invited to our Burden grandparents, or to Grandma Twombly, for Christmas "lunch" and were permitted to sit with the grown-ups. Our favorites were Daddy's parents, Grandpa I. Townsend Burden and his jolly, easy-going wife. She had been a Miss Moale of Baltimore and had a fondness for southern dishes, terrapin, crabmeat, wild duck, and always hot bread. The Moales were proud of their ancestry, which was the source of my middle name, Armistead, of Shirley's name, and that of his son, Carter. Both she and Grandpa were plump with ruddy complexions and he had a little white goatee. After a sumptuous meal in their brick house on the corner of Fifth Avenue and 92nd Street, he used to light a large cigar, Grandma Burden would tie an asbestos bib around his neck and after a few puffs he would lapse into a doze from which he would be roused and led off to bed by a footman. That is the last picture I have of him before he died.

I seemed to be Grandmother Burden's favorite, just as my

father must have been her favorite child. She was a much more likable person than my glacial Grandmother Twombly, and I returned her affection. I was ten when she was mortally ill with cancer in her apartment in Carlton House, and I was summoned to her deathbed. I remember the darkened room, heavy with the perfume she loved, her feverish but still plump hand clutching mine, and the final farewell which meant so much to her but was only dimly comprehended by me.

*   *   *

It is rare to meet any American who is satisfied with his early schooling. I certainly am not. Mother and her sisters had been taught at home by governesses and it must have been good, well-disciplined training, as mother was fluent in both French and German although she rarely used either except when in Europe. But while she insisted on my plugging away at the piano she seemed not to care whether I really learned French, and I have regretted this all my life. I wonder why. Did she have unpleasant memories of a governess who badgered her and therefore didn't want us to have a French governess?

What did happen was the formation of a class of five or six boys and girls who were taught during the mornings at our house on 73rd Street. We wrote out sentences—"Cats love mice,"—in our ruled copybooks, to shape our writing. We had a smattering of geography and memorized the countries of Europe: "Great Britain and Ireland, Norway, Sweden, Denmark, Russia, Germany, Austria, Hungary. . . ." And we added and subtracted. Our teacher was Miss Frances N. Nightingale who was to become well known as Head Mistress at the Nightingale-Banford School for Girls, which my future wife, Peggy Partridge, attended.

Miss Nightingale's class was not only my first step in formal education, it was my first regular contact with children of my own age. Among the boys were the brothers Clendenin and George Ryan, grandsons of Thomas Fortune Ryan, the millionaire, and more dear to me, Bill Harding, exactly my age with a merry sense of humor, with whom I formed a friendship which despite our separation when he went to Groton and Yale, was renewed in Washington in our mid-careers, and ended only with his death.

He was my first friend and one of our favorite pastimes after school was to go roller-skating in Central Park where the skating was much smoother than the sidewalks on Fifth Avenue. In a delightful book *Those Days*, Hamilton Fish Armstrong gives his account of what roller skates meant to the city bred:

> . . . I lived as much as possible on roller skates. From the first I had despised the wobbly rubber-tired bicycle skates affected by most of the young who frequented Washington Square. I thought them slow and sissy, and took violently to the noisier, more trustworthy and much speedier four-wheeler. Henceforth my hands smelt of oil and my black stockings always needed darning at the knees. Sidewalks were identified by their texture—some corrugated or scored with wavy grooves that would trip you, some of rough concrete that buzzed the soles of your feet, others of smooth slate that allowed maximum speed. Where there was glass in the pavement to light office basements, janitors would rush out and shake their fists at me, but on skates I could make circles around them, and returned often to do so.

After two years the Nightingale classes came to an end and mother entered me in Bovée School. She never explained why she picked the Bovée School instead of one of the better-known day schools, such as St. Bernard's or Cutler, but I can only guess that she did not want a male headmaster. Probably she also felt that there would be less athletic competition at Bovée than in the other schools, and she was right.

The school was located in an old brownstone building on East 49th Street, dimly lit in the late winter afternoons by Weisbach burner gas lamps. These were fire hazards no doubt but immensely more fascinating than the electric light of today. Boys who had done extremely well in their work had the right to light the gas lamps for a week. This involved perilously manipulating a long rod with a wax wick—somewhat like the devices used by acolytes to light candles on the sacred altar of a church—though we were no acolytes I can assure you. The trick was to turn on the flow of gas early enough to assure a successful light but not *so* early as to produce an explosion by lighting too late.

We dressed in blue suits and stiff Eton collars for special occasions, normally we wore scrubby "knickerbocker" trousers with a Norfolk jacket with belt, long wool stockings held up by elastic garters, coupled with rather scuffed brown shoes. Boys hate to be different and I was particularly embarrassed by having my shoes made by one of the few custom shoemakers in New York, a serious German named Bloch. On entering the shop one saw the men, in their aprons, cutting the delicious smelling leather, and heard the nails being driven into the sole and heel. Bloch's shoes were comfortable and allowed space for the growing feet but they were certainly no thing of beauty; they were "sensible shoes" with square toes and bulbous, not pointed, tips. My schoolmates thought they were horrors.

No teacher and no new subject particularly aroused my enthusiasm at Bovée but I definitely liked English and was reasonably good at writing compositions, essays and the like. English literature, in which I had been steeped since my early reading, I found entrancing, and continued to do so during college and, for that matter, for the rest of my life. Mathematics I found hard at the beginning.

One school activity I heartily disliked was a sort of commencement held in mid-winter for which we were all required to memorize long poems. I was never good at this sort of thing. Over the years I recited "The Charge of the Light Brigade" by Tennyson, Kipling's "Fuzzy Wuzzy," and Macauley's "Lars Porsena of Clusium," fast and nervously. What made it worse was that my mother brought Shirley and Aunt Ruth to each of these performances: Moms ready to applaud and Shirley smirking if I had to be prompted.

Finally, there were the "art" courses conducted by Miss Eleanor Bovée. Miss Eleanor was elegant to a degree; the coarser side of life did not exist for her and she suffered from the delusion that she could convert not just one or two to appreciate art but all the rather grubby little boys under her control. Shirley, who never took school seriously, introduced this deviation:

> Eleanor would often take us up to the Metropolitan Museum of Art to sketch Greek vases. We enjoyed these trips, not because we wanted to sketch Greek vases, but it gave us the opportunity for a super game of hide and seek.
>
> There were usually six of us in the class. We would pick vases to sketch in different rooms, as far from each other as possible. This made our game of hide and seek exciting but complicated Eleanor's routine. She would stay with one of us and help draw one side of a vase and then leave to check the progress of another pupil three

rooms away. As soon as she was out of sight, we would take off and look for our other partners-in-crime. An afternoon of this left Eleanor close to a nervous breakdown and her pupils flushed with the joy of the chase. As for Art, the two sides of the vase never matched.

Shirley and I were expected to be on our best behavior on our visits to Grandmother Twombly, who was what was then called "a leader of society." Physically she was small—less than a hundred pounds—autocratic, exquisitely dressed, and with a boundless love for entertaining. She was one of the "Commodore's" four granddaughters, and the only one whose husband, Hamilton McK. Twombly, had multiplied her Vanderbilt inheritance. At her command were three establishments and she filled them with guests—during the winter in her town house of red brick at 684 Fifth Avenue; "Vinland," her Newport "cottage" overlooking the sea, where she spent July and August, had fifty rooms; and the largest, "Florham," in Morris County, New Jersey, where she resided in May-June and September-October. "Florham"—which combines the Christian names of our grandparents—was in our eyes more like a palace than a country house; it had one hundred rooms, was served by a huge staff, and traditionally there were four house-parties, two in the spring, two in the fall, to which as many as fifty guests were invited, weeks or even months in advance. We went there for shorter visits and to "Vinland" for ten days in the summer, more frequently, of course, as we grew up.

The first stay which I clearly remember was in the spring vacation of 1914, when there were no other guests. I had been there earlier at the age of four when Grandfather was still living, but by now could take in the grandeur. We arrived by train at Morristown where a maroon Rolls-Royce was waiting for us. It was a great estate to which we were driven, over nine hundred acres, entirely fenced, and everything, beginning with the great gate and the half-mile-long entrance drive, was imposing. The house was of rose brick, with four, tall white Ionic columns fronting the entrance, many chimneys, and wings at either end; it was a thousand feet long, and had been built in 1896 by McKim, Mead and White, modeled on the west wing of Hampton Court designed by Sir Christopher Wren. Not until I was in college and attended some of Aunt Ruth's largest parties could I appreciate the scale of the entertainment for so many guests.

"Florham" was in the center of "the Park" and was approached between clipped lawns of brilliant green that merged into woods of oak and beech. On sunny days the scent of box and bayberry bushes filled the air and from the terrace on the east one looked down on beds of spring flowers, paved walks, and Greek statues gazing into space. At a distance was "the Farm," seven hundred acres of crops, and pasture for the large herd of Guernsey cattle.

"Florham" had thirty double bedrooms (nominal at that time for the wealthy, here and in Edwardian England). On each door was a brass frame in which the name of the guest was inserted. We always occupied the same room on the second floor, facing the drive, and I would be awakened early by the sound of men raking the bluestone gravel and the hoofbeats of a groom returning from the post office with the mail.

Shirley has an eye for detail and this is what he remembers:

> What impressed me most when I first went to "Florham" was a pair of marble lions on either side of the front door, and the front door itself. It must have been at least eleven feet high and six inches thick, made of mahogany with a

shine you could see your face in. The front and back of the door were decorated with panels and the hinges were of silver.

As you drove up the door would slowly open, like the lowering of a drawbridge to a medieval castle. Standing in the hall, in front of a seven-foot marble fireplace was a very tall, distinguished looking gentleman in a morning coat and striped trousers. This was Frederick, the Swedish butler. He wore pince-nez glasses, and his welcoming smile was chosen with care. At his right was a footman standing at attention, dressed in the Vanderbilt maroon livery, with silver buttons with the Twombly crest of a lion rampant on them.

That air of formality stayed with us when we went in to kiss Grandma, who was seated in her wing chair in the library, with her feet on a footstool. She would greet us in a dry voice. "Bill, do you like your school?" and "Shirley, you're getting to be fat." Then we'd go upstairs to change into sweaters for the out-of-doors.

Usually we were sent out to "play in the Grove," a stand of big oaks close to the house, where we once unscrewed the watering system and got ourselves soaked and scolded. But what we most enjoyed was to see the activity in the different buildings, of which the stable was our first attraction. It was half hidden in the trees, built of the same rosy brick, designed originally for forty-five horses but now subdivided. In one half there were stalls for twenty-five and a tack room, the walls covered with the blue ribbons and red won by Moms and Aunt Ruth; in the other half, large enough for many cars, were two black Mercedes, in which the grandparents had toured Europe in 1904, but rarely used thereafter, six Rolls-

Royce limousines and two Crane-Simplex limousines, Aunt
Ruth's Mercedes runabout, and a Buick station wagon for
shopping. All but the old Mercedes were painted "Vanderbilt" maroon. Every car, whether used or not, was washed
daily by the two men in high rubber boots and aprons. The
four chauffeurs were above such chores.

Next was the Orangerie, a tall, brick, glass-roofed building,
enclosing the orange and grapefruit trees, and acacia in green
tubs. Beneath it in a very large basement were the electric
generator and the heating plant which Thomas Edison, a
friend and neighbor of Grandpa Twombly, had designed. An
engineer was always on duty, and welcomed us as we stood
transfixed by the powerful, spinning dynamos. On the doors
of the great boilers, which were fired with coal, Mr. Edison
had cast the initials of our grandparents: FVT and HMcKT;
behind the boilers was a tunnel conveying heat six hundred
feet to "Florham" and the greenhouses. I remember how
warm and clean the place was, and that it supplied all the
power needed for "Florham" as well as the dairy and the
farm.

It would be nearing lunch when we reached the greenhouses, some of them hot and fragrant. We always made a
beeline for the fruit, the nectarines and peaches, Persian melons, so heavy they had to be supported in nets, purple figs and
white Muscat grapes. It made my mouth water to look at
them, but Tyson, Grandma's head gardener, forbade our
picking any; they could only be eaten at the table, and Nan,
ever vigilant, approved.

It was Aunt Ruth who made the place exciting. She had
been strikingly handsome, dark haired, with black eyes, now
was putting on weight, rather masculine, vivacious and witty.
She was younger than Moms, and played tennis strenuously

with the pro on the grass court close to the house, Shirley and I acting as ballboys. She was always on the go. "You bring them up, and I'll have fun with them later," she used to say to Moms. I admired her; I liked her colorful clothes and the smart way she drove her car. She was a fast driver.

On this visit and ever after, we looked forward to the food. Grandmother was proud of her chef; we had to be washed up, and our hair parted on time! A footman stood behind the chair of each grown-up. We ate at a side table on plain fare as Nan disapproved of our having the rich delicacies. But the fruit that came from the greenhouses, those nectarines and white Muscat grapes, and the thick cream and butter, produced by the prize herd of Guernseys were better than any we tasted at home. For Shirley who had a sweet tooth the desserts were something special.

During the summers we returned year after year to a large cottage at Coolidge Point on Boston's North Shore. Our neighbors were the Fessendens, whose daughters were beauties, with flaxen hair, the Peter Higginsons and the Coolidges, two of whose sons were at Harvard. From the beginning mother helped to make our place the center of activity and there was soon a slogan, "Come on up to Burdens." We held a field day with three-legged races, relay races and races in flour sacks. There were silver cups for the winners and it was hard for Shirley and me to understand why these were sometimes awarded to boys as young as "Pen" Higginson and slower than ourselves. On the Fourth of July we had plenty of firecrackers and torpedoes and sparklers, and that night we all went up to see the fireworks on Singing Beach in Manchester. In those years everyone made a point of displaying the stars and stripes on his flagpole or hung it from an open window. Early in the evening before it was dark enough for the fireworks, Lucien, our chauffeur, would light and release hot-air balloons which were fascinating to watch as the off-shore breeze took them out to sea, but something of a fire hazard if an east wind blew them back in the direction of the pines.

Mother had bought a wicker phaeton and a sturdy black pony we named Squaw (we were reading *The Deerslayer*). Our coachman, Lawrence Cunningham, was an amiable red-headed Irishman and when he took the reins, in his white stock and square bowler hat, we urged him to drive to Wingaersheek Beach which was wild and fun to explore in bare feet. Our one desire was to get away from Nan. We carefully explored a small pond near the house where we'd seen snapping turtles; finally we caught an angry one which we penned in under a heavy box, but he was too strong and next morning turtle and box had disappeared. Joan Higginson was one of our favorites and on low tide we would scramble down the rocks with her to catch starfish in the pools. She played on our baseball team and was plucky when she got hit in the eye with the ball.

At the outbreak of war in August, 1914, Lucien, our chauffeur, whom Shirley and I admired, was called back to the French colors and his place was taken by Harry McCabe. Harry was very skillful and he talked as he worked. I envied his efficiency with our Renault. Changing a tire in those days took time and it was fun to watch how swiftly he did it. When mother's town car developed loud noises in the rear axle, instead of turning in the car Harry himself replaced the differential gears.

The war at first seemed remote and Nan, opinionated as ever, said it would be over in a year. But after the Battle of the Marne the reality came nearer to us when Gurton, our English butler, gave notice and before long was at a training camp on Salisbury Plains, as his postcards told us. Lucien was already at the Front and he sent me a briquet, a cigarette lighter made of shell casing, such as the *poilu* used in the trenches.

Mother subscribed to the *Illustrated London News*, whose graphic, heroic drawings helped me follow the fighting. I was fascinated by the Zeppelin raids on London, and, lying on the floor, I drew pictures of the giant airship with the bombs falling. I read about the American ambulance drivers who were carrying the French wounded and the American pilots in the Lafayette Escadrille. This, and the sinking of the *Lusitania*, should have warned us that we were getting involved. But mother was so wrapped up in our domestic life that in April, 1917, when President Wilson declared war on Germany and the *New York Times* with its big black headlines reached the breakfast table, I cried, "Moms, it says we're going to war!" To which she retorted calmly, "We don't talk about that."

The causes of the war were too deep for me and my sympathies were divided. In every issue of the *Illustrated London News* was a memorial page of small photographs of young British officers killed or missing in action. I felt sorry for them, and after reading *Over the Top* by Guy Empy I felt sorry for "the Tommy." But our newspapers and magazines were flooded with propaganda which I instinctively resisted. Stephen Leacock, the Canadian, wrote about the German "soup trains" and how the soup was piped straight into the mouths of the hungry troops, which I knew was ridiculous. I thought Raemaker's cartoons were unfair. The underdog always appealed to me: I had more feeling for Hector than Achilles and had named my wirehaired fox terrier "Hector." I didn't want the Germans to win the war and yet I didn't want them to lose.

On our visit to "Florham" in the spring of 1917, Shirley and I shook hands with a French veteran who had received one of

France's highest decorations, the Médaille Militaire. This was Grandmother's new chef, Joseph Donon, a short sturdy man with a scared face, who had been given up for dead. She told us about him: how he had been trained by Escoffier, the greatest chef in the world, and then brought to America by Henry Clay Frick. Like Lucien he was called back to the French Army in August, 1914, and took part in the very first fighting at Verdun, where he was terribly wounded in the left shoulder and in the head, losing part of his jaw. He spent six months in a French hospital before he was honorably discharged, with his medals and a pension. Mr. Frick wanted him back, at his summer place in Beverly, Massachusetts, and when Donon found it impossible to use his left arm, Mr. Frick sent him to a skillful surgeon who successfully operated on Donon's shoulder and jaw. It was a heroic story that made a deep impression on us and it had a happy ending when Mr. Frick recommended Donon to Aunt Ruth. Donon was to be in our family for forty-one years, and became my friend and confidant.

That summer at Peter Higginson's suggestion Moms became an associate member of the Myopia Hunt Club. Aunt Ruth would drive over from Newport to Coolidge Point in her "Silver Ghost" Rolls runabout. It was only about ninety miles and on the way, occasionally, she would pick up her friend, Miss Eleanora Sears at Beverly Farms, who also drove a "Silver Ghost"; she and my aunt were much alike in their keen, mannish love of competition.

For years I had been wearing glasses to correct my short-sightedness but I had foxed our very old family eye doctor, Dr. Cutler, by memorizing the chart and the glasses he ordered for me were no help. As I grew taller I kept leaning over to get a better view and gradually developed a pronounced stoop. When I had lessons from the young pro at Myopia (which incidentally took its name from the fact that most of its founders were nearsighted) he was encouraging and I began to develop a serve and a strong forehand, probably because I could see the ball better, close to.

The swimming at Singing Beach was icy cold and the damp bathhouse stank of seaweed. Rather than swim we were happy fishing from the dock at Coolidge Point with handlines, using clams for bait. We fished for hours in the sun and on high tide caught flounders, sculpin, sea perch, and, rarely, a small cod. Cod was the only one the cook would clean and cook for us, but when they were biting and stealing our bits of clam it was good sport. Moms noticed our enthusiasm and at the Motorboat Show that winter she took us all over a thirty-two-foot Elco cabin cruiser, and on the impulse ordered it. We had the excitement of owning it for twenty-four hours. But when Nan said that if we went out to sea we ran the risk of being sunk by a German submarine, the purchase was called off.

During our several summers at Coolidge Point we had accumulated quite a number of pets which were cared for by Lawrence Cunningham, the coachman, during the winter. Mother had a dwarf parrot who liked to perch on her shoulder, and a large one, gray and dumb. We had two house dogs, mother's spaniel and "Nipsy," a Portuguese terrier, if there is such a breed, small, white, curley hair, who learned to stand on his hind legs and was much loved by Shirley and me. In addition we had "Woody," a black and white English setter, and her running mate "Brian Born," a red Irish setter; they were all over us and nosing around when we were on the rocks but too obstreperous to live indoors and slept in the garage.

I also spent some of my allowance on chickens—white Leghorns, Rhode Island Reds, and Bantams, and used to exhibit them in the county fair at Danvers. Moms paid me for the eggs. It was not the most profitable investment I ever made, not even on a larger scale, which came later.

In 1917 Congress was working on legislation to add an inheritance tax to the income tax which had gone into effect four years earlier, and Cousin John Hammond advised Grandmother Twombly that if she ever intended to make a generous settlement on her daughters, the time was now; accordingly a gift of seven and a half million dollars came to mother and a like amount to Aunt Ruth.

CHAPTER II

Mt. Kisco and Hollywood

ONCE mother realized that she was a rich woman she decided to leave our narrow house on 73rd Street and its sad memories, and we moved into new, more spacious quarters at 1028 Fifth Avenue, opposite the Metropolitan Museum of Art and within reach of the Bovée School. Her next step was to search for a place in the country which Shirley and I would enjoy. Personally she much preferred the city, but she knew how happy we had been at Coolidge Point.

She picked Westchester, that beautifully hilly area north of New York—Long Island was "too social"—and she and my aunt inspected a number of estates in Mt. Kisco; when they agreed on three possibilities they took Shirley and me to see them—this was to be a family decision. Most of the large houses were on the top of hills, and their owners were referred to by the villagers as "hilltoppers." In Shirley's and my eyes the one place which stood out above all others was "Uplands," belonging to Mrs. J. Borden Harriman, a big wheel in the Democratic Party, and later Ambassador to Norway. It was an estate of 190 acres, part woods, part gently rolling farmland, and what gave it distinction were the ten acres of level ground on which stood the main house, with lawns, well-laid out gardens, and a squash tennis court. We were elated when mother bought it. The main house was large and comfortable; it became the home-place where we were happiest, even in winter weekends, from July 1918 to 1931. Moms continued to buy the adjacent property until we owned four hundred acres in all.

Mr. Burnett, who had been the architect of the farm buildings at "Florham," built the auxiliary buildings we needed; a stable for eight horses—we had a pair of driving horses and several saddle horses—a ten-car garage, and a large greenhouse. Chickens were my hobby and a building large enough to accommodate two thousand was completed.

I don't think Mr. Burnett knew much about chickens for the house he put up was so damp and so much condensation gathered on the ceiling that there was a rising death rate due to pneumonia. Nor was I very successful selling my eggs. My principal customer was Aunt Ruth and two cases of Leghorn eggs went off to "Florham" each week. Donon reported that many were broken in transit and also said he preferred the eggs he purchased locally (on which he was getting a commission, as I did not know). I lost money on that deal and in fact mother paid for the whole operation—but I kept the receipts!

We lived in a small house known as "Apple Hill" while the renovation of the main house was going on and Moms, who had a number of friends in Mt. Kisco, became involved in the Liberty Loan drives, the rationing—gasless, meatless Sundays —and work for the Red Cross during that last summer of the war. The False Armistice took us by surprise and when the fighting ended on November 11, we believed, like most Americans, that with the Kaiser in exile we would have a long-lasting peace.

The construction required a work force of about fifty men. They brought with them a large steamroller to work on the roads, which they often left with some steam up at the end of the day. Shirley and I—out of sight of Nan—used to drive the monster a few feet, but fortunately never far enough for it to pick up momentum down hill, which it might easily have done.

The work at "Uplands" took over a year; there was also to be an eighty-foot swimming pool. That first autumn I said I wanted a really large dog. Mother arranged to purchase a coal-black Great Dane with beautiful yellow eyes. He must have weighed at least 150 pounds. When I went down to the stable-garage to greet this splendid new arrival, I found him crouched in a corner, his eyes glowing like the Hound of the Baskervilles. I had hardly reached out to pat him when he leapt at me and bit my cheek. It turned out that he was only doing what he had been taught, as he had been trained for military purposes in Belgium, but nobody had told us. At Nan's urging he was given to more courageous friends.

As a surprise for us Moms had Mr. Burnett prepare the foundation for a house where we could amuse ourselves in bad weather. When I became curious and asked what it was to be she said a root cellar, so the mystery continued until the roof was completed.

Within was a large, shallow stage, framed with oak beams, taken from an eighteenth-century farm that had gone to seed. The beams had rough marks that I supposed were caused by the adze but we were told that they were hacked by the sabers of Tarleton's cavalry in the Revolution. Be that as it may they were picturesque, and the stage was ideal for a marionette show. My friend, Freddy Davies, who was at St. Paul's, was a constant visitor during the holidays, and he and I produced a marionette play entitled "Mademoiselle Ponchoir" about an enticing spy who barely escaped death at the hands of the

Uhlans. She made her getaway by sea, episodes in which my model battleship, the *New York*, with its flashing searchlights and my four-stack destroyer saved her from a fate worse than death.

Adjoining the theatre was a kitchen, with one of the first General Electric refrigerators, and a stove on which we made fudge. There was a carpenter shop with a fine complement of tools, and an enclosed porch where we installed a hand press which produced quite drinkable cider from our own apples. Nan had a taste for it and persuaded us to try to ferment wine from our miserable Concord grapes. This was a disgusting failure but it left me with the suspicion that she enjoyed her secret nip and why I sometimes noticed the aroma of Lydia Pinkham's tonic (high alcoholic content) on her breath.

The troop transports began to return in the spring of 1919 and when the New York regiments, particularly "the Fighting 69th" with their famous chaplain, Father Duffy, paraded up Fifth Avenue, through a snowfall of ticker tape and between the cheering spectators, it was a sight to remember. Shirley and I were seated on the open windowsill of Grandma Twombly's house at 684 Fifth Avenue. We watched General Ryan and the troops approach, and as they drew abreast, we realized that they had deliberately left gaps in their ranks, once filled by their buddies, who had been wounded or killed. This moved me even more than the bands.

To Moms's gratification I was proving to be a better than average scholar, and, surprisingly, was awarded a gold medal for excellence in Mathematics, which I only half deserved. Plane Geometry I could picture but Algebra still gave me trouble. Kate Bovée, whom Shirley said was as tough as a Marine sergeant, was giving those of us who worked for it a sound preparation for the College Board Examinations which lay ahead. The same could not be said for my prowess at dancing school. I had a prolonged adolescent shyness with girls, and no interest in either music or dancing.

Mr. Dodsworth's Dancing School was held in a rather large old-fashioned brownstone house in the 40s and was attended by about forty boys and girls equally divided. In our blue serge suits and shining patent leather pumps we entered the large ballroom with its dangerously slippery parquet floor. The room was surrounded by a banquette on one side of which sat the girls, trying to look as appealing as possible. On the other side sat the boys, dejected and not happy at the prospect. Mr. Dodsworth, a stiff and correct gentleman, with white hair, white tie, white gloves, and a very precise attitude, was the Master of Ceremonies. He demonstrated what we were to do and punctuated his commands with a castanet whose sharp sound I have never forgotten. Mrs. Dodsworth, always dressed in pink satin, was seated on a sort of throne; the girls curtsied to her as they entered and we followed, ducking our heads in a bow. At the piano was an inconspicuous little woman who accompanied Mr. Dodsworth with loud emphasis.

When we were all seated, he with a sharp click, called us out on the floor in facing lines, to stand with our feet placed precisely on the squares in the parquet, very erect. Then we began the warmup—"Advance right foot," "Advance left foot," then two-steps to each side, as the piano indicated. Among the boys were three or four talented dancers and the rest of us ranged from apathy to rebellion. We carried our pumps in green beige bags and the rebels' favorite stunt was to mix up our street shoes, while we were making our entrance, which gave us a long time to untangle.

The girls were generally attractive, most of them good

dancers, and there was one, Marian Grey, who was willing to put up with my awkwardness. They appeared to enjoy dancing; it was their partners who were disappointing. I was not among the talented performers, and as I was slow and nearsighted I usually got one of the leftovers when Mr. Dodsworth announced, "The young gentlemen will please take partners for . . . ," and we would all rush to the girls.

The waltz was Mr. Dodsworth's favorite and our preliminary exercises led up to a trial run. My trouble was that I could not reverse—I still can't—and as "The Blue Danube" went on and on I grew dizzy and had to clutch my partners for balance as other couples whirled by me in a blur—until the castanet slowed them down. Mr. Dodsworth did not teach us the polka; he thought it a folk dance and not worthy. So we waltzed first and last, and in between we did a miscellaneous dance called the "fox-trot" which I could handle, though not well enough to be useful at Harvard.

"The Knickerbocker Greys" was another traditional organization in the Gilded Age. Formed in 1861 to instill leadership in the younger generation, "the Greys" numbered about a hundred boys (age eight to fifteen) who assembled two afternoons a week during the winter in the Seventh Regiment Armory, a huge, cold drill hall on Park Avenue and 66th Street. When I joined in 1917 the patriotic fervor made us take the drilling more seriously.

We—or rather I should say, *our* cadet officers, wore uniforms modeled on the dress uniform at West Point, with white plumes in their hats, and they carried swords. The privates, of which I was one, wore shorts and knee-length black stockings and were armed with guns.

We were commanded by an old regular, a lieutenant of infantry, long retired; he graded us on our carriage and precision, and we all yearned to be promoted. But I couldn't see much in the Armory's bleak, gray interior; I was frequently out of step and rarely managed to execute those crisp military turns which are expected of the end of the line. The only orders I fulfilled without correction were "Right face," "Left face," and "Present arms." My contemporaries who enrolled with me were all promoted to sergeants or lieutenants but it took me three years to make lance-corporal—even Shirley, who entered after I did, eventually outranked me. I was not the military type. My father, in his day, had been a lieutenant in the Seventh Regiment. It depressed me to be so awkward. When we paraded for our parents I with my corporal stripes, brought up the rear.

That summer, Moms's friends, Mrs. Josephine Potter, and Mrs. John D. Rockefeller, Jr., persuaded her to take a cottage at Northeast Harbor, Maine, where the sea is less tame than on the North Shore, and for the rest of my life this was to be my magic isle. The water is even more forbiddingly cold than that at Singing Beach, so when we swam it was in a sun-warmed pool. An exciting event for me was the presence in the harbor of a Curtis flying boat whose pilot took passengers for a joy ride at $5 a flight. I pleaded to go but Moms, backed by Nan, was adamant, and I had to be satisfied, watching it take off and disappear down the coast, and rowing around it in the harbor when no one was aboard.

Every afternoon in fair weather we went fishing with Captain Spurling, a native with a keen sense of humor. The water was alive with cod and in his motorboat we'd be on our way by two in the afternoon, heading for the fishing grounds off Baker's Island. There was no room for Nan but mother came and used a handline as avidly as Shirley and I. We would return about six, never empty-handed, and once we brought in two thirty-five-pounders, which we sold on the dock for a penny a pound. We were also learning to sail in the fifteen-foot, one-design of which Captain Spurling had a poor opinion. "Trouble with sailin'," he used to say. "Yuh can neither set, stand or lay." In Maine I learned to respect the power of the sea and the glory of being on the water in fair weather.

At "Uplands" we had a long, straight drive, and I persuaded Moms that I could be trusted with a Briggs and Stratton Buckboard, known as "The Red Bug," low-slung, made of wood and propelled by a single cylinder motor wheel. There were two seats, a steering wheel and primitive brakes. It weighed 105 pounds and you started it by pushing it down a slope and jumping in. Power was provided by a fifth wheel at the back and there was a lever by which one could raise this rear wheel and still keep the engine running during brief stops. It was my *first motor car*, and to me endlessly fascinating. With the assistance of our new chauffeur, Flaherty, six-foot four, a good mechanic but a terrible driver, the "Red Bug" was transformed into a machine powered by *two* motor wheels; with that improvement I could get up to 20 m.p.h., and I no longer confined myself to the home drive. Unfortunately, one fine summer day I lost control of the vehicle which ran away from me while I was pushing it from behind near the E. N. Potter place. It dashed to the left, went over a small stone bridge, fell into a brook, and was destroyed. With the carelessness of a rich boy, I left the wreck where it was to be picked up by Flaherty later.

To console me for the loss of the "Red Bug," Moms bought a Briggs and Stratton Motor "Scooter" which I rode with delight at Mt. Kisco. The "Scooter" was a two-wheel machine, the rear wheel equipped with power, a one-horsepower, air-cooled engine. I went around the corners of our bluestone drive at the absolute limit of adhesion, about 25 m.p.h., careful to keep in the concrete gutters and with the feeling that I was a young Dario Resta.

The year I graduated from Bovée was fortuitous. At fourteen I was the tallest boy in my class, one of the top ten in my grades, and, greatly to my relief, any thought of going on to Groton, my father's school, had been dismissed firmly by my mother. That autumn I entered Browning's Preparatory School in New York. There is always some trepidation in facing a new pecking order but I got over this quickly by being appointed editor of the school paper, *The Browning Buzzer*. How this happened I have forgotten, perhaps because of my familiarity with English fiction, thanks to Moms's reading aloud. Once in office I found that the burden of filling the paper fell almost entirely on me. I wrote short stories, anonymously, one of them placed in Italy (which I had, of course, never seen), editorials promising a banner year and essays on the Parents' League or "The Automat: Notes Taken in a Restaurant." I worked hard at improving the *Buzzer* and in so doing gained in self-confidence. My method of operation has always been never to do anything that I could effectively delegate to others, but it took me most of that year to find the few who could write effectively—and in view of my performance they elected me editor for another year.

Our science teacher, Mr. Moore, for the first time gave me an understanding of how the physical forces in our world work. He showed us the predictable results of practical, very simple physical experiments: the effect of magnetic force on iron filings, how the human eye and artificial lenses work, why an artesian well is productive, and a hundred other engrossing, practical experiments. He was a New Englander who chewed tobacco and occasionally would open the window and eject a stream of tobacco juice but we didn't laugh because of the clarity with which he aroused and answered our curiosity about physics.

With my head start, English gave me no trouble and, perhaps out of respect for the *Buzzer*, I got an "A." The regret, which I was not to realize till later was that Moms who spoke French so fluently when she was directing a maid or a waiter in Paris, never tested me at home, never tried to hear if I was acquiring a good accent, simply left me alone, struggling to conjugate those damned irregular verbs. She never imagined that I might become an ambassador or involved in international affairs.

There are strategies for those about to take College Board Examinations as Browning's was well aware. First, the student must not be rattled by the printed questions on the exam; the wording may seem tricky and complicated and the untutored will glower at it while precious time passes. But the real meaning is there: they want you to put out what you know of the subject in hand, and to familiarize us with the intent of the wording our teachers had us work through old exams of preceding years until we had lost our dread. We took the examinations at Columbia University; there were only a few of us pointing for Harvard, and my friend, Dick Tucker and I, passed our first five subjects in the spring of 1921 with no trouble. I received 99% in English; 97% in Physics.

We returned to Northeast Harbor, to a more attractive cottage known as "The Barnacles" which we were to rent for several years. Dick Tucker and Jack Degener, my classmates at Browning's came up for visits. I took them to the dances at the Kimball House, on picnics on one of the Friendship Sloops and introduced them to John and Nelson Rockefeller. I was beginning to realize that girls had their points. Sally Henry of

Philadelphia at one dance corralled me in a corner and said, "Now, Bill, you've really got to get the hang of this. It isn't so hard; let me show you," after which I felt a little more competent in the fox-trot. When we paired off in those pre-Scott Fitzgerald days the petting was restrained and the talk was always of the future, what college we were going to, and whom we were going to room with. Dick Tucker had asked me to room with him and I was eager to, but Moms had misgivings about my entering Harvard at sixteen.

That winter she had a good talk with Mr. Jones, Browning's headmaster, who agreed that although I was certain to pass the final examinations it would be more sensible for me to wait a year. I was sorry to miss rooming with Dick but I did not object; there would be free time for reading and I had hopes of getting a secondhand Ford.

I remember that summer of 1922 because of my discovery of Tolstoy. I became immersed in *War and Peace* and went on to *Anna Karenina*. When Mrs. Potter saw me on our porch with *War and Peace* on my lap, she exclaimed to Moms, "My God, I can't even get 'Beau' to read the funny papers!" At that time there were two literary figures on Mount Desert: Mary Roberts Rinehart and Arthur Train, the lawyer and short story writer, whose daughter, "Chou-Chou," was a hot number. Sally Henry was as attractive as ever, and at Bar Harbor the two Byrne sisters were beauties: Helen, the older, who was to marry Walter Lippmann, and Phyllis, who was temperamentally a gypsy. They were the daughters of James Byrne, a brilliant New York lawyer, and the chief counsel for General Motors. He was approachable and smiled at my passion for automobiles.

I had a new Eyemo movie camera and Shirley was as fascinated by it as I was. Together we planned a melodrama. We picked the girls we thought could act—Louise Ireland, who was creative and Barbara Schieffelin—we made up scenes as we went along, most of them staged on the cliff from which Annette Kellerman had once made her famous dive. This was Shirley's first venture in a field in which he was ultimately to make his reputation.

In mid-summer we went for a fortnight to Newport where our days at Grandma Twombly's "Vinland" were happy ones. On earlier visits we were tied to Nan's apron strings, now we were on our own, and for the first time Aunt Ruth took a personal interest in me and taught me to drive her Mercedes runabout! She made me practice changing gears in the driveway and when I soon acquired confidence we went out into traffic, she sitting beside me, with a reassuring smile for the cops who all knew her. I never drove alone that summer and when I put a heavy foot on the accelerator—I once got us up to 70—she would say, "Aren't you going a little fast?"

Newport in the 1920s was in its heyday as the most stylish summer resort in America. From the Public Beach to Bailey's Beach ran a two-mile promenade known as Cliff Walk, built on the breakwater above the rocks where in fair weather sightseers would stroll past, gazing at the fashionable "cottages" as the big mansions were called, which were set well back and facing the sea. "Vinland" was not as large as the (gloomy) Italianate villa of the William Vanderbilts; it was modeled on "le petit chalet" of Marie Antoinette's in the Loire, and because of Grandma's love of entertaining, for two months each summer it was certainly one of the most popular "cottages" in Newport.

At sixteen I rarely noticed architecture. "Vinland" with its fifty rooms was an attractive "cottage" and I was impressed by the stained glass windows on the stairway, depicting the Vikings and their long ships, which deflected the sunlight from the main hall. What I more distinctly recall are the flowers, the huge bed of yellow canna with a six-foot Etruscan vase in the center of the drive, and to the right of the porch the beautiful rose garden. Grandma's preference was for formal dinner parties, of thirty-four guests, and if anyone gave out at the last moment a footman would be on the telephone, requesting one of the "extras" to fill in.

The table had to be full and, thanks to Donon's magic, it usually was. In early morning Aunt Ruth conferred with him about the menu, which would be written in French and displayed on the table, and she selected the wine. Hibiscus, apricot and white, was invariably the decoration, and there would be a large gardenia in each finger bowl, with a drop of dew on the petal.

There was intense rivalry between Frasier, the gardener at "Vinland" and Tyson at "Florham." Both were Scots but Frasier grew the finer Muscat grapes and his Persian melons were so much larger (and jucier) that one was enough for eight servings. Perhaps it was the sea air but whatever the secret Frazier would gloat but never tell.

My routine was to drive to the Casino with Aunt Ruth if she had a tennis match, there I might take a lesson or rally with Jimmy Van Alen, who was my age but a far better player. For a change he tried to teach me cricket but we both gave that up in disgust. Then after eleven we would pick up Shirley on the way to Bailey's Beach where we were learning to swim. Aunt Ruth had knocked three bathhouses together to form a very popular pavilion. But I noticed how she shied away from publicity; there was usually a photographer hanging around waiting to take a picture. She told him firmly not to take her—and he obeyed.

"Tennis Week" marked the height of the season. The Invi-

tation Tournament which had been suspended during the
war was again a national attraction and we were part of the
big gallery that watched "Little Bill" Johnston win the singles.
On the Friday night before the Finals Mrs. Stuart Duncan
gave a dance for five hundred guests which lasted until dawn,
and on Saturday night Grandma had a dinner party for sixty
and they all went on to dance at Dr. Hamilton Rice's, whose
parquet floor was famous.

I, of course, wasn't even on the fringe of this yet, but I liked
to hear Aunt Ruth tell about it to Moms. Shirley and I had
our private amusement in the afternoon when, out of Nan's
sight, we caught blue crabs in the coves, using meat for bait
and a long-handled net. We'd finish up with strawberry ice
cream sodas at Loran's, one was enough for me but he sometimes liked a second.

Shirley was not happy without a little teasing. The hairdresser rode up to do Grandma's hair, and when she had finished her bike had disappeared. When Shirley brought it back
from his ride, there was hell to pay. Moms listened to Grandma's scolding until she could stand no more. "Mother," she
said, "if you really think your hairdresser is of more importance than my children, we can leave for home tomorrow!"

The prospect of marking time for a year, free from academic routine, and to read or drive as I pleased, was inviting.
In the early autumn Moms and I began to take walks on the
country roads, eight miles at a clip or more. We talked about
Harvard and for the first time she expressed her wish that I
avoid smoking and drinking until I was twenty-one. I nodded
sympathetically. To please her I also resumed riding at Mt.
Kisco, but one morning as I was backing my mare at the end
of a narrow lane her hindquarters simply disappeared into an
abandoned well that was concealed by the dense blackberry
bushes. I had the sense to climb up the horse's neck and

stepped out of the stirrups. She had no room to thrash around and when men from the garage hoisted her out with a derrick and heavy straps only her hind legs were skinned. But this freak accident put an end to my limited enthusiasm for riding.

The new garage, which was just being finished, started me dreaming: it was roomy enough for ten cars and had a pit over which a car could be placed when there was need for repairs from below. (The hydraulic lift had not yet been invented.) In it would be Moms's Phantom II Rolls-Royce town car, with a Brewster body painted green, and her Crane-Simplex limousine with a gray green Brewster body. I wondered how soon there would be one of mine.

That fall Dick Tucker invited me to Cambridge for the weekend of the Harvard-Princeton game. He roomed on Mt. Auburn Street, known as "the Gold Coast," because of the expensive dormitories and the clubs nearby. The excitement began to mount Friday night at the Copley Plaza ball, which was crowded with debutantes, undergraduates and alumni. Despite Prohibition there was plenty of hard liquor, cocktails before dinner and from flasks at the party later. Dick was drinking the hard stuff but I didn't touch it. Nor had I the confidence to dance with anyone. Despite Dick's repeated urging, I stood in the stag line watching until 4 a.m.

Saturday morning Harvard Square was thronged and by noon the crowd carrying steamer rugs began to flow toward the stadium. I sat with Dick in the cheering section and was treated to a close, magnificent game—only the second I had ever seen. The teams were even and I joined in the shouting in the tense fourth quarter. In the evening we went to another party at the Copley Plaza, where I recognized a few of the girls but still hadn't the nerve to dance with them. Just stood there again with the stags.

Sunday morning I felt seedy. Flaherty, our very tall chauffeur, had driven me up to the game in the Crane-Simplex and I thought he drove too fast for a man who lacked intuitive control of the car. On our way back to Mt. Kisco, at the top of a hill on the narrow Boston Post Road the car went into a long skid which ended as we slithered sideways to the bottom. On our drives to New York together he often let me take the wheel until we reached the Grand Central Parkway, but I didn't ask to now because I was edgy from lack of sleep and aware of a rather sharp pain in my side.

When we reached "Uplands" I told Moms who stuck a thermometer in my mouth, she found I had a fever and telephoned for Dr. Chapman, our local doctor. When he heard that I had been to Cambridge he probably assumed I had drunk too much homemade gin; he did not seem alarmed, simply ordered me to stay in bed, and there I remained till the following Sunday, the pain growing intense and my fever rising to 103°. Moms, worried and incensed, telephoned Dr. Robert Blake, the famous surgeon, who drove out immediately in his open Rolls, and I remember the ice on his moustache as he bent over to examine me. He decided to operate at once in the Mt. Kisco hospital. As he feared, the appendix had burst, peritonitis had set in, and my recuperation was slow and painful. This was not exactly the layoff I had imagined.

I was still recuperating when in the early morning of December 13th "Uplands" was shaken by a terrific explosion. Healy, the houseman (I had warned Moms that he was a half-wit), had stoked our two large furnaces to cherry heat, the water in the boilers had almost evaporated and as Healy thoughtlessly turned on the cold water the boilers erupted. The furious explosion killed our two gardeners who were in the cellar; it tore open the floor of Moms's office where she kept her accounts, blew out the windows and destroyed her desk and much of the interior. Nan said in her sepulchral voice, "Had she been sitting there, she'd have been a bundle of bloody rags."

Since we had to be evacuated immediately Moms moved us into a suite at the St. Regis Hotel, where I could be waited on while she took time to open our apartment at 1028 Fifth Avenue. We stayed on for Christmas and there, in this unpredictable year, Moms herself came down with appendicitis—it was a fashionable ailment at that time—and was operated on at St. Luke's Hospital. As I was now fully recovered I became the man of the family: I deposited a check for $2,000 she had given me, and paid the domestic staff at "Uplands" and the farm and garden personnel, surprised how much more expensive our life was than I had imagined. Going to and from the hospital I would stop by Grandma Twombly's to take messages or to report, and I remember one Sunday afternoon about 3:30 being amazed to find Aunt Ruth still in bed, with puffs under her eyes, and the appearance of what I had begun to recognize in Cambridge as a hangover. Up until that moment I had no suspicion that she was a heavy drinker. Could this be why Moms shunned alcohol? Conspicuous on my aunt's bureau was the photograph of a good-looking American officer in uniform. I had not noticed it before but a little later thought I recognized the same person in civilian dress, waiting for her in the drawing room. Of course I knew that Aunt Ruth had her beaux—Charlie Draper was one I liked— but I wondered about this stranger.

My Christmas present from Aunt Ruth was a two volume diary, bound in leather, with a key to open the lock of each. I began keeping it the day after New Year's and the key suggested that I be candid. On January 20th the entry begins: "Aunt Ruth calls for me at 9 to go out to 'Florham.' The

river was full of ice and very pretty. The *Olympic* was getting
up steam to sail at 10. Had a fine trip out over farm roads. The
country was covered with snow. Went to the tennis court
which was getting on slowly. . . ." Like most beginning diarists
I left out what was important. This was my first view of Aunt
Ruth's dearest project, which she modestly called "the Playhouse," though it was much more than that. She told McKim,
Mead and White that she wanted it built in keeping with
"Florham," the same rose brick and columned portico, and
spacious enough for the entertainment of her friends on winter
weekends. Tennis had always meant more to her than bridge
but no indoor court had been available in the city. Now she
intended to have the best, with twice the amount of space behind the base line and along the side lines. A glass roof sixty
feet high, so there would be no interference, and the surface a
special type of sand, extremely fast if watered twice a day.

Aunt Ruth showed me proudly through the interior which
was still being worked on. There was a paneled sitting-room
for the ladies with an open fire—the Chippendale furniture
and bridge tables still to come. Lockers, showers, and a passage leading to the large, heated pool, seventy by thirty feet,
surrounded by a marble floor. "Our one mistake," she said,
"when wet, it's so slippery you can break a leg. That's why
we have those mats." In the men's dressing rooms there were
electric heating cabinets for those seeking a rubdown. She had
signed up a Swedish masseur, and a capable English barman
named Woods, to serve drinks or a light lunch in the kitchen
behind the bar. She hadn't missed a thing and I felt pleased
she had taken me into her confidence.

My diary resumes: "After lunch we went for a sleigh ride in
the double cutter. It was great fun. We took 'Top' along and
drove down to the farm to see 'Torywater Warrior,' the fa-

mous Guernsey bull and some of the fine cows. Motored back to town arriving at dusk. Was most impressed by the immensity of the place. Moms was feeling well when I got home."

For her recuperation Moms wanted to go to California and the matter was settled by a long-distance call in January from our good friends, the Peter Cooper Brices in Santa Barbara, urging that we stay at "El Mirasol," a comfortable small hotel serving delicious food, where we could have a bungalow to ourselves. As the repairs at "Uplands" were far from complete it seemed an attractive solution.

We should be gone probably for two months but neither Moms nor Shirley considered this a serious setback to his schooling. He had left Bovée—"When June came," as he said of his exit, "Kate sort of looked away for a second and when she turned again, I was gone." Then it fell to Moms to talk him into Browning's. Mr. Jones, the headmaster, little realized what he was in for. He asked Moms about Shirley's "scholastic background" and she dodged by reminding him how much I had enjoyed Browning's and she was confident Shirley would enjoy it as thoroughly as I had. To his dismay he was accepted.

How can you teach a boy who can't—or won't read? There was one master who would not let up on him. To even the score Shirley devised a water pistol using an atomizer from which he removed the spray nozzle. To demonstrate its power to the class he aimed it at the door just as the teacher was entering, and fired. The drenching nearly resulted in expulsion. To restore order Shirley and one other laggard, Eric Wood, were seated directly outside the headmaster's office under the eye of an apprentice teacher. Now a change of scene Moms thought would cool the situation.

Before we left for California, Scott, the gardener, and I selected twenty varieties of giant Darwin tulips to be planted in the walled Italian garden at "Uplands." When we returned in early May the tulip beds, all one thousand bulbs were in bloom, great swatches of scarlet, yellow, white, lavender, and black. (For this I got no thanks from Moms who, oddly, wasn't particular about flowers.)

For our trip on the Southern Pacific we had all the compartments in the observation car to ourselves. Moms bought each of us cameras, mine a 3½ by 4½ Graflex, Shirley's the next size smaller, and they were certainly an insurance against boredom on the long haul from Chicago. It might have occurred to a bookworm like myself that a short history of California would sharpen our interest in what we were to see. But I made no such effort; what impressed me was the vastness of the prairies, and I spent hours and many rolls of film taking prosaic pictures of Kansas wheatfields, of Indians selling turquoise bracelets at our stops in Arizona and of our waiter serving us fresh trout that had just been taken aboard. As the weather became warmer we rode outside but unless one needs sleep as Moms did, four days, even on a crack train, can become a bore.

In the soft air and dazzling sunlight of Santa Barbara we all relaxed. One of the most exciting things to Shirley and me, accustomed to gray tones of winter, were the masses of semitropical vegetation, golden acacias, bougainvillea, poinsettias, orange and lemon trees laden with fruit, the rows of almond trees now in blossom, wisteria and mimosa. The low buildings were of pale ivory stucco with red tile roofs with striped awnings for the shoppers in the marketplace. When we needed exercise I played tennis with Shirley, beating him so badly, 6-1, 6-0, that he quit. He said my forehand would knock the teeth out of an elephant. (He got even a year later by challenging me at dusk, trimming me as he pleased.) Our bungalow at "El Mirasol," was pleasant enough and from it we set forth to see the old Spanish missions in an open Cadillac, driven by a dismal young man who knew nothing and seemed to care less about California. We went on to the Yosemite and then to the famous grove of sequoias, whose height and age awed me. I continued to photograph like mad, stopping the car continually as I shot from twenty-five to thirty pictures a day, which must have tried the patience of Moms and Shirley.

According to my diary there were three high points in our stay. First, the time I spent on the polo field at Santa Barbara where a barnstorming pilot kept a J.N. IV biplane, a "Jennie," in which he took passengers up for short joy rides. I was forbidden to go so made it my duty to photograph this fascinating machine on the ground and from every angle.

The three of us watched an exciting automobile race at the new Beverly Hills race track under a blue, cloudless sky. Everything was colorful—the brand new wooden track with highly banked corners which the drivers took at full speed; the cars, brilliantly painted in scarlet, bright blue and yellow, and the large crowd in light clothes. The track was 2½ miles in length and the race was for a hundred laps—250 miles. The cars were American built, all Millers and Duesenbergs, with a piston displacement limit of two litres (122.04 cubic inches). Consequently they were very small.

The best American drivers participated—Jimmy Murphy (later the first American to win the twenty-four-hour LeMans road race in France with his Duesenberg which had very efficient four-wheel hydraulic brakes); Ralph DePalma, who won the Indianapolis 500 twice (once in a Mercedes), Jim Hill and Harry Hartz.

From the start these four drivers stuck together for a long time until Hartz dropped out with engine trouble; then DePalma blew a tire, and Murphy finished first only six feet in front of Hill,—remarkably close for a 250 mile race. The average for the 250 miles was 115.8 miles per hour, a new world's record for the distance. All records from 50 to 250 miles were broken —a fine race. Afterwards on the way out we were caught in a jam of spectators in a narrow tunnel, and some of them started to panic. With my height I saw what was happening, and I shouted, "Take it easy! Take it easy!" which surprisingly quieted them down.

Although I did not realize it Shirley was movie struck and what was uppermost in his mind was to meet Douglas Fairbanks and Mary Pickford. Our friends, the Brices, knew the Fairbanks well and arranged for us to visit the United Artists Studio where Douglas was shooting "The Gaucho" with Lupe Velez. When he wasn't busy he told us about the pictures he had made and actually performed some of the stunts for which he was famous. We went on to the Universal Studio where Lon Chaney was starring in "The Hunchback of Notre Dame." We were entranced by the set, an enormous castle with a formidable gate and portcullis. As we watched, the massive drawbridge was slowly lowered, the portcullis raised, and beneath the great arch emerged the small figure of Charlie Chaplin. With happy unconcern he picked up a milk bottle and put out the cat.

Neither Moms nor I appreciated the magnetic effect of all this on Shirley. What I brought back after our six weeks in California was my huge assortment of photographs and my secret desire some day to own a Duesenberg. What Shirley retained was more significant. Here was a place of everlasting sunlight and beauty, a fabulous industry, and people who didn't bother whether you could read or not.

I was always deep in books and had become a fast reader.

On our train ride to New York from Mt. Kisco, of an hour and a quarter, I skimmed through two hundred pages of Boswell's *Journey to the Hebrides*. On this trip beginning with *Soldiers Three* and *The Light That Failed*, I had been reading a good deal of Kipling, and in Los Angeles I ordered a complete set of his works and one of Robert Louis Stevenson's, to be bound in three quarters Levant, at $495 a set. The volumes followed me home as an expensive postscript.

Miraculously on our return home, I began to see the world clearly for the first time. All through our Western trip my frantic photography had been complicated by blurred vision. My glasses were so inadequate I began to wonder if I were going blind. Our family ophthalmologist, old Dr. Cutler, whom I had tricked by memorizing the charts, had retired at the age of ninety-three and young Dr. Krug, who had taken over his practice, was a no nonsense guy. He listened to my confession, then fitted some trial lenses on the frame; the numbers on the chart suddenly sprang at me and he burst into laughter. He said they suited me to a T. "Have your oculist follow these directions," and I was out of his office in ten minutes. Flaherty drove me to town to get the new spectacles and I had them on as I got back into the front seat of the car. Glancing up at the rearview mirror, I exclaimed, "My God, is that the way I look!"

I became conscious of the beauty I had been missing in Mt. Kisco as Moms and I resumed our long walks. She reminded me of how fortunate it was for her and for me that Cousin John Hammond had urged Grandma to make the large gifts to her daughters before the inheritance tax took effect. Moms said she was giving me an allowance of $25,000 at Harvard. She would take care of the tuition, and my room. Later, on another eight mile hike to Lake Byram and back, she said, as she had earlier, "Bill, I know you don't drink—and I hope you won't until you're older. I'd like to set up a prize of $1,000 if you promise not to smoke or drink until you're twenty-one. Will you try?" Well, I hadn't been strongly tempted yet, so again I nodded. But after that promised allowance I wondered if a prize of $1,000 would really keep me away from temptation.

In New York, before I went to Harvard, I used to haunt the agencies of the best European automobiles: Rolls-Royce (in which I was never much interested); Isotta-Fraschini, who built a beautiful runabout for Rudolph Valentino with a silver cobra on the radiator cap; Mercedes and Benz, which at that time were separate companies; and Minerva, a beautiful car but unfortunately with a sleeve valve engine which was never very reliable at high speeds.

All these agencies were generous in giving demonstrations, and I would ask if a representative would take me in one of their cars to the Long Island Motor Parkway, which was in part the old road built for the Vanderbilt Cup Races. It was thirty-five miles long from the start at Mineola to Lake Ronkonkoma. There was no speed limit and the corners were banked. The road was quite adequate for the speeds of that day (the best sportcars could make 100–120 m.p.h.) and it was thrilling to drive from one end to the other, and back again, particularly in the winter, in the sharp winds. Whenever a car would fail to complete the course satisfactorily (the Minerva, for example, froze up after a few miles) the salesman would naturally be embarrassed. In the Parkway I usually did the driving with him riding alongside. This was an initiation, which prepared me for the joyous time in France when I watched the European Grand Prix at Lyon in 1924.

"Beau" Potter, the son of Moms's close friend, wandered

"Florham"

Lindsay, Shirley, Oscar and I at Coolidge Point

The Playhouse at "Florham"

Aunt Ruth

over on his first day home on summer vacation and began boasting about a secondhand Ford which he had stripped down; he thought he could get it up to eighty-five miles an hour. "Maybe," I said, in disbelief and with the suspicion he wanted to sell it to me. No sale. But if he could soup one up, so could I and at a favorable moment I confided to Moms my plan to buy an old Ford, remove the body and convert it into a two-seater. She seemed noncommittal. But the following day after breakfast she said, "Come, I want to show you something." Flaherty drove us down into the village and we parked beside the Cadillac agency. On the floor of the showroom was a single beauty, a gray-green V-8 touring car. "That's for you," she said, "I bought it yesterday." I had a license now and I drove it every day with bliss, and as fast as possible. My new glasses reinforced my feeling of confidence; I knew I was a good driver and I enjoyed racing "Beau" Potter in his cut-down Ford and leaving him far behind. On one trial as we approached a narrow corner side by side at accelerating speed we encountered a limousine filled with the Elder Generation —including Cousin John Hammond. We avoided a catastrophe but that afternoon they visited Moms and stated sternly that such wild driving had to stop at once. Moms was courteous—"Thank you very much. I am responsible for my son's driving," and she served them iced tea.

That summer I saw a lot of Freddy Davies who visited us at Northeast. I first met him—he was always called Freddy, not Fred—in New York when I was about nine. Mrs. Davies was an acquaintance of Moms and Mr. Davies—who died young —had known my father and been a close friend of Alfred Gwynne Vanderbilt. Freddy was a warm, amiable, attractive boy with a great sense of fun. When he was at boarding school I saw less of him but we always got together in vacation. I was a class ahead of him and when my admission to Harvard was postponed we happily agreed to room together. By now he was six feet one and a half inches tall, well dressed, a beautiful dancer and susceptible to girls. I saw him through a series of infatuations, serious on his part, though he never seemed to progress beyond a point.

My arrival at Harvard two weeks before college opened was made miserable for me by my mother's and Shirley's presence at the Copley Plaza in Boston, determined to help me prepare our rooms. Moms still regarded me as her ewe lamb whom she was hurling into the evil flames of Harvard (and in a way she was) and she was very reluctant to let me go. James Smith Hall, now part of Kirkland House, had an imposing red brick exterior but was dingy within. Hence the last-minute ritual of buying furniture.

The problem was this: our suite—two bedrooms and sitting room—had minimal furniture provided by the college: a couple of uncomfortable iron cots, two battered desks and two resistant wooden chairs, no curtains, a beat-up carpet. Together we bought some medium priced dowdy copies of antiques, a stuffed sofa, arm chairs, new carpets, curtains, etc.—still in the dark brown shade which my mother loved so dearly. (What was done was plushy enough to stamp me as "different" in what was a conformist society.) But before they were installed Moms borrowed a bucket and brushes from the janitor and she and Shirley were on their knees scrubbing the floor, to my mortification. I walked out hoping no one would look in as the new stuff was arranged in the room by my brother and Moms. Freddy had sense enough to absent himself too until the job was done.

The day after my family departed was a Sunday and I remember the joyous independence with which Freddy and I decided that we would not go to chapel—not only *that* Sunday but *any* Sunday in the future—*ever*. This was a sharp break with my past as I had diligently recorded the titles of the sermons in my diary all summer. I had attended St. Thomas's regularly, gone to Bible Class, been confirmed—and now rebelled!

Since we were not going to church we took the next step of independence by renting a Model T closed Ford (Freshmen were not allowed cars) from the Harvard Square Garage. It was a glorious fall day. We drove into the country to a wooded embankment, had a most innocent nonalcoholic picnic lunch; photographed each other with my French Sept movie camera (film now lost); and returned to Cambridge, childishly happy.

CHAPTER III

Harvard College

I entered Harvard eager and innocent, without a father or grandfather to advise me; a teetotaler, sexually inexperienced, a non-athlete and uninformed by the bull sessions which prep those in boarding schools. I had an extravagant allowance but no intention of throwing it around. I wanted to make a place for myself and I intended to do well scholastically.

The first meeting with my faculty adviser, Dean David Little, took place in the granite severity of University Hall and could not have been more cordial. He explained that the college divided one's courses between the subject in which one wished "to Concentrate"—English literature was unquestionably mine—and those courses in "Distribution" which covered a wide range. For the Freshman year the choice was limited: one had to choose between Economics A and History I, from Charlemagne to the Versailles Peace Treaty (the Dean highly recommended the latter because of the brilliant lectures by Professor "Frisky" Merriman); a foreign language, and as I had passed my French for admission, I elected German, and the third obligation, English "A" which called for a theme a week. When I told him that I had edited the *Browning Buzzer* for two years he said I might be exempt from that course by mid-years. For my fourth course I thought I ought to know something about government, so I chose Government 2, taught by Professor William B. Munro.

Within a fortnight Dean Little invited me to have supper with his charming wife "Hengie." There were two or three other Freshmen present; Mrs. Little's cooking was delicious and afterwards we sat talking, well-fed and relaxed. Unhappily the Dean had trouble with his eyes and was compelled to retire in the spring. I felt it as a personal loss and I was not the only one who was never to have as sympathetic an adviser.

Dick Tucker, the Sophomore with whom I might have roomed, looked me up that first week, when Freddy happened to be out of the room, and we had a good talk. He commented on my "swell" furniture, and went on to speak about the Final Clubs. He told me that his father and uncle had both been members of the Porcellian; he was what was called a "legacy" and he hoped to be elected before Christmas. If he was he said he would do his best to get me in next year. "Thank you, very much, Dick," I said, "but my father and grandfather were both in the A.D. and that's where I'd like to go."

Early in September the *Harvard Crimson* published a call for candidates for the manager of Freshman football. The manager of the varsity in his senior year earned his "H" and was one of the most respected men in his class, and I decided to give it a try. In sneakers, old pants and a T-shirt I reported to the Field House right after lunch, one of forty classmates eager to make themselves conspicuously useful during practice; we fielded balls for the punters and place kickers, threw passes, tended the water buckets and sorted out the jocks and sweaty uniforms for the drying rooms, menial chores imbued with team spirit as one came to be recognized by prominent players on the squad. Knees and ankles are the early injuries and I helped a couple of the limping wounded to the sidelines;

this may have brought me to the attention of the team physicians, Doctor Nichols and Doctor Richards, his assistant, for after the first cut I was assigned to their office. Dr. Nichols, about to perform a sudden operation, told me to sterilize the instruments, and, never having done so before, I put them into the sterilizer without removing the cellophane covers; I realized something was wrong when I received a swift kick in the pants from the irritated surgeon. Thus ended my candidacy on Soldiers' Field.

Of course I felt chagrined. Until I was cut I had not realized how much I enjoyed the sweaty experience of being a handyman to the squad. It had rubbed off some of my shyness. It had also caused me to miss the opening of Aunt Ruth's "Playhouse" on October 12, 1923, a Saturday when both the Harvard varsity and Freshmen had games. That was the largest bash ever given at "Florham," as mother and Shirley kept reminding me when I came home for Christmas. Six hundred guests were invited, many from out-of-town being put up at the neighboring estates in Morristown and Bernardsville. There was a mixed doubles tournament in the afternoon on the new court, which was very fast, and as it was a perfect day, many went swimming in the big pool with the impeccable John and his assistants serving drinks. Then after the dinner parties the guests returned to dance in a big marquee and to enjoy the champagne and the buffet which were served until 3 a.m. Donon outdid himself, and as the "Playhouse" was four hundred yards from "Florham" his hot dishes, the delicacies and ices were continually replenished by two station wagons, shuttling back and forth. With "Florham" blazing with lights, an excellent orchestra and a full moon it must have been a night to remember.

Sunday morning Aunt Ruth said to Donon, "I don't see how you did it. I could never imagine such perfection," and she gave him a purse of $20 gold pieces. That afternoon the finals of the tennis tournament took place, and the cups presented to the winners. I wish I had been there.

Institutional food soon begins to pall and by October the meals in James Smith Hall seemed to me tasteless, and often lukewarm. It was said that a wealthy graduate had endowed our dormitory with a legacy to provide two servings of ice cream a week and, true or not, it was the only dish we looked forward to. We had to pay for our meals but were not compelled to eat them. When the menu became unbearable Freddy and I would head for the Georgian Cafeteria where the rare roast beef and hot corn bread were a change.

Besides, I had an advantage, thanks to my father's friends, Peter Higginson and John Saltonstall, who invited me down to their country places on the North Shore for Sunday dinner, so I hired a Ford and drove the thirty miles with anticipation. I was offered sherry but declined; what delighted me was the charm and spaciousness of the houses, you were offered second helpings and the questions about college were informed and encouraging. Harvard's proximity to Boston and its suburbs gives one the chance to enjoy a familiar atmosphere and to meet girls who will soon be making their debuts. And in my case there were affectionate allusions to a man I wish I had known, my father. They helped me form a picture of him. To Higginson he was an inspired leader at school and college, a powerful athlete whose tackles repeatedly saved Harvard in the scoreless tie with Yale when he was captain. John Saltonstall recalled how deeply influenced he had been by the Rector at Groton and said he was the most devout Christian in their class. I wondered what father would have thought of me who cared more for beautifully built cars than for athletics—or the Church.

I was only temporarily dismayed by my fiasco at the Field

House and not long after I joined the candidates for the man-
agership of the crew who in early afternoon reported at the
varsity Boathouse on the bank of the Charles. There were
fewer competitors and less for us to do than at the Stadium.
The coxswains wiped off the cedar shells at the end of practice; our job was to wipe off the oars, clean the slides, help
with the launches, and, of course, sort and dry the wet shirts
and jocks. It was indicative of my ambition that I, who had
always been surrounded by servants and never did any work I
could pay someone else to do, should volunteer again for such
genial drudgery.

Before coming up to Cambridge I had taken dancing lessons from a Mrs. Hubbell in New York and dancing alone
with her to a Victrola I had gained confidence in the fox-
trot. I really felt what fun it was to dance and began to use my
height to advantage at one of the first social events in Cambridge, the Brattle Hall dances for the sub-debs. Freddy and I
went to all of them; they were informal and friendly. The orchestra was mediocre but this was a sort of trial run for the
Freshmen who composed most of the stag line. There was a
link between the hostesses at the Brattle and the mothers
whose daughters would be coming out a year hence. It was
important to be on the Boston list of invitations. I remember
two or three of the girls who were already touched with glam-
or and that few of my classmates showed signs of liquor. As I
wasn't drinking I may have missed those carrying flasks but
to me the parties were fun without booze.

Autumn is the glory of New England and I relished the
brisk walk through Harvard Yard on my way to class. The
old dormitories of red brick with white cornices (occupied by
Washington's Colonials early in the Revolution, and now reserved for the Seniors), the green turf under the old elms and

the seated statue of John Harvard in front of University Hall, the flood of students and faculty with the green baize bag of books (carried over the shoulder) formed a picture of unchanging Harvard I was never to forget. Duckboards were laid on the walks when the snow came and those Sophomores who were being initiated into the "Dickey," were conspicuously on the run, dressed like Pullman porters, and with a pocketful of sharpened pencils ready for their inquisitors.

One gets used to what is called "Harvard Indifference," which is really an aspect of Yankee reticence. The man sitting beside you at lectures might nod as he passed in the Yard or simply look the other way, and being fundamentally shy myself I didn't mind. It just takes longer to know those you want to know. Athletes are the first to become conspicuous in Freshman year and our big tackle, Leo Daley, was one I liked. In our dormitory I enjoyed eating with Lammot du Pont Copeland (who would one day be the president of the Du Pont empire). Freddy Davies wore well as a roommate; he had been popular at St. Paul's and his friends came to accept me; from St. Paul's, Bill Wister and "Ducky" Harrison, from St. George's, Cecil Lyon, "Teddy" Gross (one day to preside over Lockheed), and Alexander Cassatt, a Philadelphian of great charm. They had their school loyalties which made me envious. I remember a stranger, Bob Magowan wandering in. On my table was a photograph of the Rolls-Royce my mother had just bought. Magowan said, "My, that's beautiful, I hope one day to have one." (And he did when president of Safeway Stores.) I thought he was rather rough and as he was leaving I said, unfortunately in his hearing: "Gee, he certainly isn't a gentleman." He asked me why: I tried to explain, made a hash of it, but we became friends.

Freddy and I went to the theater constantly. Boston was

then ideal for tryouts and here, or in New York, we saw the Barrymores in "The Circle" by Somerset Maugham, Joseph Schildkraut in "Liliom," Katherine Cornell in "The Outsider," Beatrice Lillie and the lovely Gertrude Lawrence in "Charlot's Review." We would dine well at the Touraine, where one of the headwaiters looked out for us, expecting a lavish tip. As Freddy's allowance was so much less than mine, I paid the tab. He was deluged with invitations which he would open and stack on our mantelpiece; this irritated me— I thought it ostentatious—and was probably jealous.

I enjoyed the freedom and the challenge of Harvard. Merriman was positively brilliant in History I. I never missed his lectures and though the reading assignments averaged at least one hundred pages a week I could cope and often read more than what was required: this must have been evident in the Hour Exams and the Finals, for I got a "B" in the course, and with my excellence in English was put on "the Dean's list." Professor Munro's course in Government, on the other hand, was so full of theory that I found it a bore—I prefer dealing with reality.

In view of my love of books it seems odd that I resisted the impulse to try out for one of the Harvard publications. I guess I was just too lazy to want to get embroiled in as much editing as I had done for the *Browning Buzzer*. Besides my compelling attraction was for motors. The Boston airport was opened during my first month in Cambridge and I read all the columns about what this meant for the future. Somewhere I heard that Edward P. Warner was giving a course on aviation at the Massachusetts Institute of Technology; I drifted in to listen to one of his lectures, was fascinated, and would have gone to more had I not been laughed out of it by Freddy and his friends.

I had not yet got the taste for alcohol and privately was a bit disgusted by those who couldn't get enough of it. Lanny Pruyn, one of Freddy's friends, had been captain of the St. Paul's hockey team and could have been a star at Harvard had he kept training. Now, free of restraint he made such a noisy business of getting tight that I felt sorry for him.

On my homecoming in June I returned on the famous "One O'clock," which in those happy days used to pay a rebate if it were more than five minutes late in arriving at Grand Central Station. We were right on time, and to my surprise there was Moms at the gate waiting to greet me. She did not fuss over me after our shy kiss, and on the drive out to "Uplands" she told about our trip to France; the four of us (including Nan of course), would be sailing on the *Aquitania* in ten days. Shirley had grown taller and better looking, though I did not say so; despite a casual handshake he seemed glad to see me. Together in my long-idle Cadillac we went for a quick spin before supper, checking on what we needed, especially for our cameras.

It was to be expected that Nan was not happy about the trip as she took a dim view of all "furriners." Moms said that Grandma and Aunt Ruth always stayed in their favorite suite at the Paris Ritz; she had reserved one like it, and had asked that a Renault and a chauffeur, recommended by our cousins, the William Kissams, be ready for our arrival. She spoke of the trips to Europe in her girlhood in such a matter-of-fact way that I guess she was planning this journey more for our pleasure than for herself.

The Cunard liner was a model of British efficiency and everything about it was novel. People on the pier waved farewell as we slowly backed out into the Hudson; then came the rhythmic throbbing of the ship's engines as we got underway, the first meal with the enormous menu, our deck chairs and our eagerness to go forward on the promenade deck for the view of our prow cutting into the open sea. Shirley and I shared a double cabin and were in it as little as possible during the voyage.

On the day of our landing at Cherbourg we were up at dawn and from the promenade deck saw a beautiful sunrise as the fair, green low shore of France came to life. (The great dock at Cherbourg had not yet been built.) After the customs' formalities all the passengers descended to a lower deck where we crossed the narrow gangplank to large "tenders," steam-powered boats, a hundred and fifty feet long, which were to ferry us and our baggage ashore. During this operation we were catapulted from the highly disciplined atmosphere of a British ship to the highly emotional atmosphere of a French landing. Much yelling and waving of arms were standard procedure, with altercations, and many a "Mon Dieu!" Despite apparent confusion the baggage did reach the pier. Mother and Nan each were carrying a small overnight bag and Moms checked all our trunks straight to Paris, assuming they would accompany us on the boat train. This was the first time in her life she had to make such a decision, and it was a mistake.

I think my infatuation with France began when we boarded the gleaming boat train to Paris. I had often ridden on the Merchants Limited from New York to Boston which was exceptional in service and speed. But this French express was spotless and comfortable; instead of standing in a draughty, swaying corridor waiting for a seat in the diner, we were given tickets in advance for "le premier service," or "le deuxième." This was my first French meal; it took up much of the three-hour run and beginning with the fresh, crisp French bread and Normandy butter it was served with a style and seasoning so different from Pullman cooking. During the four or five appetizing courses I was fascinated by the French countryside, a man fishing in a canal, a distant château, the long straight roads between the poplars, the picture-postcard villages—and then the outskirts of Paris. We entered the St. Lazare Station with that shriek characteristic of French locomotives, coasted to a quiet stop and there waiting to meet us was a smartly groomed chasseur from the Ritz to whom in French Moms presented our baggage stubs. After a short interval he reappeared, his hand eloquent in apology. "Il n'y a pas de baggage, Madame. Mais c'est sûr demain." No trunks.

Our drive to the hotel was through boulevards, to me the most beautiful in the world, totally unlike any I had seen. The very broad avenues and the open cafés with couples sitting at tables drinking, the gendarme directing the pell-mell traffic, the flower stalls and the little tin cabins by the curb (when I asked what they were, Moms said, "Toilets. Forget it."), the soldiers in the horizon-blue uniforms, the widows in black, and the cripples who had lost a leg or an arm in the war —all this colorful life, as we swept past the majestic public buildings, was a scene I was never to forget. Our car turned into the Place Vendôme and came to a stop before No. 15, the hotel which set a standard for all other capitals, the Ritz.

There was a formality to our entrance, as the top staff had assembled to receive us. Mr. Ritz, the founder, had died long ago, and in his place was the short, impeccably courteous Mr. Auzello and beside him a tall Polish aristocrat, Mr. Zembrzuski, equally impeccable in his cutaway and striped trousers. But here we were, without any baggage, and this was disturbing, not only to the management but even more to the maids awaiting us on the second floor, ready to unpack and expecting a big tip. Clearly we were not living up to form, and to make things worse Moms had apparently forgotten that distinguished clients (or even undistinguished ones) *never* shake hands with the manager—or the staff. She, being an inherently friendly soul, and Shirley also, shook hands with everybody, including the elevator man and the bus boys—and I followed suit. I don't think this democratic gesture added to our stature.

It had been a long day for all of us and Moms, having nothing fresh to change into, took us down for an early supper in the main dining room; Shirley had to have the menu translated and he reveled in a new dessert, Crême Brulée. Afterwards we went up for a blissful sleep in the double room we shared.

We slept late and our trunks had arrived and Nan had unpacked before we went down for breakfast. It was a perfect June morning and Shirley and I were eager to get going. We stepped out into the Place Vendôme and I stopped, dazzled by the splendor of the cars parked before the Ritz. They were all of foreign make, some I had never seen before; the bodies, as I soon learned, were custom-built by the most famous coachbuilders in Europe. There was a large Rolls-Royce in the center which the doorman told me had been specially built for the Aga Khan. He also pointed out an elegant Hispano-Suiza belonging to King Alfonso of Spain, which he said the King himself had driven from Madrid to Paris in record time.

Paris traffic has a frenzy and color all its own. As we strolled along the Champs-Elysées I was drawn again and again to the show windows of those beautiful cars—the Farman, Hispano-Suiza, Minerva, Isotta-Fraschini, Voisin—only the Renault was familiar. Across the street, closer to the Arc de Triomphe, were displays by the famous coachbuilders, and around the corner I found the showrooms of Bugatti, Rolls-Royce and the only American—the Packard. Most of these French cars had their agencies in New York which I had visited, so I made the same approach here: talked to the English-speaking clerk about the model on display, price, speed, improvements—and got a catalogue. Shirley, who had no such curiosity, grew impatient. "Come on, Bill. Let's get going!" That afternoon he discovered and devoured the patisseries at Rumpelmayer's and henceforth this established our favorite destinations: the sweets for him, the cars for me.

Having completed our tour of the fabulous "automobile row" we might stroll on to admire the Rue de la Paix or stretch it to the Rue St. Honoré, site of the United States and British embassies, and the Elysée Palace, the beautiful residence of the President of France. With Moms we went to the Louvre and to the Eiffel Tower. Shirley and I were more attracted to architecture than museums, especially Notre Dame, with its stained glass windows, and Versailles—but those vast, bare rooms were disappointing. Sightseeing works up an appetite and Moms took us to dine at two special restaurants, "La Rue" and "Tour d'Argent," where I thought the cooking was almost as good as Donon's.

We liked our French chauffeur who handled the Renault with such confidence that the other cars gave way. He drove us to Verdun and we spent the night with a French family— of whom Nan was suspicious—and next morning we followed an English-speaking guide through the battlefield, through the trenches, down into an abri and a pillbox for a machine gunner. He pointed out one famous trench where he said an entire company was buried alive by a land mine, with their bayonets sticking up through the ground—and I disbelieved every word of it—like the propaganda, it was just another war story.

We drove out the Route Nationale on our way to see the châteaux in the Valley of the Loire. Moms kept saying, "Vite! Vite!" until the car was touching 80 m.p.h., a new record for me. We must have inspected about twenty of those famous old buildings; personally, I was less impressed with the musty interiors than the beauty of the façade with lake or river in the background. Azay-le-Rideau, one of the smaller, we thought was the most stylish.

But at Lyon we came back to the twentieth century when at my urging we watched the European Grand Prix, the first road race I had ever seen. The chauffeur placed our Renault at a strategic spot from which we could see a long straightaway approach and one of the more difficult, unbanked corners. The complete circuit was about fifteen miles, with the cars going over 100 m.p.h. on the straightaway, and what added drama to the event was the introduction of the supercharged engine by the Fiat team. The supercharged, straight-eight Fiats were leading for a large part of the race but then they all broke down and the race was won by G. Campari in an Alfa Romeo. The spectacle was enlivened by the enormous French crowd, now shouting with joy, now in despair over the fate of the nine or ten French cars and very much "en fête" as the wine began to flow.

I can still hear the whine of the Fiat superchargers as they appeared like small dots and came flashing, whining by in a matter of seconds. Our pictures were just a blur. We had brought along a wonderful French picnic lunch, and the hotel had added a bottle of claret; no wine for us, of course, but the chauffeur drank much of it by himself sitting in the front seat, beside him his small black puppy, "DiDi Chocolat," a schipperke, to whom he fed bits of his sandwich.

Our last two days at the Ritz were mostly consumed by

Freddy Davies and Susie Scott

Shirley at the time of "The Silent Enemy"

shopping and packing; in my trunk Nan stowed the Charvet dress shirts, initialed handkerchiefs and a crimson necktie of beautiful silk which Moms insisted on ordering for me. Shirley and I went for a last stroll along the Champs-Elysées and I remember studying the full-length portrait of Guynemer in the show window of the Hispano-Suiza. He was the most famous French ace, credited with fifty-two victories before his death in 1918; he was said to be tubercular and looked very pale in his black tunic which was covered with decorations. The flying stork, the emblem of his squadron, had been adopted by Hispano-Suiza for their radiator cap. The night before departure we stayed up late by the window listening to dancers in the garden restaurant fox-trot to the tune of "California, Here I come!"

*   *   *

In early September I drove up to Cambridge in my Cadillac. There is a feeling of exuberance in being a Sophomore; the best things in college lie ahead. I was more interested in crew than I had been in football, and rather pleased with a new gray suit with a double-breasted waistcoat which Dunhill's had fitted for me. Freddy Davies was not arriving till the day college opened so to my annoyance I had to supervise the moving of all our stuff to the suite we'd be sharing in Randolph Hall. It relieved my irritation to dump Freddy's old invitations, still stacked on the mantelpiece, in the wastebasket.

In the evenings I paged through the catalogue looking for the courses that appealed to me, taking care to avoid any course meeting Saturday mornings. I definitely intended to take, as part of my "Concentration," Professor Kittredge's course on Shakespeare—"Mon., Wed., Fri., at 10 a.m." George Lyman Kittredge, the leader in what was then the finest English Department in the country, was said to be a taskmaster who made one memorize long passages, and was a strict marker. I was keen to work under him and checked it. As a counterbalance why not the History of the Printed Book by Professor Winship? It only met twice a week and was rumored to be a snap. (Actually it was fascinating and well taught. About ten of us met in the Treasure Room of Widener Library and under Winship's guidance examined the rare and beautiful books.) Dick Tucker had recommended Fine Arts 1A, a history of sculpture and painting from the Greeks to Picasso. Lectures and many slides in a half-darkened lecture hall. If you'd had a late night it was a place to drowse. O.K.

The Club system in the 1920s was a kind of progression which for those elected came to a climax before the Christmas holidays of one's Sophomore year. The first step was election to "The Dickey" (the name a relic of the DKE fraternity which with other frats had been ruled out by President Eliot). The candidates were chosen in groups of ten; athletes and those who achieved prominence as Freshmen came first. I was in the fourth "Ten"; I "ran" for a week in a porter's shirt, was the butt of mild hazing, and on the night of election had no alternative but to swallow the gin fizzes and orange blossoms until I was drunk. That kissed good-bye to Moms's prize.

At the same time there was election to either of the two "waiting clubs," the "S.K." and the "Iroquois," whose houses were side by side on Mt. Auburn Street. I made the former and with some twenty-five classmates regularly attended the appetizing luncheons, talking airily and pretending to be unaware that each of us was being looked over critically by upperclassmen in the Final Clubs.

The steward of "S.K." made his own (passable) gin and I

drank an occasional cocktail before dinner, or at the "Punches," usually on Sunday, which the Porcellian and the A.D. hosted at some attractive place away from Cambridge such as The Country Club in Brookline or the Myopia Hunt. It was a rather nervous sociability and I noticed that the Grotties or those from St. Marks or St. Pauls gravitated together. I wondered if I were being thought of as "a legacy" by the A.D. I had set my heart on it, and I knew my father's friends would be pulling for me. My handicap was that I was so little known by those from the big boarding schools. Perhaps my work for the crew would help.

As the week when the bids would be sent out approached, Freddy and I opened our mailbox each morning with expectation. But no word came and when we could tell from the elation of those in the dormitory who had been elected we realized that we'd been passed over, and were sunk.

It was impossible to hide from each other how hurt we were and the rebuff drove us closer together for parties of our own away from Cambridge in my Cadillac. We knew that individuals occasionally were elected to a Final Club in Junior year, and held on to that hope, but it was slim. I admitted my disappointment to the family at Christmas and Aunt Ruth blamed it on my double-breasted waistcoat—and that I didn't drink enough. She even had me pass the champagne at a big dinner at Grandma's to show what a good sport I was.

In January when the oarsmen returned from vacation they rowed indoors on the machines and I observed the training more intently. Rowing depends on team work, calling for sturdy oarsmanship, coordination and stamina; the oarsmen practice five months before the formal races and it surprised me to watch how a long-armed 180 pounder from Iowa who had never before sat in a shell, under careful coaching, could begin to acquire the rhythm and power to unseat a man who had rowed for three years in prep school.

I turned deaf ears to the course on Fine Arts and was to regret it. Professor Edgell's opening lectures were on Greek sculpture and for the slides to be effective the auditorium in the Fogg Museum—well named—was so darkened that I daydreamed; while he was explaining how to recognize a head by Scopus I was choosing between a Duesenberg and a Mercedes, and in the second term when Professor Chase in his subdued, mousey way was trying to make us appreciate the Renaissance, I was doodling. I was completely unaware that a member of my class, Lincoln Kirstein, son of Louis Kirstein, the philanthropist and head of Filene's department store, was creating fresh attention to the arts in his magazine, *The Hound and Horn*, and by his enthusiasm for the ballet. Kirstein formed a group of those who shared his interest in contemporary painting and they met regularly with Alfred Barr, then teaching in Wellesley but later to be the distinguished director of the Museum of Modern Art in New York. Had I been aware of his circle then I would not have had to wait another decade before my appreciation was awakened by my wife Peggy.

Even in my chosen field, English, the reading I did privately, *The Dance of Life* by Havelock Ellis and *Remembrance of Things Past* by Marcel Proust in the superb translation by C. K. Scott Moncrieff was so much more absorbing than the tedious updigging of word-roots in the course on Anglo-Saxon.

In the spring the crews went out on the water and with my motion picture camera I took slow-motion films of all three, both in practice and in the varsity races. What good they did I never knew but the English coach, Bill Haynes, was grateful and my initiative helped me survive the cut; I was one of the last four candidates in the competition and in early June we accompanied the three crews to "Red Top" on the Upper

Thames, the lovely training camp for the races against Yale.

For us four competing slaves it was a charmed life. We took part in the games of croquet which was the traditional relaxation. With the coxswains we waited on table, and learned that shirred eggs are dangerous to serve—the metal platter must be 150°. We fussed over the launches, cleaned the slides in the shells, shared in the rising tension, and helped lay out the stakes that marked the course. After supper we were free, and thought up dirty tricks, like painting a large "H" on a shed in full view of the Yale quarters at Gales Ferry.

"Red Top" is a place and a legend. The fifty acres with its fine oaks, and a quarter of a mile of shoreline had been purchased by Harvard oarsmen back in 1881 and at that time the crews and coach lived in one large frame house on the bluff overlooking the Thames: meeting room, dining room on the ground floor, kitchen in an ell and all sleeping on cots in the big loft above. In 1910 it became more habitable with the erection of three portable houses, the largest for the varsity and J.V., a second for the Freshmen, the third for dining quarters and kitchen, with cots for the manager and his assistants.

Peter Higginson told me that in the days before the automobile when he was rowing, the crews and shells were transported from Boston to the wharf on the Thames in a river steamboat. There was a thrill to one's arrival at "Red Top" and to the oarsmen the charm of the place interspersed with hours of intensity in that final fortnight before the races, were an unforgettable reward for the many months of training. All of us had to bone up for those Final Exams which were not scheduled until *after* our departure from Cambridge but crewmen are above average in scholarship and writing their papers at "Red Top" didn't phase them.

Occasionally we "managers" would drive in to New London for an evening on the town and return to "Red Top" in a somewhat inebriate condition. On one such trip Lansing Pruyn joined us very drunk and with some sort of an allergy which caused his face to swell up. He came back to the quarters with me. Probably a mistake for the crew doctor hauled him up before every one, flashed a bright light in his face and said, "Look at this object. He is a disgrace to Harvard!" Unfortunately this castigation did not have the slightest effect on his drinking habits.

Yale had an almost unbeatable coach in Leader and his crews had run up a succession of victories almost as remarkable as that of the Harvard eights today under Harry Parker. But in 1925 hope was undiminished that this at last might be Harvard's year.

In those days yachts flying Harvard and Yale colors came in to anchor on either side of the course for several hundred yards toward the finish. J. P. Morgan's magnificent *Corsair* was the finest and one of the great treats for the crews and managers was to be taken for a sail on it. We were all warned that we must be spotlessly clean, because the slightest bit of dust would not be tolerated on this gorgeous yacht. I took the trouble to buy a new pair of sneakers for the occasion but unfortunately as I was running for the tender I stepped on a mass of tar. It was too late to change, so I went on board and sat on the fantail with its wonderful red baize cushions with a big gob of tar on the sole of my sneakers. Harry Morgan was so horrified that he was about to eject me but I pled to be allowed to continue in stocking feet, and carried my sneakers ashore in my hand.

Despite our toil and our hopes the Fates were against us: Yale made a clean sweep, winning all three races. And that evening I learned that I had not won the competition. Win or lose, it had been a priceless experience.

Harvard College in the late-twenties was drastically different than it is today. It was governed by the last of the autocratic presidents, A. Lawrence Lowell, and the strictures were as much a matter of form as of rules. Married undergraduates were frowned upon and a rarity; any student involved in a sexual scandal that reached the press was expelled. Radcliffe was regarded as a nunnery of plain, earnest girls; they did not appear in the Yard, were not admitted to Harvard classes, and socially were ignored.

Students were neatly dressed, a few made a point of being fastidious; neckties were worn with pride, club ties were conspicuous, also the various patterns of crimson and black which designated members of the varsity teams. Everyone wore hats: a beat-up brown felt, or even a derby for everyday, and for those who were ushers at coming-out parties, a collapsible silk opera hat completed the full dress of white tie and tails. No one went bare-headed before May. Blue jeans and turtleneck sweaters were unheard of. I never knew a classmate who was on drugs, and doubt that there was one.

As our elders defied Prohibition so did we. Wine was inaccessible; we went for the hard stuff, homemade (bathtub) gin, disguised by orange juice or grenadine; a bottle of bootleg Scotch was a prize to be finished off as soon as possible. One carried a full flask to football games, and to dances, as a precaution if the host was stingy.

Of the well-to-do upperclassmen, I among them, were a number who owned Cadillacs, Stutz Bearcats, Amil cars and Voisins. The cream of the crop belonged to Hollis Hunnewell who drove a Duesenberg, Model A, with a straight-eight engine and hydraulic brakes, the first American or European motor to have all these features. The runner-up was Peter Brooks, who sported a supercharged Targa-Florio Mercedes, which was one of a kind. None of these were limousines which would have been handy in a New England winter with a girl aboard. A sporting car was more essential to an undergraduate. My Cadillac was adorned with a silver coiled cobra for the radiator cap, a fire-engine siren, a whistle on the exhaust and a cut out.

Speed was in our blood; the roads were narrower, the curves sharp yet on my innumerable drives back and forth to New York on the Boston Post Road, often after midnight, I never had an accident. True there were fewer cars or police on the highway. But, unhappily, the combination of hard liquor and fast driving accounted for the deaths of some of the most attractive men in college at my time: Johnny Tudor, Lawrence Dickey, Bill Elkins, to name but three. Oddly, I cannot remember any socially prominent girl being injured in a crash; it was generally the driver. But by far the greater number of casualties were those who, notorious as hard drinkers in their clubs, could not shake the habit afterwards and became hopeless alcoholics, or dead, before forty.

Freddy and I could afford to patronize a fairly reliable bootlegger and his bottles had the prestigious labels even if the contents had been cut. We did not realize any more than our elders that such deliberate defiance of the Law as the "speakeasy" provided a respectable foothold to the Mafia, whose tentacles today reach deep.

The changes in the "well-brought-up girl" were more subtle. The novelty in dress began on the tennis court where the shorter skirt and smaller girdle—or none—set a new fashion. The length of the skirt rose to the knee—or above—and a girl's knee is one of her least attractive features. It takes a straight, beautifully articulated leg to stand that much exposure. The bosom was lashed flat, to achieve "a boyish form" (and a skillful "petter" began by undoing that absurdity). Hair was bobbed; the use of cosmetics, scent as strong as "Chypre" numbed the nostril. The drawings by John Held, Jr. are a not-too-exaggerated caricature of what the "flapper" of that period looked like.

The chaperone was on the way out which meant that a twenty-year-old had to decide on her own defense. "Petting" or "necking" was a summer temptation, as I suspect it has always been—but even among those who were really attracted to each other there was a usual stopping point. It was part of the upbringing: girls flaunted a great deal but were afraid to give very much. As observed by me at Harvard—and I was not typical, for I was not aggressive enough to pursue the possibilities of girls of my own class—I should say there was very little premarital intercourse on the part of "respectable girls." I would have thought five percent a very high estimate.

Some of us enjoyed limited sex by picking up Boston shop girls, "chippies," "bags" or "broads," as they were called: they were game for a drive out of town to a roadhouse for a good dinner with gin in some form and would sport with us on the back seat on the way back, the soberest male being at the wheel. Both sides regarded it as casual fun and here too there was a usual stopping point.

The lasting effect of college is not what one commits to memory but the unforgettable recollection of one or more brilliant teachers. The man I most admired was George Lyman Kittredge. He was revered and feared by those graduate students struggling for a Ph.D.; to us undergraduates he was that distinguished-looking man in the Yard. In his suit of light gray flannel, a blue tie setting off his cold blue eyes and his glorious white beard he challenged attention. English 12, his famous course on Shakespeare compelled us to absorb three of the great plays a year (he always chose three different ones the following year for those who wished to repeat); he read the magnificent passages in a sonorous voice and he dwelt on the dramatist's choice of words, their Elizabethan meaning, the puns, the political jibes, their humor and beauty. He was quite an actor and when moved he would suddenly be Lear grieving over Cordelia, or Falstaff or Hotspur. We were required to memorize long passages and be ready to quote them in the Finals; I have always found memorizing difficult but, remembering his interpretations, I found it a pleasure. In his class, and it was a big one, he would tolerate no coughing and would pause and stare down the victim until the hacking ceased.

Kittredge and Mrs. Kittredge held open house every fortnight: conversation, which he would not permit graduate students to monopolize, and cups of cocoa at nine o'clock. We were all invited but I never went, and now wished I had.

Another fine scholar, though not as inspiring, was John Livingston Lowes. A very tiny man, with a very deep voice, he wished us to appreciate Coleridge with the intensity and insight of his finest book, *The Road to Xanadu.*

Finally there was that original maverick, Richard C. Cabot of the famous Boston Cabots. He taught a course on what today would be called "social science." Frankly I took it because I had been told that it was a snap, but it turned out to be one of the most fascinating courses in the University, and Cabot and I became great friends.

It involved a number of study trips to typical institutions in Boston which gave the students an idea of the problems of a modern city in a way that they could not have acquired in any other manner. We visited the infamous Charles Street Jail and saw firsthand the horrors of an antiquated prison and the ineffectiveness of the current attempts of rehabilitation. It is still one of the most overcrowded, hateful institutions in New England.

We visited a mental hospital and were horrified by the hopeless plight of those inmates stricken with schizophrenia (who constituted nearly half of the inmates) for which there was at that time no cure. We saw them huddled pitifully in the corner of their cells—and it really was a cell.

We were given a more encouraging view of the famous and effective Perkins Institute for the Blind.

The subject of the first long paper assigned to us was "The effect of the automobile on American society." I received the highest mark for my essay which mentioned, among other things, that one of its more familiar uses was as a "comfortable and convenient whorehouse on wheels." Cabot had a grasp of reality and I liked his sense of humor.

Where I stumbled was in Middle-English which I thought a bore, and in Chaucer. If the music in Chaucer's lines can be pronounced as meaningfully as Professor Robinson had done in the recent past, the *Canterbury Tales* spring to life but our teacher, the renowned scholar, Professor Tatlock, lacked the magic. Bill Wister who was having as much trouble getting interested as I did, took his father, Owen Wister, then an Overseer, to one meeting and when we emerged the novelist said, "That man has ruined the course!" I was halfway through Senior year when this occurred and I was shocked to discover that if I did not pass Chaucer I would not get my degree.

Accordingly I took quick action. (I was always an activist and still am.) I had special tutoring at "the Widow Nolan's," that cramming establishment across the street from the Yard, and not only passed that crucial course but in June graduated with honors.

The decision to "Concentrate" in English was a happy one. It broadened the horizon of my reading and quickened my pace, so that even during the war years in government when we were working fourteen to sixteen hours a day I still found time to read an average of at least two new books a week. Harvard's system of distribution required that I take at least one course in science. I hesitated between astronomy and meteorology and finally chose the latter: it proved to be easy, the professor was devoted to his subject, and amusingly, in 1943 when I became Assistant Secretary of Commerce for Air, the Weather Bureau came under my supervision, which I think might have made him smile.

In our Senior year we all roomed in the Yard; we had had three years in which to get to know each other and there was a congeniality in those ancient dormitories. In one of them, Hollis, Professor Copeland would welcome us to his Readings or introduce us to some of the famous pupils like Max Perkins, Scribner's great editor, or Walter Lippmann. Alex Cassatt was the most popular man in our class, Leo Daley and Izzy Zarakoff, our best athletes, Lincoln Kirstein, the most original. It was too early to recognize in "Chip" Bohlen the Russian expert and future Ambassador to the Soviet Union, or in Charlie Wyzanski, our most audacious judge.

Some of Freddy's friends had become mine, too: "Hootie" Whitman, good company, amusing when tight, an inveterate "sponger" which one forgave; Eddie Weld, that proper New Yorker, who worked hard to prepare himself for Law School, drank with the best of them and had a dry, cynical wit, "I'm going to town," he once told me "to lunch with my grandmother, she's deeply religious and a God-damned bore"; Natty Hamlen, the rugged hockey player, with whose family in Needham I spent many a pleasant Sunday; and the polished, endearing Cecil Lyon, who was to find his happiness in diplomacy. Lawrence and Harold Coolidge had made me feel at home in their country place in Beverly Farms. Harold was my mentor. "Bill," he'd admonish me, "you mustn't leave your money lying about that way on the bureau. It's too great a temptation for the servants!" Or, "Bill, you shouldn't send such lavish bouquets (they were always orchids) to Lydia (or whomever). It isn't done. People will think you're engaged."

At the age of seventeen Shirley abandoned any hope of academic progress. He went through the motions of taking the College Board Examinations at Columbia but except for his signature at the top of the first page the papers he handed in were blank. Reading still defied him; his aptitude seemed to be for photography and he had installed a fireproof projection booth in the "theatre" of the Playhouse at Mt. Kisco to show the homemade films we made during the summers at Northeast Harbor.

In the autumn of 1926 he had an unexpected opening. Our first cousin, Douglas Burden, who was five years my senior, and who lived at Bedford not far from us at Mt. Kisco, was a writer and naturalist. Doug had been deeply impressed by the two documentary films, "Grass" and "Chang" which Merian Cooper had shot in the Far East on an incredibly small budget and both of which were successfully promoted by Paramount. With this inspiration Douglas had raised the capital for a documentary he had written about a small Indian tribe in northernmost Canada whose existence depended upon the annual migration of the caribou; he insisted on the utmost fidelity, the actors were all to be Indians, including the hero and heroine, and knowing of Shirley's passion for photography Doug invited my brother to join the company. The experience, as Shirley recalls, was rather trying at the outset but it was to have a lasting effect:

I was just getting settled at our base camp near Lake Temagami when my cousin Douglas came to me and said, "Shirley, as you know, we have been looking for some time for the perfect Indian to play the lead in *The Silent Enemy*. Well, I think I've found him: he belongs to the Blackfoot tribe; he is an all-around athlete; he writes, and he has a wonderful figure. I want you to go to New York and sign him up. You can find him at the Cosmopolitan Magazine office."

By the time Douglas finished I felt as if I had been kicked in the stomach. "Douglas, please, just a moment," I said. "Remember, I never went to college—I've had very little experience away from home—I'm not a talent scout. Just how do you expect me, at my age to negotiate a motion picture contract with an American Indian in the office of Cosmopolitan Magazine?" I knew Douglas, but not well; little did I realize, "No" was not part of his vocabulary.

The following morning I was on my way: first, by dog sled, then by train to New York, to meet, and if possible, sign up Chief Buffalo Child "Long Lance." I was pretty low when I started, but the freezing air, the beauty of the vast expanse of frozen lake, the snow-laden trees, and the enthusiasm of the dogs as they pulled, barked and puffed clouds of steam, lifted my spirits.

When I reached New York I called the Cosmopolitan Magazine office and arranged a meeting with Long Lance the following day. I spent most of the night rehearsing what I might say, or what I should say, with uncertain results.

The office was high up in a huge building that took up most of the block. I found the elevator, the floor, and the office number, without too much trouble. At each stop my heart beat faster. When I finally opened the door, my heart stopped. In front of me was a small counter; behind it there was nothing but space—space larger than a football field. No floating partitions, just space, every square of which was fitted with desks, and behind each desk was a beautiful girl, busy doing something. I wanted to go home, or hide some place, anything to get away.

The door closed behind me, and a sophisticated young lady appeared at the counter. "What can I do for you," she said. My heart started beating again, and the cat gave me back my tongue. "I want to see Chief Buffalo Child Long Lance," I said. "And what is it about?" she asked, charmingly. The girls in the front rows had stopped typing and were listening. "I am Shirley Burden from Burden Pictures and I have an appointment with Chief Long Lance," I said. That did it. All the girls looked up from their work, they smiled, and some of the bolder ones were laughing at me. The girl at the counter had vanished.

The next thing I knew, a young, well-dressed Indian appeared, accompanied by three forbidding executive types. They all looked at me as if I were some sort of a joke. Long Lance stepped forward and offered his hand. I explained that my Cousin Douglas Burden and I were producing a picture called *The Silent Enemy*, in Canada, the story of a tribe of Indians searching for food. We wanted him to play the lead. Would he be interested? He asked how long it would take. I told him I didn't know, it depended on the weather. He asked about money, a contract, etc. I told him my Cousin Douglas was really the man to discuss that. Looking back on it, I'm sure the executive types were getting pretty fed up. Long Lance turned to them and said, "I think Mr. Burden and I will take a walk. I'll get back to you later." Then he turned to me, "How about a walk in the park. I want to hear more about the picture."

We found a nice bench in the sun by the 59th Street Lake. I felt more relaxed now, and Long Lance was a great listener. I told him more about the story. I told him of Douglas's interest in the American Indian and that he was a trustee of the American Museum of Natural History. I told him whom we had signed up to play different parts in the picture. I explained Paramount Pictures were interested in releasing it when it was finished. I told him Ilia Tolstoy, a relative of the famous writer, was in Alaska shooting pictures of migrating caribou for certain sequences we had planned. I did a lot of talking and a lot of praying that morning.

It was worth it. We left together a few days later for Canada.

When Shirley was in the frozen north that winter, I was invited to be an usher at several "deb" parties in Boston and New York: it made you feel responsible for what was going on. I remember one dance at the Somerset Club where undergraduates who had drunk too much passed out on the long leather couches. I helped two of them down to the men's room where cold water and hot coffee got them back in shape to shuffle around again to the music, or leave.

One can never forget the gracious hospitality of the Boston town houses. I think particularly of the Sears and the Thayers, on opposite corners of Beacon Street. Jean Sears was the most beautiful of the Boston debs with Katherine Roche and Mabel Thayer not far behind her. In New York Libby Woodward and Betty Bliss were my pick and in Philadelphia, Sally Henry, who first taught me to dance at Northeast Harbor, was not only ravishing but the wittiest of the lot.

There was a private source of elation for me that spring when Lanny Pruyn told me the unexpected good news that I had been elected to the A.D. I had long given up hope but as I learned later the pressure of my father's friends, the urging of my intimates, Courtie Gross, Cecil Lyon, Alex Cassatt, and, surprisingly, the approval of younger members had silenced the opposition. It was the most heart-warming reprieve in my life. My grandfather, Hamilton Twombly, had been president of the A.D., my father was beloved and a leader in the Club, and now I was the third in succession and immensely happy at the thought. I would have the chance to prove my loyalty to the Club in the years to come. My election made no difference in Freddy's affection for me or mine for him; it must have hurt him that I alone was elected but he never showed it. I took supper quite regularly at the Club and often stayed on talking to those I wanted to know better.

With Commencement in sight I drove a foursome from the A.D. down to New York for a debutante's ball; it was a good party and afterwards in the soft spring night we made the rounds, ending up for a nightcap at our apartment. We were then living on the corner of 63rd Street and Fifth Avenue, and our big living room with three overstuffed sofas and comfortable chairs seemed very restful. As they finished a last drink, the boys stripped off their stiff shirts, and stretched out. Morning came too soon, and this is what Shirley discovered:

> Our living room was exceptionally large, with windows overlooking the Central Park Zoo. In one corner Moms had her desk, and like most antique desks the writing area slanted forward and was too narrow to write

on easily. Each day Moms would go religiously to her desk and write in a very small book how much she had spent the day before. She really didn't have to worry about such things but it gave her pleasure.

I was fast asleep when the apartment was invaded. After a leisurely breakfast I wandered into the living room. It looked like a battlefield: there were bodies everywhere. In those days, men always wore tops when they went swimming. These bodies wore no tops and some of them, no bottoms. The noise of snoring and the smell of alcohol were everywhere.

I was trying to figure out what to do when the door to the living room opened, and my mother walked in. Moms was never a prude, but the consumption of alcohol was not one of her strong points. She didn't look to the right, and she didn't look to the left; she walked straight to her desk, opened the mirror door, took out her small notebook, placed it on the desk, sat down and started making out her accounts. . . .

It was quite some time before the first body came to. There was some grunting, then the fun began. One by one they came to. None of them focussed very well, but they all saw my mother, they got to their feet. They walked. They ran. The room was soon cleared; my mother never looked up once from her accounting.

Lunch was rather strained that day. Everyone was dressed; hair, ties and coats were all in place. Moms was really a great sport.

One collects a number of sentimental mementoes in college and after Commencement I made a ruthless discard as I packed my clothes and the books I prized into the back of the

Cadillac for my drive home to "Uplands." I was quite uncertain about my future and when I tried to share my problem with Moms, asking her what she thought I ought to do for a living, she said, emphatically, "Well, we'll never have a penny more than we have today—$125,000 a year!" which left me still wondering.

My father after his graduation in June, 1900, had gone on a world tour with three friends, Peter Higginson, John Saltonstall, and John Jay and there were photographs of them mounted on camels beside the Pyramids, or in Peking, and on the Acropolis before they returned to Paris and London. I wanted to follow his example; Moms thought it a good thing to do and so did I. Freddy jumped at the opportunity.

Freddy's mother and mine were both encouraging. Moms busied herself securing letters of introduction to American and British diplomats and had the help of the distinguished Henry White who had served as Second Secretary of the American Embassy in London and more importantly in the United States delegation to the Versailles Conference. At the age of seventy he had married my wealthy, amiable and scatterbrained Aunt Emily Sloane. I remember his giving the packet of letters to me from his sick bed at "Elm Court." He was dressed in an immaculate old-fashioned nightgown, and his magnificent wide-swept mustaches were perfectly trimmed. Moms failed to remember Joseph Grew, a friend of my father's, then our Ambassador in Turkey, but otherwise we were well supplied before we left.

Mrs. Davies took it upon herself to arrange our travel itinerary, not with Raymond Whitcomb who were the best in the business, but with the Geyelin Agency in Philadelphia and Geyelin's schedule proved to be punishing. To begin with he booked us most of the way on the Dollar Line, whose ships

were named after our Presidents. This sorry collection of slow
boats had the simple virtue of calling every month at the major ports, but otherwise they were stuffy, served mediocre meals,
and naturally carried far less attractive travelers than the best
French or British liners.

Again, it was Geyelin's idea to over-schedule us—the more
we traveled the larger his commission—so despite our energy
we found ourselves exhausted and began cutting sizable and
sometimes the most interesting sections out of our itinerary.

I had convinced Moms that we ought to have a Mercedes
touring car in which I'd drive the three of us on our next holiday in Europe. She liked the idea, so I made the arrangements.
I ordered a Mercedes K, 6-cylinder, 160 h.p., supercharged,
the chassis to be built in Germany and shipped to Bridgeport,
Connecticut, where the body, black with green striping, would
be designed and fitted by Le Baron, the total coming to about
$11,000. It was finished in the fall of my Senior year, was as
distinctive as I had hoped, and a joy for long drives as I demonstrated to Moms.

As the day of our departure from San Francisco in August
drew near she became more nervous about the tour. She
feared that I, to whom she had devoted so much of her life,
might run into trouble and her fears were played on by Nan
who predicted that I would come down with malaria, or be
held for ransom by one of the Chinese warlords.

CHAPTER IV

Grand Tour: 1927-1928

WERE I asked to advise a grandson planning a round-the-world trip today I could give him some pointers although I doubt if he would listen. Don't try to take it all in one gulp. Decide what you want most to see—the Far East or Africa or Rome, Turkey and the Greek Isles. Talk to those who have been there; read a few edifying books like Edith Hamilton's *The Greek Way*, and get letters of introduction to those living on the spot, especially our Ambassadors.

In the carefree 1920s, before the transcontinental flights, a debutante accompanied by her maiden aunt went on a world cruise, every stop, almost every meal, arranged in advance. Young men went as they chose. Neither Freddy nor I made any serious preparations; we read little if anything for guidance though we did lug along a handful of rather heavy books including *Mother India* by Katharine Mayo, which was hardly an invitation to that ghastly country. I know we expected to enjoy ourselves, especially in Japan, China and Egypt—good food, plenty of native brew, yes, some sightseeing, and the companionship of glamorous girls, not strictly chaperoned.

We were to be gone eight months, following a schedule far more strenuous than we realized. Freddy and I made friends easily, we shared the same likes and dislikes; and we were hedonists with an awakening interest in history and foreign affairs. Neither of us cared for shooting, for the obvious reason that our fathers had died when young and we had never been taught to shoot. We had our sights on attractive girls, and plenty of money with which to amuse them.

I can hardly exaggerate our excitement when at San Francisco we boarded one of the small boats of the Dollar Line. As we headed out through the Golden Gate we were busy scrutinizing the thirty-four fellow passengers in First Class. Not one beauty among them. But in the bar before dinner we began chatting with a couple of Navy wives, on the way to join their husbands at Pearl Harbor, who seemed happy to lap up our cocktails. Fun but not flirtatious.

Honolulu was our first stop. In 1927 there were only two hotels on Waikiki Beach: the old wooden Moana in which my mother had stayed on her honeymoon in 1904 and the brand new Royal Hawaiian, owned by the Matson Line, which was truly luxurious. It was one of the most beautiful hotels I had ever seen—vaguely Spanish in design and the dominating interior tones were green and blue, a restful combination. Our room faced directly on Waikiki Beach and had a pleasant screened porch. Waikiki was a surprise—I had always imagined it to be immense. Actually it is so narrow that at high tide the waves come right up to the hotel. The great rollers, however, were most impressive. They sweep in straight from the reef to the beach with wonderful swirling crests twenty or thirty feet high. The water is so shallow that they have comparatively little force and are ideal for surf boarding. Prohibition was theoretically in force, as at home, but there was a native distilled liquor "okoleao"—or "oak"—made from sugar cane, pleasantly sweet with the kick of a mule, and we soon became fond of it.

We had letters to the Walter Dillinghams who were then living in their beautiful, hilltop Italianate house, "La Pietra." The Dillinghams were one of the five "Colonial" families, descendants of missionaries, whose fortunes were founded on real estate and sugar cane. Mr. Dillingham was a fine looking man, six feet four, athletic and an ardent member of the A.D. He left Harvard in 1900, became a leader in the community and was now the richest man in Hawaii. He drove us to the other side of the island to see their ranch of several thousand acres where he raised cattle and polo ponies for the Dillingham team—the best on the island—consisting of his three sons and himself. His oldest son Lowell proved to be a business genius who increased the family wealth dramatically, beginning with the dredging operation with which he cleaned up Pearl Harbor after the Japanese attack.

According to Mr. Dillingham of the 300,000 people who then inhabited the group of islands, nearly 100,000 were Japanese and Chinese, and only about 20,000 were native Hawaiians who are fast dying out. Most of the rough work in the plantations and ranches was done by the Japanese. The Hawaiians themselves are the most simple, likable people in the world, but they have not taken kindly to civilization. The beach boy, for instance, is a perfect example of carefree indolence, existing from day to day on the tips of tourists and the fees from swimming and surfing lessons. But he is hopelessly pugnacious and quite unscrupulous in a fight. What is more, he will take whatever appeals to him—especially if it happens to be liquor, for which he has a very decided preference. At heart he is a very likable fellow.

We were eager to have a Japanese dinner and were told that Mochizuki's Restaurant was the best. A lovely spot it was, with an elaborate Japanese garden, separate little tea

houses and a carp pond, beloved by the proprietor. The food
was very good, sukiyaki, which is thin-sliced, delicately fried
beef, seasoned with vegetables, and washed down with sake.
About ten o'clock we thought it might be fun to tease the carp,
using my watchchain as a line and Freddy's gold collar-pin as
the hook, baited with a bit of raw bacon. The trouble was that
the chain wasn't long enough to reach the water, and the proprietor objected to our molesting his pets.

A day or so later we rented a twenty-six-foot sampan to go
fishing off Diamond Head. The skipper was a little Japanese
about four feet high and his assistant, a Hawaiian, with no
fingers on one hand and three on the other. The tackle was
much the same Shirley and I had used at Catalina. About
half a mile out I struck a 30 pound mahimahi (dolphin) that
put up a terrible fight and in reeling him in I lost several
pieces of knuckle. He had a high sail-like fin and a forehead
like a ram. His color was green, shading into yellow with a
number of pretty silver spots, altogether a monumental fish.

Later, we drove out Pearl Harbor way and I had no idea
that Hawaii was so thoroughly fortified. Apparently we had a
large percentage of our standing army here together with a
big detachment of submarines and destroyers. The road is
well paved and winds between great fields of sugar cane and
pineapple. We stopped at Wheeler Field where the "Mait-
land" and "Heggenberger" flyers complained that they only
got obsolete planes; I wondered if this lack of funds is typical
in our military and naval posts. We lunched at Haleiwa, a
pleasant spot had it not been for a machine gun detachment
which was having target practice at an imaginary landing party.
Eight guns were in action; the noise was deafening as they tore
up the water. The next war, I thought, will be a terror.

On our return visit to Mochizuki's Restaurant we brought

with us a couple of shark hooks, determined to do a better job on the carp. The fishing was splendid, everyone had been feeding them bread for the last decade and all we had to do was to drop the shark hook with a bit of roll on it into the pond; they fought for it and we caught five beauties before Fumiko, the proprietor's daughter, put a stop to it.

It did not seem important to us to visit the "outer islands," possibly because by now we had made friends with the beach boys. With their enthusiastic support and seven gallons of the best "oak," we hired a hall and invited the town to a farewell "luau." Hawaiian music, played by the beach boys on their steel guitars and ukuleles, was something new and we had the best performers on the island. They had beautiful voices and sang with real feeling, "The Song of the Islands," "The King's Serenade," and dozens of others. Then, Winona Love danced. I described her hula in my diary:

> It was perfect—the prettiest young Hoppi Hula you could conceive of, with grass skirt and ginger leis and dancing a gracious
> Melania Mo
> Melania Oi

> First to the right and then to the left, first to show it this way, and then to show it that way. She was the most famous hula dancer in the islands and she well deserved the title. I have never seen anyone use their hands and arms so meaningly. Her expressions were perfect, natural and utterly sophisticated. She was refined, yet savage, and conveyed everything that the Hula could possibly do without obvious coarseness. The beach boys, the musicians, are crazy over her and they outdo themselves when she dances. It was a sight no one could forget.

Our next to last morning I lunched at the University Club, where I met Mr. Dole, the "pineapple king," who put up the prizes of $35,000 for the race from Oakland, California, to Hawaii. He told me that of the sixteen original entries two cracked up on the narrow take-off at Oakland, eight started, and only two finished the 2400-mile test. The winner was the "Woolaroc," a single-engine Travelair monoplane, piloted by Colonel Arthur Goebel and navigated by Lieutenant William Davies. Second money went to the "Aloha," a Breese monoplane, piloted by Captain Paul Schluter and navigated by Martin Jensen who had never flown before! He hit the islands by dead reckoning, no small feat, with only four gallons of gas left. Two planes were lost at sea.

*   *   *

With heavy heads we boarded a President liner for Yokohama. It was a gloomy boat on a ten-day voyage but we had smooth sailing and the routine was restful: deck tennis in the morning, luncheon, reading, cocktails and, after dinner, cards, either "21" or poker. I finished Lotte's *Japan*—well written though confined to only a single city, Nagasaki; Franck's *Glimpses of Japan*, which told more about the Japanese character and Cooper's *Nippons*, which struck me as too romantic. Also zipped through a number of Louis Bromfield's novels, the best being *The Green Bay Tree* and *Possession*.

We tarried at Yokohama long enough to see the great bronze Buddha, thence to Tokyo which was decked out with foliage and flowers to celebrate the birth of the Empress's daughter. We were among the first guests at the Imperial Hotel, built by Frank Lloyd Wright, the brilliant American architect (of whom we had never heard). He had been commissioned to construct an earthquake-proof structure after the devastating earthquake of 1923 had left many hundreds dead and thousands homeless. Actually the area within miles of the hotel was depressing and still being rebuilt.

We approached Japan looking for what was aesthetic or good fun and despite the incessant rain what attracted us most on our short trips away from Tokyo was the inherent beauty of Nikko: the majestically beautiful cryptomerias which reminded us of our California redwoods; the red lacquer shrine of the first Shogun, the masses of pilgrims and the Sacred Horse which they paid to feed, the great Drum Tower, and the pervasive atmosphere of the town which gave us a feeling of something *very different* from the West.

The trains were a delight: spotlessly clean, on time to the minute and provided with box lunches, purchased on the platform, with perfectly cooked rice, fish raw or well cooked, octopus or shimi, garnished with delicious seaweed, and to be eaten with chopsticks, which Freddy and I were beginning to master.

We left for Fujiyama on a foggy day, but at last we came into the clear and suddenly got a good view of Fuji without a single cloud. It really lives up to its reputation. The stations were crowded with troops on their way to the maneuvers around Fuji, so we elected not to climb the mountain preferring to spend a night at one of the famous inns, several thousand feet up its slope. That inn was fascinating: we enjoyed its excellent food, its hot baths, and indulged more than once in massages, administered by the famous Japanese blind masseurs. While we were being massaged we read to each other from an English-Japanese phrase book which we found in the inn. It had been printed in the early 1880s and it included some rather weird phrases, such as the Japanese translation of "We need help. Our postillion has been struck by lightning."

—which must have been an odd occurrence even in the nineteenth century.

Then on to Kyoto where I remember our visit to Yamanaka's main store with its wonderful stock of screens, prints and sculpture—and how I lacked the confidence to buy anything significant for Moms. That evening we went to one of the Tea Houses where we were entertained by two pocket-size geisha girls. They were only twelve years old but were all dolled up and to us had the dignity and sophisticated bearing of an old woman of fifty. They put on a couple of classical dances that were a treat—especially one that was supposed to represent a lion admiring the peonies that bloom in the spring. Afterwards we all joined in Japanese games—variants of Blind Man's Bluff, Peas Porridge Hot, etc. Quite childish and having the consumption of sake as a forfeit. At this sort of thing they were very natural but the contrast between their age and their getup was irresistible.

At every opportunity we took photographs. I had a 3×4 Graflex and a French "Sept" movie camera, weighing only five pounds. The "Sept" consumed masses of film which were sent ahead to our various ports. We ended up with hundreds of stills and several thousand feet of motion pictures; I sent them back in installments to Shirley who put them together and had evening shows for our staff, neighbors and tenants numbering about sixty. He wrote me that whenever I—"the laird"—appeared in the film everyone dutifully applauded.

We were a little too conspicuous when we reached the Inland Sea, for at Shimonoseki, where, unknowingly, we had been filming a Japanese Naval base, two secret service men (in the late 1920s all Japanese secret service men wore white rubber soled tennis shoes and were easily identified) became intensely interested in our activities. They didn't actually arrest us but they followed us on the boat across the Sea of Japan and by rail through Korea to the Chinese border (no doubt having submitted a lengthy and suspicious report on our activities).

Safely inside the Chinese border we stopped at a small station and bought from peddlers several bunches of beautiful white grapes and ate them avidly en route to Peking. Later when we met the head of the Peking Hospital (a gift of the Rockefeller Clinic) he sternly warned us that eating fresh grapes—unsterilized—was the kiss of death. But we were young and enthusiastic. We had not been in Peking more than twelve hours before we realized that this—in sharp contrast to Tokyo—was really a "fun city," and went out to make the most of it.

On the overnight train to Peking, an impressive American Army officer came aboard who turned out to be Colonel Newell, in command of our troops at Tientsin. We asked him into our compartment and he gave us some interesting dope about the disorganization in China: "Bolsheviks to the South, Brigands to the North, and one powerful dictator who strictly minded his own business; every leader out for himself—you can buy a General for $2000, and an Army for $20,000. The people are untrustworthy; trouble is caused by the young students who have picked up revolutionary ideas abroad. We get sentimental about a free and united China but the possibility is remote."

In Peking, where we had planned to stay a fortnight, our letters brought a prompt invitation to our Embassy. The Legation Quarter seemed extremely attractive. After the Boxer Rebellion the Chinese were ousted and the larger powers built quite pretentious establishments surrounded by high walls and guarded by regular troops. In the British Legation part of the

old wall remains—bullet scarred, and inscribed "Lest We Forget." About three in the afternoon we called at our Legation
which is guarded by very efficient-looking Marines. Ambassador MacMurray was away and we were received by "Buzzie"
Hewes, the Second Secretary, who took us to watch the polo.
They play on a field absolutely devoid of grass and mounted
on tiny Mongolian ponies; the game was quite fast and fun to
watch. There I met Roy Chapman Andrews who attained
world fame as the discoverer of the first dinosaur eggs in the
Gobi Desert; he turned out to be charming, with an eye for
the ladies. He spoke frankly about the Chinese situation which
rankles like a thorn in the heart of every man who knows the
country. He agreed absolutely with Colonel Newell.

Cocktails and an excellent dinner with Hewes, where I sat
between Andrews and a Miss Duer; Andrews was telling us
about his experiences—the time when he camped in a perfect
nest of puff adders, and another time when he watched "the
death of a thousand cuts" in Tientsin, a traditional form of
torture. Present also was a German princess who had been bit-
ten by a chipmunk and was afraid of getting hydrophobia.
Andrews suggested that she make up a list of the people she
was going to bite.

On the third day we had the sad news that we would have
to depart tomorrow. To dodge the civil war one had to go by
train and boat to Shanghai, and American Express could only
get us passage from Tsingtao. We decided to cram everything
into the remaining hours. Piloted by a rickshaw man who
spoke English and French, we went to the Forbidden City.
For two miles runs an absolutely straight road—straight as an
arrow—to the Dragon Throne. The throne room itself is perfectly proportioned and of immense size. The richly decorated
ceiling must be sixty feet above the floor. In the center stands

that miracle of workmanship—the Dragon Throne. Twenty feet square at least, it is carved of red lacquer with stairs and railings to the seat itself, where once presided the Manchu emperors.

It is not hard to imagine the majestic procession of Mandarins and court officials in their ceremonial sables, filing majestically along that glorious avenue through courtyard after courtyard, between the royal bodyguard to the very throne room itself, there to prostrate themselves before the living embodiment of the celestial Empire. And today the rightful occupant of that throne lives in a tawdry set of rooms in a tawdry city protected by the foreigners who insured his downfall. He is the most tragic figure in the world: Henry Pu-Yi.

In the afternoon we went down to the Peking Club and had a little tennis—the first in nearly two months. Just before dinner we drove over to the Legation to say goodbye to our friends, and with them went to dine at a Chinese restaurant. The food was amazing: perfectly black eggs which had been buried for three weeks before being hard-boiled, shark fins which were excellent and birds nest soup I thought insipid, followed by about twenty other dishes, most of them allegedly aphrodisiac. The "pièce de résistance" was Peking Duck which is done in a perfectly delicious way and eaten with pancakes in the manner of caviar aux blini.

Afterwards we set sail for a nightclub, "The Alcazar," a large vanlike structure with a pretty good orchestra and an excellent Russian basso. Here we ran into the famed Russian girls for the first time . . . and I'm inclined to believe that the Revolution has done a great thing for the East. Of course the great majority of them are duds. I spotted Barma, a blonde with lovely hair and eyes. Her English was adequate and she didn't dance badly. However, she became a bit of a trial.

About two o'clock Freddy and I suggested that we might take her home (purely platonically). She got quite upset and said that she could have gone home at 12, but not at 2. As we argued, I unintentionally insulted the première danseuse, a very majestic lady who was in the midst of a rather erotic classical dance. Out of the goodness of my heart I threw all my loose change at her. It was the thing to do, but unfortunately it consisted entirely of coppers.

Apparently it is the ultimate insult to offer coppers to an artist. There was an uproar. The lady walked off the floor and Barma was sputtering. To propitiate the injured genius, I hit upon the happy expedient of changing a dollar Mex. into dimes, and sending them to her one by one. After about sixty cents she was ameliorated. After the last one she was beaming.

On the roundabout train and boat trip to Shanghai we slept. I kept wishing we'd had more time in Peking; in Shanghai we had no connections and the contrast was bleak. At one of the famous nightclubs I spotted a Russian who was an absolute knockout. Dark, of medium height, perfect features, close cropped black hair, alluring black eyes, a charming way of talking, and dressed with a simplicity that set her apart.

I asked her over to the table, and before I knew it, discerned that she was truly beautiful. In repose, her features were perfection, when animated each expression seeming more fascinating than the last. She had a distinct air of breeding. Her story was the usual one. . . . Her father and mother died when she was ten. . . . Her husband, a White Russian, was killed fighting the Bolsheviks. . . . She then accompanied a girlfriend from Harbin to Shanghai. (When other girls told me the same story I did not believe it; true or not, as far as Maria was concerned, it hardly mattered to me.)

Time flew in her company, Freddy went back alone to the

hotel, and we did not leave the nightclub until 6 a.m. We went out the next night to another and did not return until 5 a.m.

We planned still a third party, but unfortunately Maria confessed that she had eaten so much Japanese food that she felt unwell. I took her back to 4 Astor House Road—the most disreputable of the Russian lodging house district. If someone with plenty of money should marry her and turn her out in the style she deserved she might have been a famous beauty. What a pity! We said goodbye, and when I turned at the foot of the lane, she was still standing at the gate, waving.

It was one of the most moving moments of my life.

It was at this point that our schedule became more binding: from Shanghai to Hong Kong, where we barely had time to be fitted for some light clothes for India and Egypt before we boarded a charming little Dutch boat, to Java and thence to Sumatra. In a bar at Surabaja Freddy was captivated by a big game hunter who described, drink by drink, the thrill of killing a banteng. He said a banteng was even more dangerous than the African wild buffalo. If we could spare three days he'd be glad to arrange for the porters and outfit us. Neither Freddy nor I had ever handled a rifle but our hunter sounded so plausible that Freddy was wild to try; it was his party and I went along.

With our porters, cook and two ominous 30-30 rifles— Freddy and I decided to take turns—we followed Mr. Intrepid who led the party through the bush to the beach of a small lake where we were to spend the night on a large platform in a tree. On the way the hunter who was also carrying a light rifle urged me to take a practice shot. I aimed at a small yellow bird in a treetop and to my surprise killed it.

We went light on the whiskey before supper and the campfire kept the bugs away but when we settled ourselves in our treehouse the hoardes of mosquitoes added to our discomfort. Intrepid said we must be very quiet—crush the bugs not slap them. Sleep came in snatches and through that hot, thirsty night we neither heard nor saw a banteng. Three days of this were enough for us, and enough for our "white hunter" (who proved to be a half-caste) out to extract as many American dollars as possible from two naive young travelers. The canary was our only trophy.

*   *   *

Our next destination was Singapore where we remained for over a month but of which I saw little. We had rooms at Raffles. The day after our arrival I felt very feverish. Freddy took my temperature, found it was 104° and called a doctor. A red-faced Englishman in a dusty morning coat, after testing my blood, pronounced that I had tertian and quartan malaria. I could expect alternating chills and fever for quite a while, but he assured me, humorously, that I would not die, and hired two beautiful Australian nurses to apply cold compresses around the clock. In our "de luxe" suite there was a W.C. but in place of a bathtub stood a huge stone jar on a stone base. When the nurse poured water over my red-hot or shivering frame it produced an incredible itching. No fun.

I begged for ice cream but the doctor forbade it, "a barbarous dish invented by Americans." During my slow recovery the nurse, the doctor and his sexy daughter, who was carrying on with Freddy, would gather in my room before lunch and dinner and endeavor to cheer me up by downing gin slings, which, of course, were prohibited for me. They pointed out that the cold compresses wrapped around my head gave me a striking resemblance to Suzanne Lenglen, the French tennis champion. Freddy's nightly account of his erotic adventures did not improve my morale either. Fortunately his reassuring cables to Moms had stopped her from attempting the 12,000 mile journey to my bedside. But my protracted misery (which Nan had predicted) canceled our plans to visit Bali and French Indo-China and it was five weeks before I was fit to travel. I had lost twenty pounds and was in no mood to enjoy our next country, India.

We debarked at Calcutta, India's dominant port, and my first impression that it was the most overcrowded, odoriferous city I had ever lived in never changed. It had grown to be the capital of British India until 1912 when the administration was shifted to New Delhi, deeper in the interior. It was still the center of the jute industry whose mills, surrounded by thick walls and barbed wire, were spacious and clean in revolting contrast to the slums in which the workers dwelt. There seemed to be hundreds of thousands of men without jobs, beggars everywhere, women scooping up cow dung for their fires, and the multitude of undernourished children. In going around Calcutta I asked myself, "Can anyone be held accountable? Is change impossible? Aren't the British appalled?"

Our rooms at the Grand were comfortable enough and the only unpleasant hangover from malaria was the itching which overwhelmed me after a bath. Against my better judgment I consulted another English doctor whose sole comment was that it was the usual after-effect, nothing could be done. *Ça passe.* He seemed to take a ghoulish pleasure that it happened to an American.

Freddy and I had letters to some impressive dignitaries and one of the first invitations we received was to attend a regimental banquet for the Cameron Highlanders in Mandalay.

The Cameron headquarters were quite elegant for an "up

country" station. Just what the regiment mission was in this little hill town we never learned, perhaps on guard against "China across the way" as the song has it. At any rate there were two dozen or so officers present, relaxed and most hospitable, the young subalterns of the same age as Freddy and I. Many were handsome and all splendidly attired in dress uniform which put to shame our white mess jackets so hurriedly fitted at Hong Kong.

The long mahogany table was graced with the superb, beautifully polished regimental silver gathered together over two centuries of the regiment's existence, and I seem to remember regimental flags adorned with battle honors at the end of the room. We were served by well-attired Indian servants headed by a marvelous white bearded Sikh majordomo who was honored by being allowed to wear the regimental badge on his turban.

The evening began with prolonged drinking of (warm) pink gin or whiskey. Then the dinner, elaborate, lengthy and mediocre. According to William Hickey's diary Indian cooking was terrible in the eighteenth century and it had not improved by 1927: roast beef (overdone), Yorkshire pudding and Gorgonzola cheese (a long way from home), an item so ripe that the slogan "unleash the Gorgonzola" was apt, savories, etc.—all of which was accompanied by four wines, sherry, hock, claret, and champagne in copious amounts. With the champagne came numerous toasts to the King, to the President, to the regiment and to anyone else we could think of. Then we moved on to serious drinking of port, accompanied by excellent cigars, followed by a superb cognac. Then back to Scotch whiskey and the singing of many songs, some beautifully traditional regimental ballads, others rather pornographic.

The whole business lasted five hours, from 8 p.m. to 1 a.m., and in this rivalry between Harvard and Regimental capacity no one passed out or became "sick" to use the elegant English phrase.

When activities reached a climax about 1 a.m., the more enthusiastic subalterns decided it would be great "fun" to throw the septuagenarian butler through the open window into the garden some six feet below. Despite the dismay of the democratically minded Americans the officers proceeded with their task: "One, two, three and away we go." Minutes later he emerged much crumpled, his immaculate white costume covered with dirt. He did not seem unduly upset. I suspect he had been subjected to this ignominious treatment many times before. But I doubt if the act contributed much to the long range future of Anglo-Indian relations. We were to awaken next morning with frightful "heads," treated, rather effectively, as in Wellington's time, with the "hair of the dog," and our misery was alleviated by the cries of "stout fellahs" with which our new found military friends had bid us farewell.

We had a therapeutic lunch at the very traditional Mandalay Club and afterwards Freddy and I fell asleep in arm chairs flanking the slumbering form of Congressman Tinker from Massachusetts, an avid big game hunter, returned from an exhausting expedition.

Calcutta became our springboard to places of greater singularity.

Our British friends said if we saw nothing else in India we must see the Khyber Pass and the Himalayas which involved a thirty-six-hour train trip to Rawalpindi. We had a wonderful view of the Khyber Pass and were promised an even better view of the Himalayas should we care to face a six-hour donkey trip to the famous "Tiger Hill." Freddy did the trip and was lyrical about what he saw. I felt too lousy and did not go.

The British officers stationed in the Khyber Pass to whom we talked said they were constantly involved in Afghan guerrilla warfare and described the Russians as wanting to take over the whole country—all news to Freddy and me. Kipling was right in his picture of the Russian, "the bear who walks like a man."

We visited Udaipur with its marvelous white marble palace in the center of a small lovely lake and Jaipur with its sugary pink palace. Occasionally we traveled by elephant, probably the most uncomfortable beast to ride on except the camel. The elephant's defect is that he lacks shock absorbers going down hill. Each giant stride downward produces a jarring shock which rises undiminished from his feet through the rider's spine.

We went to Benares, the holy city on the Ganges, and were horrified that such shocking pollution existed in India for thousands of years. And to us, the Taj Mahal, unsophisticated as we were, was too "pretty" and not really a great work of art.

In Calcutta we were introduced to a tall ex-State Department character named Don Springer who had resigned and was now working for one of the Standard Oil subsidiaries. He enthusiastically invited us to go "hunting" with him, but hating horses, and loathing to get up early (The Hunt, as I remember it, involved getting up at 5:30 a.m.), we both declined. However, we did thank him for putting us in touch with a barber who was so beautifully trained that he could shave us perfectly and completely in bed *without* waking us up. What luxury! What bliss!

At the outset we thought of India as Kipling had pictured it in his magnificent stories of that glamorous period when the country was a picturesque, subordinate part of the British Empire. In Katharine Mayo's book we learned for the first time of the cruelty of the caste system, of the Hindu religion which made reincarnation so much more sacred than life on earth. Now we saw its seamy side: the sacred cows which befouled the city and could not be killed for the much needed food; we were aware of the dung, the urine, the degradation.

But December was the big month for Calcutta in British eyes. The Viceroy and his retinue were there for Christmas and "Boxing Day" (when children "boxed" their second-best presents for the poor). At the formal balls attended by the Maharajas and the British and Indian officers, bemedalled and in full dress uniform, we in our tails and white ties had our first impression of the "raj," the caste system imposed by the Empire. For more than a week we had a gay time, at the dances and the innumerable race meetings where we were more attracted by the elegance of the scene than by the horses.

On Christmas Eve our Standard Oil friend, Don Springer, invited us to a fancy dress affair given at a big American owned jute mill on the banks of the Houghly River. Some sixty couples, English and American, were present (no Indians of course), the food was excellent, the consumption of alcohol fantastic and by sunrise there were a number of casualties, not including Freddy and myself. But it was really fun and after a few hours sleep we were restored by that wonderful drink, "black velvet," half stout, half champagne.

We went on to New Delhi where we were privileged to be guests of the Viceroy, Lord Irwin (later Lord Halifax), for five days. Lutyens great palace for the Viceroys was in the very early stage of construction and the Viceroy's quarters were in the process of transition. The vast ménage was living in tents waiting for their permanent quarters to be finished. But what

tents! The one Freddy and I were assigned to (and we were
the most junior members of a huge house party of at least a
hundred people in January 1928) was 50 feet square with
bathroom facilities and hot water brought in by a half dozen
bearers to fill long Edwardian tin bathtubs. Tremendous
wardrobe for clothes and above all two magnificent turbaned
Sikhs in glorious scarlet uniforms with hip high patent leather
boots, white leather gauntlets, gold turbans, glorious swords
and very tall lances—a really impressive ensemble.

We of course had our own bearer to take care of our clothes
on top of all this. I cannot remember how many tents there
were but the total "encampment" must have amounted to at
least fifty, many of them far larger and more luxurious than
ours. A huge dining hall had been built where we attended a
"state dinner" for at least a hundred persons.

White tie was de rigueur. Freddy and I with no rank and no
decorations were the lowest of the pecking order; the only one
seemingly lower was the distinguished Professor G. P. Gooch
who was engaged in writing a history of India. I don't remember much about the dinner except that it was long, dull and
the food mediocre—that execrable combination of imitation
English cooking (bad enough at the best) cooked by Indians.

The mediocrity of the wines (not improved by being shipped
and stored under tropical temperatures without air conditioning) was saved by the excellent and liberal potions of port—
which appears to be invulnerable to climate—and the excellent cognac (brandy to the British) which one then found at
all British outposts.

The morning after the big formal dinner we were informed
by an ADC that Lady Irwin would be happy to play tennis
doubles with us and a capable young Englishwoman tennis
player for a fourth. We were cautioned politely that Lady Ir-

win always *insisted* on winning and that she was not above calling balls that were patently out—by six inches or even a foot, *in*. We were told that we should not question any dubious calls. Nor did we. She won and everyone was happy.

The next time I met Lady Irwin was some eighteen years later in Washington when her husband, then Lord Halifax, was the British Ambassador. We again played doubles together on the excellent court in the Embassy grounds; she still cheated on the calls, and I still recognized her prerogative, and she again won.

Her husband, the Viceroy, was of course far above my head. He was a devoted Catholic and a convinced pacifist and young as I was I thought him rather sanctimonious and wildly unrealistic.

We spent some time in New Delhi with George D. Widener of Philadelphia, a handsome, delightful man, much older than we, owner of one of the leading racing stables in America, who was enjoying himself in India, riding, shooting and at every function. What impressed us at the time was how impeccably he was dressed. His shoes and boots always shone and his white bow ties for evening were exquisite. When I complimented him he said it was all due to his English valet Johnson whom he then loaned to me, and I made a mental note. What, of course, we could not foresee was that Freddy would one day marry George's stepdaughter.

At the end of two months we embarked from Bombay to Alexandria on one of the famous P&O steamers. On our last morning ashore we said farewell to our Singalese bearer who deserved a big tip. Only when we were at sea did we discover that he was as crafty as he was efficient as he had stolen a small sapphire Buddha.

The P&O steamship line had long been a British institution,

every boat, coming or going, crammed with civil servants and
the military. These were its characteristics:

1. The menus and the cooking were entirely British and
the quality of both awful.
2. Wine was practically nonexistent. There was, however,
an astonishing consumption of gin and bitters, Scotch and
water, without ice.
3. No air conditioning. During the long hot passage through
the Red Sea many slept on deck.
4. There was a rigid caste system. High level civil servants
rarely spoke, much less ate with the lower level. The high
ranking military formed a caste of their own.
5. On the lowest level were British businessmen. The un-
touchables were stray Americans, snubbed with a brutality
of which the British, at that time were masters. They tried
it on us until word got around that we had been guests of
the Viceroy. This and our winning tournaments in deck
tennis raised our standing.

*   *   *

After the oppressive cruise on that all-too-British steamer,
Egypt seemed like Eden, the weather was warm, the ambiance
semi-European—and free from caste! But our punishing travel
agent had conscientiously booked us for a side trip to Palestine
and from the sunshine of Alexandria we passed into bleak, cold
rainy days and when there was a recurrence of my malaria in
Jerusalem I said the hell with this and as soon as I could totter
we headed for Cairo.

We had reservations at the famous Shepheard's Hotel, Victo-
rian and comfortable, a delightful bar and a huge terrace on
which to enjoy one's drink and watch the life of Cairo go by.

The trouble was we arrived two days ahead of schedule and every room was taken. A magnificent tip to the reception clerk produced an arrangement that two cots for Freddy and myself would be set up in the spacious ground floor "ladies room" provided we agreed not to sleep before 3 a.m. The Cairo night clubs being what they were this was no problem. We slept comfortably and late as "the ladies" was not open for use until lunch.

Once we got unpacked in our permanent suite the fun began. Freddy had a letter to a very amusing Foreign Service officer, named Winfield, who introduced us to some interesting Egyptians and aroused our interest in the Cairo Museum. Tutankhamen's tomb, recently opened, the pyramids and the much smaller Sakkara pyramids, beautifully preserved with their painted bas-reliefs made a deep impression.

I remember seeing three Hispano-Suizas, all Egyptian owned, one of them the famous 37.5 HP sports model with a boat-shaped tulip wood body and driven by a chauffeur wearing a dashing red fez. From the sublime to the ridiculous I was reminded of the new Ford Model A which I learned was available for test driving in Cairo. The Ford dealer amiably lent me one and it accelerated easily although the brakes seemed inadequate. I was soon bowling along at seventy-five on the road to the pyramids, which is elevated some fifteen feet above the surrounding sandy fields. Suddenly about twenty feet in front of me a huge camel leaped up into the road. I couldn't stop; all that was possible was to take evasive action which I did without going off the road, and so lived to tell the tale.

Very soon after our arrival we "picked up" two very lively American girls. Freddy's Kitty came from Greenwich, Connecticut, dark-haired and tolerably good-looking; mine was a rather ruggedly built divorcée from Indianapolis. She dressed terribly, was far from good-looking but had a grand sense of humor. If not the most cultured traveling companions they were certainly the most amusing we ran into on our entire journey. They were booked as we were for a leisurely trip up the Nile. The food and service were excellent and with our amusing, compliant companions life was delightful indeed. We traveled only by day and usually stopped to see one or two fascinating temples. Excellent picnics were provided and on shore there were other amusements such as donkey or camel races, a fair proportion of which either Freddy or I won. I don't remember the temples individually but I certainly recollect being overwhelmed by the majesty and beauty of Thebes.

About half way to Assuan romance got the better of me. Everyone dressed for dinner and this particular night there was a full moon. The Nile looked particularly romantic.

Tied to the stern of our steamer was a very large rowboat on which the passengers went ashore when we could not tie up to a dock. In my hearty mood I neglected to remember that the boat was at least twenty feet long, very heavy, made of steel, and when rowed to shore in the daytime required at least six strong Egyptians wielding very long oars to propel it.

My imagination excited by an excellent dinner with appropriate wines and a companionable girl also in a very romantic mood, I decided that it would be a wonderful idea to go for a row on the Nile by the light of the moon. *Time: midnight.*

We leaped lightly into the boat. I cast off the painter without looking at what equipment was available in the boat. Much to our surprise the boat took off like a rocket downstream propelled by the current. Our mother ship seemed to be vanishing rapidly upstream.

I quickly reached for the oars but found to my horror that not only were they great heavy sweeps at least ten feet long but even worse there were *no oarlocks*. (The oarlocks had been removed by the sailors to protect the rowboat from theft.) Rowing a twenty-foot steel boat with heavy oars and without oarlocks is no easy job even for two healthy young people. In fact, it was impossible. We worked out a method of hooking one knee over the oar to keep it more or less in place and this arrangement enabled us to row after a fashion but it soon became evident that we could not overcome the current. We shouted but no one heard us.

I took off my dinner jacket; she took off her dress; luckily she was a strong young woman and we went over the side on opposite sides of the boat to attempt to push it up current to the diabeah. Much to our surprise we found ourselves up to our knees in the squishy, filthy mud of the Nile bottom. Near the shore where we were, the river was not over four feet deep.

We huffed and we puffed making, it seemed, not more than ten feet progress upstream every half hour. But we persevered and about 4 a.m., well before dawn, *we made it*, tied the dinghy painter to the stern of the diabeah, stumbled up to the deck, frightfully dirty, disheveled and exhausted. Fortunately everyone was asleep and we were able to steal into our respective cabins unnoticed.

From then on for the several weeks we were together my girlfriend from Indianapolis was nicknamed Cleo and I Tony (after Shakespeare's famous pair), for we had braved the Nile successfully and *survived*. I learned a lot from this bizarre and amusing experience: Make a careful study of the practical problems that face you before embarking on a major enterprise.

*   *   *

Our trip up the Nile—the temples and picnics by day, the frivolity by night—came to an end at Assuan. The girls were going on; we gave them a farewell dinner of Egyptian quail and burgundy and ourselves took the sleeper on the long slow ride back to Cairo. Egypt had been delightful; we had no letters to any ranking official and did not trouble our minds about the political problems of the country of which there were plenty just around the bend.

I was particularly eager to get on to Rome where Moms's new touring car, our Mercedes, would be waiting for us. My brief touch of speed in the Ford Model A—never mind the camel —had given me a longing to get my hands on a really fast car. So we canceled our scheduled visit to Khartoum and a motor drive around Sicily, and luckily got staterooms on a Cunard boat bound for Italy. The Mercedes with its beautiful black body by LeBaron had arrived without a scratch, and as Freddy was feeling seedy I hired an excellent guide and, at his suggestion, conscientiously saw every "sight" in Rome which had one star or more in Baedeker's, quite the most educational stint thus far, despite my having so little knowledge of Italian history.

Freddy was still under the weather when we set forth for Florence in the beauty of the Italian spring, planning to drive through the "hill towns," beginning with Orvieto. We had reached the town of San Gimignano and were lunching after seeing the marvelous Giotto frescoes, when Freddy suddenly collapsed and begged: "Bill, get me to Florence as quickly as possible. I feel terribly ill." I never needed any encouragement to drive fast, which was a real pleasure in the Europe of those days when the roads, though far from perfect, were almost empty. Using a "cut in cut out" supercharger as often as possible, we roared over hill and dale for the thirty-four miles with that little bit of extra power and that marvelous amount of extra noise. In forty minutes we drew up before the very comfortable Grand Hotel in Florence, eliciting the obsequious bows of the manager, the concièrge and the doorman who felt that two eccentric American millionaires had arrived for a long stay. In fact the "Grand" was to be my home in that loveliest of Italian cities for almost six weeks.

Freddy's illness did indeed turn out to be serious (perhaps encephalitis his New York doctors thought on his return) and it was certainly beyond the understanding of the leading doctors in Florence to whom we had access through my letters to the leading Florentine family, the Guerardeschi, one of whom was married to my cousin.

I didn't take Freddy's illness seriously enough. Life was too pleasant for me in Florence—lots of pretty American girls available, residents in schools or travelers; an excellent cuisine, the marvelous countryside; and my car with short trips to Venice and to the Adriatic. Perhaps it was also psychologically a way of "getting back" at Freddy who had had such a grand time with my doctor's daughter in Singapore when I was flat on my back. Meanwhile he was in bed with a high fever, watched over by a bevy of depressing nuns whose appearance did not cheer the invalid.

I only became seriously worried about his condition when I had drunk the last bottle of Chambertin 1906. (There were three cases in the hotel cellar when I started.) At about that time Freddy rose from his bed and said: "If I stay here much longer, I will die. Bill, I want to get out of bed and go to the Riviera."

So we left. He picked up along the way and when we arrived at Monte Carlo he had apparently recovered.

We stayed in the south of France for awhile, then a couple of weeks at the Ritz in Paris, and then, suddenly, both smitten with homesickness, we went to London to be fitted for new suits, shirts and shoes, and returned to New York in mid-May.

I doubt if either of us was much the wiser but my movies and the thousands of stills reminded me of the highlights in Peking, New Delhi, the Nile, and Florence. I had brought home gifts for

Moms, Aunt Ruth, and Shirley, but the one most talked about in family circles was the sari of cloth of gold which I purchased in India for my Grandmother. She seemed most appreciative and had it made up into an evening gown.

What did I learn from my Grand Tour? It stirred my interest in international affairs and widened my understanding of what the world was really like. I thank my lucky stars that I had the experience and had not invested the same amount of time in a graduate school at Harvard. Our trip was certainly different from that of the serious tourist. We were on the outlook for a good time which meant parties and girls—after all we were only twenty-one years old—but more than that I now realize we were acquiring the background, perhaps in India even the perception, of events to come.

CHAPTER V

Bachelor at Large

WHILE I was abroad Shirley had shaped up into a young man of eagerness and charm. The time he had spent in Northern Canada working on Douglas Burden's film had given him an incentive. He had always gotten along easily with people and the experience of being tossed into an Indian tribe, of living with Long Lance who had become his friend, and the professionals from Hollywood had matured him. When the shooting was completed on "The Silent Enemy" he suggested that the editing and cutting of the film be done in our playhouse in Mt. Kisco. Dick Carver, a film editor, chose the equipment that was needed, and Shirley supervised the installation of two 35mm projection machines, and a larger screen for the stage. The only thing missing was "sound," which was about to transform the movies and of course "The Silent Enemy" had been produced as a silent film. Shirley bought two turntables, installed speakers on either side of the screen, purchased some appropriate records, and synchronized them skillfully to the action in the picture. It was, of course, only an approximation, but it was enough of an innovation to impress the few who saw the early rushes, such as Walter Wanger, a producer for Paramount Pictures, and Jesse Lasky, the head of Paramount, who had originally given Douglas a release contract for "The Silent Enemy." The critical question was whether Doug's film would qualify for "block-book-ing." Whatever the professionals may have thought, what struck me was Shirley's competence in a medium about which he knew so little at the time I went abroad.

My cousin, John Hammond, who had taken a personal interest in me since my father's death, was a lawyer, a partner of Cravath, Swaine and Moore, and the counsel for the well-established investment firm of Brown Brothers. He foresaw that in time I would inherit a considerable fortune, and after my graduation we had a cordial talk about the care of money, in the course of which he advised me to begin as a student with Brown Brothers in the autumn. It made sense and I told him that I would be ready in early September.

I had joined the Racquet Club and it was there, lunching with Alexander Cassatt and Cecil Lyon, both of whom were working in the Cassatt firm in Philadelphia, that I got a lively account of how the stock market was booming. Alex, who had been buying on margin with astonishing success, was evidently quite rich and confident of the future.

I listened attentively for on my twenty-first birthday I had come into money of my own, inheriting a third of my father's estate—some $70,000—and had been given by my grandmother a generous present of half a million in gilt-edged preferred stocks. Grandmother suggested that I keep it in a trust fund. "No," said Moms, "let him use it as he pleases." So far I had been very cautious.

The months abroad had left me a compulsive traveler. I collected countries the way a stamp collector buys stamps, checking off those I had seen and making mental note of those I next wanted to visit. When Moms proposed a trip to Europe and a leisurely tour through Belgium and Holland I readily agreed although I'd been home less than two months. The Mercedes

Freddy and I had driven in Italy would be waiting for us in London.

We landed in Southampton on July 5 and registered at Claridge's that afternoon where the Mercedes was parked. One of the luckiest things that ever happened was when I bumped into Bob Buell, an agreeable foreign service officer, whom I had met in New Delhi, and who had subsequently been transferred to the American Embassy in London. I told him we were in town for a few days and that we would be grateful if he could introduce Shirley and me to a couple of attractive girls. This he did at a cocktail party in his flat. Both were Americans and the most beautiful, Peggy Partridge—Margaret Livingston Partridge— greeted Shirley affectionately; she was his age and they had danced together at Bar Harbor and at parties in New York. ("You snake," I said to him later, "you've been holding out on me.") She was warm and intelligent and on the impulse I asked if I could see her the following afternoon. She must have supposed that I was taking her somewhere to dance for when I called for her at the Marble Arch Hotel she appeared in high heels and a picture hat, but I had different ideas.

My friend, Amherst Villiers, who had designed the supercharger on the 4½-liter Bentley, was constantly urging me to try it; the car was capable of 125 miles an hour, and I thought this would be a splendid opportunity to impress Miss Partridge. As I drove through Hyde Park I felt that I had one of the handsomest cars in London and beside me one of the most beautiful girls anywhere. I told Peggy that I was going to test the car in the Brooklands Racetrack, which was banked and safe as a church. When we got there I stepped on the accelerator and we had climbed to 110 m.p.h. before I noticed what a time Peggy was having with her hat. As we slowed down I felt contrite when she said that she detested fast driving. I apologized; said that tomorrow was our last day in town and perhaps she'd like to go dancing then.

After that the three of us left London, taking our car across the Channel and spending the night at a comfortable inn. Ever since the German invasion in 1914 Belgium had won the admiration of the Allies for the valor of its troops against hopeless odds, and the tenacity of King Albert and Queen Elizabeth who kept their colors flying in an uncaptured fragment of their little kingdom. We drove direct to Brussels, the capital, where I discovered to my delight the supremacy of the Belgian restaurants. Here in the famous Place, dining, which begins in earnest at 9 p.m., is an art and had it not been for Moms's disapproval of alcohol I would happily have lingered for more than one night. We paid our respects to the British war memorial at Ypres and the Cathedral of Louvain, so beautifully restored by the American architects, Whitney Warren and Charles D. Wetmore. And we caught tempting glimpses of the Belgian châteaux which, because of the damp climate, are famous for their flowers and the incredible shooting parties in the autumn (as I was to learn first-hand later in my career).

My remembrance of the Dutch was not of delicacies but of the glory of their paintings by Bruegel, Rembrandt, Vermeer and Rubens. We visited the museums in Amsterdam, and The Hague, boated in the tiny canal in the pretty little town of Delft and sat in the open cafés watching the swarms of bicyclists—the flaxen-haired girls with pretty legs—peddling home at day's end. Then (two more countries in my collection) we headed for the European city I love best.

When we checked in at the Ritz in Paris, I had had enough experience abroad to appreciate the people and the service which made the hotel unique. 15 Place Vendôme was originally the town house of the Duc de Lauzun, greatly enlarged by the purchase of the garden and the adjoining large building on the Rue Cambon, the two being joined together by a very long corridor. The princely clients, including us, had their rooms on the Vendôme side, the less princely on the Cambon side.

There were a number of Ritz characters each of whom ruled his private domain. In a hidden nook near the front door was a cluster of fin de siècle telephone booths, presided over by André, a short dark man who was always about to pounce. When he saw a client who looked as if his French was not very good, or as if he wanted to make or was expecting a telephone call, André offered his services. If there was a delay in the call and the client went up to his room for a nap, André would interrupt every thirty minutes until the call was completed. If the person wanted was out, André would repeat this information at intervals and when the call was completed, a tip in proportion to the endeavor was expected.

The regular Ritz telephone staff which served the room telephones was completely bilingual, and of course capable of taking messages, but André gave the impression that he alone managed the phones.

Several ranks above André was Michel, the concièrge. The concièrge of any good international hotel must be fluent in five languages. He must be able to handle three telephones at once: the first call asking for theatre seats, which would require a brief delay; the second phone, cocked under an ear, with apologies between the outbursts of an impatient client; and the third call placing an order for some hard-to-get delicacies, fresh truffles or large Belgian strawberries.

Not far from the reception desk in a small room of their own and behind an impeccable counter sat two impeccably dressed young men—everyone at the Ritz was impeccable—whose days were devoted to cashing traveler or personal checks. Behind them presided a more eminent official (as I remember he remained for thirty years) who was entrusted with larger amounts—he once gave me $5,000 without the flicker of an eyelid—if a customer was in a hurry for cash he would be given as much as he wanted, the amount being entered on his bill. To the right of his desk was a huge walk-in safe, with dozens of small private safes in which the really rich clients stored their important jewels.

Perhaps the most stylish of these personages was Olivier, the greatest of all maîtres d'hôtel. It was he who waited personally on Marcel Proust, at large dinner parties, or when alone; and when Proust was unwell Olivier went to his bedside. Before I appreciated his rank, I once had the effrontery to attract his attention by snapping my fingers. His back was turned to me, but he reversed stiffly like a Colonel of the Guards and with an expression on his face similar to that of King Edward VII when disgusted. I never did it again.

When our stay in Paris came to an end we returned to London to pick up the clothes Shirley and I had ordered and sailed for home. In mid-September wearing my new Davies suit, with a boutonnière of corn flowers I presented myself at Brown Brothers. I went down to Wall Street by the subway as seemed appropriate for a beginner, and continued to do so for several weeks. Cousin John was there to welcome me, introduced me to the partners, and I was then led to the cashier's cage where I was to emulate the head cashier. Standing all day long was a new ordeal and by five o'clock as the saying goes, "my feet were killing me." I reverted to my most comfortable old shoes and it gradually occurred to me that if the cage was to be my station for some months I might as well spare myself strap-hanging in the subway and let our chauffeur drop me off in the family's car.

The cage was humdrum but as a student I couldn't complain. Sooner or later I'd get my teeth into something more exciting. Meanwhile I made the most of my time away from the office. I played racquets and court tennis at the Racquet Club, often with Freddy, but my hours with Peggy were what I most looked forward to. Peggy's father, William Ordway Partridge, was an eminent sculptor; he had imbued her with a love of art and she was surprised by how little I knew or cared about it. She took me in hand: on Saturday afternoons we visited the Metropolitan Museum and the Frick Collection and in January, 1929, attended the opening of the Museum of Modern Art in small, rented rooms in the Heckscher Building that were blazing with Cézanne, Gauguin, Seurat, and Monet. My correct cousin, Emily Hammond, spotting us in the crowd, called, "Bill, I'm glad to see that Peggy is at last educating you in painting!" (The education stuck.)

For my part I was educating Peggy in what to order at my favorite speakeasies, improving her taste for wine, and sharing delight in the theatre, which in music, drama and comedy, in Shaw, Noel Coward, Somerset Maugham, Eugene O'Neill, Gershwin and Kern, was so vastly superior to that of today.

I drove her out to see—and be seen—at "Florham." Her beauty and her manners made a conquest of my grandmother. We played tennis before lunch, and Peggy played well, with Aunt Ruth watching (and wondering "if she was quite sporting enough"). I thought she would be impressed by the great house with all its grandeur, but Peggy said quietly as we were driving home, "Bill, that's not the way I *ever* want to live."

Shortly after I took up my job in Brown Brothers, a classmate called on me at our apartment to see if I would buy him a seat on the Stock Exchange. The tab was $600,000, which he promised to repay within two years. He had no financial background and I questioned very much whether he would have been able to pay it at all should the market decline—though no one believed that possible. I turned him down.

There were many ways of making money in 1928; never had

there been a better time for getting rich and people knew it. 1928 was the last year, according to John Kenneth Galbraith, in which Americans were buoyant, uninhibited and utterly happy. Certainly from what I observed in Wall Street this was so. In 1928 Radio went from 85 to 420, (it had never paid a dividend), Du Pont went from 310 to 525, Montgomery Ward went from 117 to 440, and Wright Aeronautic from 69 to 289. All in one year and quite a satisfactory performance for the bulls.

In March, 1929, I emerged from the cage and became a staff member of Brown Brothers, at a salary of $3,000 a year, assigned to do research under Henry C. Brunie, ten years my senior, an able, attractive executive destined for success. He appreciated my enthusiasm for aviation and encouraged me to explore the possibilities of investments in that new field, which was emerging as a bonanza in the wildly excited market.

Shirley twits me that I always have to read about what I propose to do. Well, one book I had read was *Common Stocks as a Long Term Investment*, regarded as a Bible in 1928, and it left me cold. What caught my admiration and what I had been reading avidly was General "Billy" Mitchell's challenging statements to the press that our air force left over from World War I was too small and obsolete and that the country must have modern fighter planes and bombers if it was to be properly defended. His criticism outraged Secretary of War John W. Weeks. But Mitchell proved what he was saying in June, 1921, when his bombers sank the German light cruiser, "Frankfurt," and a day later, the 27,000 ton battleship "Ost Friedland" off Hampton Roads, before three members of the Cabinet and the military high brass. The Navy had maintained that the battleship was unsinkable. And in 1923 the same bombers sank two of our obsolete battleships, the "Virginia" and the "South Carolina." General Mitchell risked his career in the harshness of what he was saying. Secretary Weeks denounced him as "a headline hunter," stripped Mitchell of his rank and young fly- ers who supported him, like Arnold and Spaatz, were repri- manded. But further proof was not long in coming.

The flight across the Atlantic had been tempting pilots ever since the end of World War I. One of our Navy Curtis Flying Boats, the NC-4, had made it with jumps in May, 1919, flying from Rockaway Beach to Plymouth, England, with stops for fuel at the Azores and Portugal.

But the ultimate test was set up by Raymond Orteig of Paris who, early in 1920, speaking through the Aero Club of America, offered a prize of $25,000 to the pilot making the *first non-stop flight* from New York to Paris, or vice versa. This resulted in a flurry of activity and I read every account of the contestants. The first to try was France's famous ace, Captain Nungesser, who with his co-pilot Coli took off from France in a Farnum but, bucking the head winds, was lost at sea. A second French pilot, Captain René Fonck, flying a S-35 Sikorsky, and presum- ably over-loaded, crashed on his takeoff from Roosevelt Field, Long Island, September 21, 1926. The two crew members were burned to death but Captain Fonck and his navigator, Lieuten- ant Curtin of the U.S. Navy escaped injury.

There was no restriction to the size of the crew and because of the weight of gasoline required the odds seemed to favor a solo flight in the spring of 1927 when a number of competitors were busily preparing. In early April Lt. Commander Richard Byrd, U.S. Navy, cracked up the Fokker monoplane "America" in its first trial flight. On April 26, two other Navy fliers, Lt. Commander Noel Davis and Lt. H. S. Wooster, practicing for the long flight to Paris, were killed while testing their biplane, "American Legion."

Then, May 20–21, Charles Lindbergh, in his single engine

monoplane, "The Spirit of St. Louis," barely clearing the trees in his takeoff from Long Island, and fighting off sleep through the dark hours, flew to Le Bourget airport, 3,610 miles in 33 hours and 30 minutes, winning the prize and the reputation of being the world's most resourceful pilot.

Lindbergh hastened his flight lest he be beaten by Clarence D. Chamberlain and Charles A. Levine (who financed their venture), in the Bellanca monoplane, "Columbia." On June 4th and 5th they flew nonstop from New York to Eisleben, Germany, a distance of 3,905 miles, their takeoff having been delayed a fortnight by a legal squabble with Bellanca.

Finally, but belatedly, Lt. Commander Richard Byrd on June 29–30 in the Fokker land plane, "America," made the successful crossing only to crash in the sea off the French coast, none of the crew being seriously injured. These exploits thrilled me and I read everything I could get my hands on. I was aware that American novelists, Hemingway, Fitzgerald, dos Passos and Sinclair Lewis were then attracting international attention, but my interest in fiction began to wane in contrast to the daring reality of aviation.

I remember precisely where I was the afternoon of May 21, 1927, when I heard the news, "Lindbergh has landed!" I stopped to buy an "Extra" opposite Schwarz Toy Store on 58th Street and those columns of type thrilled me as nothing had ever done. As Carl Solberg says so eloquently in his history, *Conquest of the Skies*: "Lindbergh's epochal solo flight evoked a mass adulation unique in all history. It was as if he personified the release of man's bondage to earth—to the French who mobbed him that night at Le Bourget, to the English who lifted him high in London, to the Brussels bourgomaster who said, 'in your glory is glory for all men.' "

In the good will flight he made to our forty-eight states and to Mexico he further demonstrated his command of the airways, and with his bride, Anne Morrow, as his radio operator, he explored the air routes and created the confidence, the opportunity and inspiration which were to bring our airplane builders international prestige.

I believed in the future of commercial aviation, and that it would come fast: Colonial Airlines were making preliminary flights, Boston to New York; Boeing Air Transport, Western Air Express, were pioneering; and Juan Trippe in Washington, D.C. was buying up landing rights and acquiring United States mail contracts, laying the groundwork for Pan American Airways to link the North and South American continents. Shirley was right, I was reading omnivorously, clipping articles from newspapers and magazines about Pratt & Whitney, about Curtis and their competitors—everything of enterprise in the sky. I found an advisor when Edward P. Warner, whose lectures on aviation at M.I.T. I had briefly attended, gave up teaching to become Assistant Secretary of the Navy for Aeronautics in 1926.

Naval aviation was then in the ascendency, and Warner with his swift mathematical mind and brilliant technical ability supplied the momentum Admiral Moffett was looking for, even if at times the gold braid resented being talked to as a student. In 1929 Warner left Washington to assume the editorship of *Aviation*, published by McGraw-Hill in New York. When I heard this I made up for lost time. I went to his office, introduced myself, explained my interest in aviation, and that I'd like to talk to him about its financial prospects. To my delight he was encouraging, invited me to lunch and so began a lasting friendship, which eventually included Peggy, when Ed and I were working together during the war. He was broad shouldered, very approachable, with one of the keenest scientific minds I have ever known. He wore well-tailored suits but never had them pressed and usually looked like an unmade bed.

Robert Lovett, one of the partners of Brown Brothers, and

like myself a nut on automobiles, had begun to take an interest in me, and my statistical reports came to the attention of another partner, Ellery Sedgwick James. In the spring of 1929 there was considerable speculation in aviation stocks; a proposed merger between Curtis and the Wright Aeronautical Corporation was in the wind, which I naturally checked out with Ed Warner. Mr. James told me that the firm was seriously considering whether or not to participate—what did I think? I was certainly no authority but I felt I knew more than he did and I said I wouldn't touch it with a ten-foot pole. Why? Because I believed Curtis was in deep trouble. A few months later that proved to be the case and my reputation went up a notch or two as the partners congratulated themselves on their caution.

That summer Peggy invited me to spend a long weekend with her family in Bar Harbor and I decided to fly up. The seaplane I hired from the Curtis Flying Service made the run to Bangor without a hitch and a taxi took me to the Partridge cottage. During my stay I came to admire her mother but saw little of her father who was in failing health and confined to his bedroom. Peggy showed me through his summer studio, which was next door and crowded with large plaster casts. She told me that he'd been educated at Columbia and at the Sorbonne where he shared rooms with Bernard Berenson. He was only twenty when his work was first exhibited at the Paris Salon.

It was my impression that William Ordway Partridge was a versatile romantic for he wrote poetry, published three novels, and the sculpture which made him one of the most distinguished artists of his day, was heroic: the equestrian statue of General Grant in Brooklyn, the bronzes of Thomas Jefferson and Alexander Hamilton at Columbia, the bust of Beethoven in the Metropolitan Opera House, the romantic Shakespeare in Chicago, and "The Pietà" in St. Patrick's Cathedral on Fifth Avenue.

Peggy said his commissions were large—$50,000 for General Grant—but so were his expenses, and he loved to spend. It was Mrs. Partridge who held the purse strings, as he aged.

I enjoyed every hour of our time together, the picnics, the sailing, the dances and best, when we were alone. I knew I was getting in deep, and when her mother asked me to stay on for two more days I wired the office that I was. But my flight back was a fiasco. A cylinder head blew off as we were taxiing out of Bangor and we put in to the nearest cove. After a considerable delay my bag and I were transferred to a single-motor, Consolidated landplane which conked out in Boston. It was Curtis's boast that it delivered its passengers by air no matter what it cost the company and the third relay finally did land me on the airstrip at Mt. Kisco at 8:00 p.m.

In Galbraith's book, *The Great Crash*, it is his thesis that the American people believed through the 1920s that they were predestined by luck, an unbeatable system, divine favor or access to inside information, to become rich without work. But on Tuesday, October 29, 1929, the most devastating day in the history of the New York Stock Exchange, that myth was punctured. The dismay on Wall Street was so thick you could cut it with a knife. There were temporary spurts of recovery but the down-drag grew steadily worse. The news on the ticker made those who had been buying on margin shudder, as Peter Arno illustrated in his book, *Where are the Customers' Yachts?*

My only gamble had been to invest $25,000 in bonds issued by the City of Hamburg, supposedly paying 8%, which of course became valueless. Another acquisition at this time was my first valet, Johnson, who had turned out George Widener so handsomely in India and who came with George's bland recommendation. On our tour I had one old suitcase plastered with stickers of every hotel we stopped at; I knew this wasn't done but I

wanted to keep it as a souvenir. On his very first morning Johnson spotted the bag and scrubbed it clean—and I didn't have
the heart to scold.

Johnson was a Scot, mousy, thin, and about forty. I liked
him and he began to tell me stories about his early life. It was
the ambition of many boys of his class to serve in the great English country houses. He started at thirteen and his first job was
to iron the newspapers in the early morning—it was inconceiv-
able that his Lordship or the guests should face a rumpled *Times*.
His efficiency commended his service to wealthy aristocrats
and eventually George Widener brought him to America. It
did not occur to me till later to wonder why George had let
him go.

My uncle David Dows, who had connections with W. R.
Grace & Co., thought it would be a good idea for Shirley and
me to take a cruise on one of the Grace ships down the West
Coast of South America, cross the Andes by train, and have a
pleasant time in Buenos Aires and Rio. It would be their summer and we would have the opportunity to visit the family properties in Peru and Ecuador. Why not? New countries to con-
quer, and with the market in the doldrums, my presence in the
office would not be missed.

We sailed from Havana on the "Santa Maria" on December
31st, Moms loyally waving us off as she always did. I shall only
touch on the high points because for much of the time I was
half-hearted, the other half remaining with Peggy in New York.
I knew I would miss her but I didn't realize how much.

The "Santa Maria" was a trim ship, logging along at 12 knots
and with a moderately good cuisine. This was the first time I
traveled with a valet, and it was a relief to have Johnson pack
and unpack and attend to the fussy details.

The passengers were largely businessmen. What saved the

voyage for us was the delightful company of Luis Valverde of Ecuador, his mountainous wife and their beguiling sixteen-year-old daughter Julie, a jeune fille who despite elaborate chaperonage, contrived to flirt with Shirley. To her he was an American dandy; her eyes would widen at his approach, and her questions and laughter would hold his attention. When we were in our stateroom I would tease him about Julie, never suspecting she would one day enter his life. He would tease me back about Peggy. "For God's sake, Bill, instead of moaning and groaning, why don't you propose to her? You know you love her." I had been on the verge of doing so at Bar Harbor but held back out of shyness. I wrote her that I liked to think that the gulls which followed our ship were messengers carrying her love.

The West coast of South America is desolate, far less interesting than the East, as an example I give you Antofagasta in Chile, the port for the great nitrate fields which were to be of such importance to us in the Second World War. On a roasting hot day Shirley and I motored up to one of the largest mines. The fields were as barren as a desert, as there is practically no rainfall. At the mine several hundred Indians were extracting the nitrate with steam shovels and loading it on cars that would carry it down to the harbor, a simple operation, supervised by two white men, one a Scot, the other American. We had a sultry lunch with them; they seemed to hate each other as much as they loathed the job, for there was nothing for them to do when not working—no town, no movies, above all, no women.

One was a teetotaller who spent his pay buying tickets on the Chilean lottery and would sit glued to the radio, hoping his "number" would come up with a prize large enough to free him from this ghastly existence. The other spent all his money on spirits, drinking alone (so we gathered) and falling into bed night after night, without a word to his fellow prisoner. Shirley and I were glad to depart before knives were drawn.

Our stay in Santiago was more agreeable. The weather was balmy, January is their summer, and we were treated to their delicious seafood, the erizoes (sea urchins) and langosta (lobsters without claws) large and tender, caught off the island of San Juan Fernandez where Alexander Selkirk, the model for *Robinson Crusoe* was marooned. I liked the Chileans, handsome people with not a little English and Irish blood, and at that time, before the Communists, they had the Briton's love of clubs and horses. They entertained us as did the British Ambassador, Harold Caccia, who was quite popular, as he was on his later appointment to Washington. He showed off his athletic prowess in after-dinner feats, such as Indian wrestling, etc., but whatever he did Shirley could do just a little better.

Having taken a look at the single-motor Fairchild which was to have flown us over the Andes, I decided it would be safer to go by the trans-Andean Express even though it took two days longer. The train left at 10 a.m. and as we were going to a Chilean dinner party I thought how lucky we were to have Johnson to do the packing and have breakfast ready for our departure. We returned, slightly intoxicated at 2 a.m.

What we did not know was that Johnson had found a blood-brother in the Chief Engineer of a ship in the harbor. They sat all night long over their native brew and it was the hotel servants who aroused us at 9 o'clock. Johnson, fully clothed was snoring loudly on his bed. We stripped and doused him in a cold tub, flung our things into bags, paid the bill and supporting Johnson between us barely caught the Express. His seat was behind ours and as the train began its climb to 12,500 feet, I noticed his face turn pallid. The inhalation of oxygen is the best cure for a hangover, but the reverse is also true and the higher we went the more miserable Johnson became. He finally staggered to the W.C. where he remained until we were over the peak and approaching sea level. Contrite and exhausted he promised it would never happen again. But it did.

We had been told that Buenos Aires was "the Paris of South America" which, of course, we disbelieved. It is certainly not favored geographically as it stands on an absolutely flat plain with no water nearer than the beaches of La Plata. Its many handsome broad boulevards, such as those in Paris, are partly responsible for the slogan, and besides there were sophisticated shops, restaurants which specialized in the fantastically tender Argentine beef and stylish night clubs, with the best tango music.

The American Ambassador, Robert Woods Bliss, was a classmate of my father's of whom he spoke with affection. He and his wife Mildred were our most elegant representatives in South America, and the dinner they gave for us—food, wine and flowers—was perfection. He was an authority on Pre-Columbian art and had a superb collection of jade, gold and crystal, the history of which, as Bliss related it, was fascinating.

Uncle David had given us a letter to Louis Lacey, an Englishman long resident in Argentina, who next to Tommy Hitchcock was the finest polo player in the world. Lacey invited us to lunch at his club in Hurlingham, some forty-five minutes out of the city, and when we stepped off the train we stepped into a replica of the village of Hurlingham, outside London, where polo is king. Here the houses were British in appearance, the atmosphere in the Club stuffily British and the cursing in the polo match we watched, furiously British.

Rio de Janeiro has an incomparably beautiful harbor and to enter Rio during Carnival in 1930 as Shirley and I did, fresh from Buenos Aires, was to pass from the extreme of elegance to the extreme of gaiety. "Cariocas" is the slang name for those carefree inhabitants of Rio who love to sing and dance, and the Cariocas do both with wild energy for four successive nights in their annual Carnival before the beginning of Lent. The Cariocas maintain their boundless energy on a minimum of alcohol. It sounds implausible but while they are at it they drink very little.

We arrived in early morning, after the first night of the Carnival was over and it seemed as if most of the adults and older children were just beginning to recover from last night's revelry. There was a repressed excitement in the air and on our way to the Copacabana Hotel we drove through the famous Avenida Rio Branco, Rio's main boulevard, where the festival takes place. It appeared that a good many business firms lining the Avenida had vacated the upper floor which they rented to wealthy families who moved in with beds, furniture, chefs, and maids. Picture Fifth Avenue in New York undergoing such a transformation.

Shirley and I needed costumes and as we were shopping for white sailor suits and hats, we decided that we also needed partners. By a stroke of luck we ran across two free-wheeling American girls we had noticed on the "Santa Maria." They were happy to join us, the tall one for me, the shorter for Shirley. We planned to dine together and they went off to get their make-up.

Properly elevated by cocktails and champagne we set forth at twilight drawn by the pulse of the music on the Avenida and were soon part of an enormous crowd, dancing the samba, the Brazilian national dance—to a very catchy tune. We had never danced it before but the girls helped us pick it up, and danced so well they were cut in on freely by the Brazilians. Many men and a few girls carried atomizers of ether which they squirted on those they wished to dance with, it felt cooling in such heat.

At the height of the evening the long boulevard was a gorgeous sight, tens of thousands of dancers in fantastic costumes milling around, singing, dancing, pausing only for the parade of elaborate floats, decorated by clubs striving for the grand prize. Everyone may have been sober but I suspect there was plenty of young love for sale or given away. On the last night the prizes were awarded for the best song and most beautiful float, the winners went wild, and the Carnival ended with a great ball in the municipal theatre.

Our journey reached its high point with the Carnival. Our partners went on their way, and a two-mile walk I took on the beach, clad only in trunks, so blistered my hide that I was in agony for forty-eight hours. We decided to return via Italy, expecting a week in Venice, but shortly after we landed in Genoa a cable saying Mother was ill with tuberculosis made us rush to catch the *Bremen* for our passage home.

March is the stormy period in the Atlantic, and this was the roughest crossing I ever experienced. On the second day we covered but fifty-eight miles. The *Bremen* was practically empty, only fifty in first-class, one of the passengers being Bill Coolidge with whom we had grown up on the North Shore; on the third day out there were just the three of us in the restaurant, and the maître d'hôtel had collapsed. We got in two days late. To our relief the worry about Moms's tuberculosis had been a false alarm and her flush of happiness at Shirley's and my return dispelled anxiety. It felt good to be back. I telephoned at once to Peggy and sped to her apartment where it was bliss to have her in my arms. After any separation I am always struck by her blonde loveliness. To be honest that was one trip I was happy to have behind me.

In answer to her questions, I told her about the Valverdes and Shirley's flirtation with young Julie. I described the perfection of the Bliss's parties at Buenos Aires and the exuberance of the all night carnival at Rio. Peggy burst into laughter when I swore that never again would I walk the Copacabana beach in the blazing sunlight of a Rio summer, clad only in bathing trunks.

I persuaded Moms to give a fancy dress party at Mt. Kisco. Susan Scott, Peggy's best friend, came up from Philadelphia and they both appeared in gingham dresses with bare legs which caused Nan to call Peggy "an adventuress." Freddy Davies and his fiancée, Diana Dodge, were there and many of my friends from Harvard. The music was good; there was much cutting in and by midnight Moms was surprised how quickly the whiskey was disappearing. She suggested to Hoskins, our English butler, that the bar be closed, to which he replied, "But, Madam, I cannot have the young gentlemen 'harrguing.' "

I was pleased that Mr. Brunie, my boss, was genuinely glad to have me back. At Harvard I had subscribed to *Aviation* and *The Journal of the Royal Aeronautical Society*; now for my research I added the *Aero Digest*, *The British Aeroplane*, *Flight*, the French *Les Ailes*, and *The International Interavien*. The Navy and Juan Trippe were still demanding flying boats, but I put my confidence in the rising interest in the construction of land planes for commercial flights in the United States. The books, magazines, and press clippings overflowed my tiny office downtown and I moved the file home. I was one of the very few in finance who was making such a thorough collection.

CHAPTER VI

Honeymoon

AS summer was approaching, Peggy and I conceived the idea of a motor trip through Europe, with Shirley, and Mrs. Partridge as chaperones. Mr. Partridge had died, his widow needed a change and the idea was to visit places Peggy had never been. (I had reached an amicable understanding with the office that I'd prefer an occasional holiday to a raise.) We sailed on the *Bremen* in July, landed at Cherbourg where the Mercedes was waiting and on the way to Paris the road rules were set . . . Bill not to exceed eighty m.p.h., unless there was an exceptional open stretch. At the slower pace, Shirley and Mrs. Partridge amicably continued a running discussion about religion, of which we in the front heard snatches; it seemed to be interminable with many approaches and no finality. Don't all discussions on religion have the same result?

We received a warm welcome at the Ritz and dined that evening at the "Tour d'Argent" on "Canard à la Presse" with a Romanée Conti 1906, "Crêpes Susette" for dessert with Schloss Vollards, Trockenbeerenauslese 1921 (which Mrs. Partridge sipped) and then Cognac of 1848 (which she declined).

There was no objection to my rather "conservative" driving through France. But when we approached the winding Swiss Alpine passes which often had cliffs a thousand feet high bordering the road with no guard rail, and some roads so narrow that if we had to back up a distance to let a post office car (they have the right of way in Switzerland and other traffic must pass on the *outside*) or a school bus pass, it was quite hair-raising even to an experienced driver like myself. Moreover, our open touring car did not provide much protection from the wind, even when the side curtains were up. Mrs. Partridge took it all very gamely.

It has always been my habit to make reservations far in advance at every place we spend the night, which amused Peggy and her mother who were accustomed to taking pot luck.

One amusing incident occurred when I had planned to end up at a small Swiss inn, world famous for its food and the view of the very beautiful lake of Thun. Unfortunately that day's drive was long and rough and made more unpleasant by pouring rain. To make things worse both Mrs. Partridge and Peggy were suffering from really terrible colds. As we approached the town where we expected to stay we had the misfortune to see a large but very dubious looking hotel, brilliantly lighted. This produced a palace revolution. Peggy and her mother stated emphatically that they had had *enough* and we were going to stay at *that* hotel no matter how charming the little inn that Shirley and I had set our hearts on. They went straight to bed and had their supper sent up. Of course they were quite right and we submitted. However, Shirley and I did dine at the little inn which was delightful and returned to the big hotel to sleep and protect our charges.

However, we had our revenge, if one can call it that, at Freudenstadt in the Black Forest. Peggy and her mother stood firm against making reservations, and we bowed to their wishes.

But Freudenstadt in August was jammed to the roof with tourists of every nationality and when we arrived there every hotel was completely full. After an endless search we found a nice German family who took care of Peggy and her mother. Shirley and I slept the night in two bathtubs at a fourth rate joint—such is travel, and in love as in marriage one must compromise.

We had a marvelous time in Austria. Mrs. Partridge was not a strict chaperone, especially in Vienna, which was full of romantic memories of her own.

One evening Peggy and I set forth to a dinner à deux in the famous Grinzing Hills, about thirty miles away. These hills have a magical charm with a view of the Danube on one side and the Wienerwald on the other.

There are a number of small, enchanting restaurants in a delightfully sentimental atmosphere, specializing in the Heurigen wein, the wine of the year's vintage, which has a romantic appeal to young lovers. The food is simple but delicious and there is always a romantic tenor singing Viennese folk songs to the lilting tune of the zither.

The combination was irresistible. One song seemed especially for us and we fell in love with the tune "Drunt in der Lobau," a romantic lyric about two lovers on an island in the Danube. Immediately on hearing the first few bars, we recognized that this was to be "our song," and we have had it played by a Viennese orchestra at our annual New Year's Day party for the past fifty years.

Drunt in der Lobau

Wo die Donau mit silbernen Armen umschlingt
S'Letzte Stückerl vom träumenden Wien
Wo die Einsamkeit winkt wo die Nachtigall singt
Und das Heimchen noch nested im Grün
Dort lacht das Glück aus tausend Zweigen

Dort ist der Blühtenduft so eigen
Am stillen Waldrand wo ich mein Glück einst fand
Drunt in der Lobau wenn ich das Platzerl nur wüsst
Drunt in der Lobau hab ich mein Mäderl geküsst
Ihre Äugerln warn so blau als wie die Veilchen in der Au
Auf dem wunderschönen Platzerl *in der Lobau*

which may be roughly translated as:

Down in the Lobau

Where the Danube with silver arms
Embraces dreaming Vienna,
Where solitude beckons, where the nightingale sings
And the home nestles in the green.
There happiness smiles from a thousand branches,
There the fragrance of the blossoms is so delightful,
At the quiet edge of the forest where I once found my happiness
Down in the Lobau well I remember the place
Down in the Lobau I kissed my sweetheart
Her eyes were as blue as the violets in the meadow
On that beautiful spot *Down in the Lobau*

Throughout our travels and on the returning voyage I had
not found the perfect moment to propose, though we were going
on as if I had. Then one early autumn afternoon in Peggy's
apartment out popped the words, "Peggy, *when* will you marry
me?" "I was wondering when you would ask that," she said.

After I met this beautiful girl in London and fell head over
heels in love with her, swept off my feet and deliriously happy,
I came to realize what an extraordinary human being she was,
intelligent and perceptive without being an intellectual blue
stocking, with the warmest of hearts and an infinite capacity
for love and understanding.

Peggy and I at the Wedding Reception

Easter Parade, Fifth Avenue

Peggy had never gone to college, nor had any of her close friends, but during her travels in Europe with her parents she had become more fluent in French and Italian than I could ever be. And she had that rare combination, imagination and courage; without her imagination, her willingness to try new things, and her belief in me, I doubt I would have entered government service in 1941—which changed my life.

Now we had the fun of telling our family and friends (who were not overwhelmed by surprise), planning the wedding and the honeymoon, and looking for an apartment. Her mother announced our engagement in October and we set the date for the marriage, February 16, 1931.

In 1929, I had placed an order for a Duesenberg sports sedan, with a Rollston body, painted black, no chrome visible, and upholstered in pigskin. It became my favorite, prompting a New York debutante to exclaim, "I am wounded by the beauty of your Duesenberg."

*   *   *

Bob Lovett, one of the original proprietors in the new apartment house at 10 Gracie Square, urged us to look it over and we were charmed by what we saw. This was to be our home until we moved to Washington. Our apartment fronted on the East River with a corner view of Gracie Park and the Gracie Mansion; there was a large living room, a small library (all too soon stacked from floor to ceiling), guest quarters in the duplex, rooms for ourselves, an English cook and butler, and the hopefully sober Johnson. As my collection of books on aviation approached 3,000, Moms rented two separate rooms for them in an empty apartment.

In planning our wedding party Peggy invited her best friend, the lovely and brilliant Susie Scott of Philadelphia, to be her

maid-of-honor, and her four bridesmaids were Helen Thorn-
dike from Boston, Jane Gates, whose husband Geoffrey was an
usher, Pyrma Pell and Isabel Thatcher, all from New York.
Shirley, of course, was to be my best man and my twelve ushers
were Harvard classmates, including Freddy Davies, who was
married a few months before us, Eddie Weld, Hootie Whitman,
Tony Cassatt and Nattie Hamlen. I held the ushers' dinner at
Mt. Kisco, and gave them each gold cufflinks, with their initials on one side and my initials on the other (platinum for
Shirley and Freddy). There was limitless champagne, the first
toast to Peggy and the glasses tossed into the fireplace, followed
by affectionate and ribald ones thereafter.

Our wedding took place at St. Thomas's in the late afternoon. The aisle for the first time in its history was illuminated
by candles, mounted for each pew in wooden holders designed
by Mrs. Partridge. (They were very effective and have been
used many times since.) Peggy in ivory satin and a family lace
veil entered on the arm of her cousin, John Livingston, then
Susie and the bridesmaids in orange chiffon, followed by my
straight-faced ushers who had sworn on a stack of Bibles to remain sober.

Peggy and I left the church in our green Rolls-Royce town car
driven by our towering chauffeur Flaherty, swelling with pride
not only on the importance of the occasion but on the fact that
he, for the first—and last—time in his life had a police escort.

The reception was held in the ballroom of the Colony Club.
As the long line came to an end the dancing began; there was
champagne and wedding cake, and the rising voices, so appreciative and affectionate on such occasions. Outwardly the bride
and groom were pleased and responsive, inwardly longing for
the seclusion to come.

Peggy and I were of course on cloud nine. We danced together, photographs were taken and then we made a quick getaway to pack our bags for the first delight of marriage, the honeymoon, and our heavy luggage for abroad. I picked Peggy up in my new Duesenberg, the best looking car I have ever owned (Peggy thought so too) and we set off for "Florham," the seven-foot long hood and powerful headlights piercing the darkness. I had made that trip at least a hundred times but on this very special evening, when the tires spurted the bluestone gravel of the long front drive, I was glad we had the great house to ourselves.

At the door we found the smiling Irish figure of Esther, the maid in charge, a very conservative lady of sixty, who was to be responsible for our care. She led us to the best guest room, which I'd never occupied before, here by the open fire we enjoyed a light supper and a bottle of champagne in its frosted bucket (ordered by Aunt Ruth). There stood the big four-poster, eighteenth-century bed with a canopy to keep drafts out and privacy in.

Peggy has always had a very healthy appetite, so what was more natural than only a few moments after opening her eyes on the second day of our marriage she said cheerfully, "How about some breakfast?" My grandparents never got around to the idea of a telephone in the guest rooms. If you wanted breakfast you rang a bell and a faithful footman walked through miles of corridors, up and down innumerable stairways to take your order. In time the faithful Esther appeared and could not conceal her shock at finding Peggy and me in the *same* bed but fifty years of training prevailed: she took our order and eventually appeared with two superb "Florham" breakfasts, beginning with hot-house Marshall strawberries, deep red and juicy, thick cream, and croissants from the magic hands of Donon.

After dressing leisurely, Peggy—in a particularly smart tan and black dress, and a chic black tricorn hat—and I motored slowly back to New York and, having picked up our heavy luggage and kissed the family farewell, we boarded the "Roma" of the Italian line. We trans-shipped at Gibraltar, and after a most uncomfortable night in a miserable hotel took a small boat bound for Tangier.

Marriage enables one to see life through the eyes of a partner and this second-sight was a fresh delight for both of us on our honeymoon in Morocco, Spain and Portugal, all new to us and fascinating to visit in the spring. Peggy's judgment of persons, places and paintings is not as abrupt as mine and causes me to reconsider, a habit that has grown through the years.

We chose to begin in Morocco because of what the French, under Marshal Lyautey, the admirable Governor General, had done to make it more approachable. They had completed a chain of chic "Atlantique" hotels from Dakar to Marrakesh, with efficient French management, and connected by fast, well-built highways. In Lyautey's words, "Morocco is a cold country where the sun is hot" and Marrakesh, on a high plateau with the snow-capped Atlas mountains in the background, was not springlike in early March—it was damned cold! That does not trouble honeymooners as much as others; they have their own insulation. We rented a car with a driver to my liking and we were both attracted by the lovely house belonging to Mrs. Moses Taylor (which was to be the headquarters of Churchill and FDR at different times in the war to come).

Fez seemed to us the most truly native city and we were intrigued by the *souk*, the native market, completely hidden from the sun by thatched mats covering the narrow streets, far too narrow for vehicles, and inhabited solely by Moroccans, a secret place, out of "The Arabian Nights," stirring to the constant native music, and thronged by women with their faces veiled. One wondered what really went on behind those clay-walled houses.

Rabat, the French administrative capital, was very orderly, officers in French blue with scarlet kepis much in evidence. Once again I wished I had had the sense to get letters of introduction to that great pro-consul, Lyautey, as we could have done. Nor had I any to our Embassy people although we were so absorbed in each other's company I doubt if we'd have used them.

Morocco was the perfect appetizer. We then boarded a small commercial ship bound for Barcelona where our faithful chauffeur Joseph was waiting for us with a new car. Joseph was one of Mercedes best drivers, cheerful, intelligent, and an exceptionally able mechanic. He had driven with me every year since my tour with Freddy in 1927–1928 and I shall never forget how skillfully he had welded the crankcase which I had cracked forcing our way through a landslide.

Now he was at the wheel of a new 7.7 litre Grosser Mercedes, a model designed especially for Hitler and his staff on ceremonial occasions, which did not deter my desire to own one. We drove down the Costa Brava, that famous coast, now overbuilt, but at the time, except for a few old-fashioned hotels, hundreds of miles of beautiful empty beaches, illuminated in the evening by an orange moon.

The road to Valencia and beyond was good and I was so infatuated with the new car that I drove it as fast as possible. Out of habit I had made reservations at the Prince of Asturias Hotel at Malaga, a famous Spanish summer resort—but this was March and much too nippy for bathing. It turned out to be a huge caravansary with accommodations for about fifteen hundred guests. There were perhaps twenty in residence when we arrived, and we dined in a tiny corner of the vast dining room, with a few tables shut off by screens. So Peggy had the last laugh.

After that long drive we had a good night's rest and the next day set out for Cadiz, a more grueling run. After about four hundred miles I looked down and saw that Peggy, utterly exhausted, had slumped *under* the instrument panel.

"Can you make it, darling?" I asked. There was literally no place to stop. "I guess so," she sobbed. I needed this reminder that six hours of driving was about her daily limit; I could go on for ten if I were sure there was a good restaurant at the end.

Fortunately, on the following day it was only a short distance to the "bodegas" of the great shipping establishments of Jerez de la Frontera, where sherry is made. In the early morning and in our innocence we were unaware that the great houses also make their own brandy, equal in strength to French cognac. We found ourselves faced with rows of "copitas," the tasting glass, of the sherry to be sipped with delicious Spanish hors d'oeuvres and *followed* by four or five different brandies—in total, quite a twist of what the British call one's "head."

When we got back in the car and had not gone far, Peggy leaned toward me and admonished, "Bill, after all that sherry and brandy, I can't see anything. I hope you can but I doubt it. So slow down!"

From Cadiz we motored to Lisbon and I will never forget the dramatic ferry ride across the Tagus (the bridge from Almada to Lisbon was not built until years later), gazing at the blood-red setting sun, and the multicolored buildings of Lisbon. Our large Mercedes was an object of curiosity and admiration, and as always seems to be the case in Latin countries, the handling of freight, the parking of vehicles, and the setting forth of any boat necessitates a good deal more shouting than one hears in America.

Portugal was a surprise to us, both because of its individuality and its profusion of color. It has been dominantly seafaring ever since the voyages of Henry the Navigator established its empire overseas, and the principal buildings of pinkish sandstone are decorated with maritime motifs—scallop shells, rudders, fish, designs of twisted rope—as in no other European country. The harbors still maintain their fishing fleets and near the Tagus river the streets of Lisbon were given a picturesque charm by the young women in peasant costume, balancing trays of gleaming fish on their heads.

We spent four days in a charming hotel sampling the delectable fish restaurants; one day we drove to Coimbra, the seventeenth-century university town where we spent hours in the unique, green-paneled library, adorned with many globes and ancient, beautiful maps going back to the earliest explorations. The weather was warmer and on that trip we took a picnic lunch; along the way, as I happened to glance back, I caught Peggy energetically raiding the basket. When she was hungry she wanted to eat then and there. She had made quite a dent before Joseph and I had our turn.

We decided to take the train to Madrid, leaving Joseph to come by road, which he did with such speed that he was awaiting us at the Madrid Ritz when we arrived. This was the perfect base for a number of our excursions. We went first to El Escorial at the foot of the Guadarrama Mountains, a monastery-palace erected by Philip II as a memorial to his father, Charles V, which ever since has been the burial place of Spanish kings. It is built on a grandiose scale, but placed in such a barren setting it is only at close range that one appreciates the architectural details, the gardens and the patios. There is a striking contrast between the small bare cell in which Philip chose to die and the exquisite carpets and tapestries with which his successors decorated the huge edifice, with its sixteen courts, three chapels, close to a hundred fountains and three hundred rooms.

Much more to our liking was the walled city of Avila, fought over by the Moors and the Christians until Alfonso VI rebuilt the town and walls to bring it permanently within Christian control. In my opinion Avila is superior to Carcassonne which I think was ruined by Viollet le Duc's confectionary restoration.

At Seville we witnessed the solemnity of the Easter Festival. The immense crowds on their knees, murmuring as the image of the Virgin Mary, carried under an embroidered canopy, passes by, the various Madonnas, dressed in capes of satins or damask encrusted with jewels, are carried by hooded penitents wearing cowls of scarlet or gray. The unrestrained devotion was impressive, even to an agnostic like myself.

Madrid's color appealed to us: the buildings of pinkish sandstone have so much more warmth than the granite we were accustomed to at home, and the innumerable flower boxes are cultivated with the same gaiety one remembers in London. We went to the Prado Museum with its superb paintings by El Greco, Goya and Velazquez, which I enjoyed the more because of Peggy's comments.

King Alfonso XIII was dethroned during our stay, to the alarm of our families, who read of the violent riots, etc., but the fact is that we never saw a trace of them, perhaps because we were so often out of town.

In Madrid we went to one and only one bullfight. Peggy averted her eyes through most of it and never wanted to see another. It was not until years later that a friend of ours, David Levy, a psychiatrist, explained its significance. He had been to dozens of fights and was fascinated by the spectacle. It is of course not a fight, he said; the bull is foredoomed to die, but only after an elaborate drama. The mounted picadors taunt him and wear him down, and it is the matador with his cape and his sword who brings the drama to a close. I realized the danger to which even the most skillful matador is exposed when my brother Shirley had the famous Dominguin to stay at his home in Los Angeles in the 1940s. Almost every inch of Dominguin's body was covered with scars, some so large as to indicate a major operation.

We sailed for home on the *Bremen* and by chance Nelson Rockefeller, whom I had known since my boyhood at Northeast Harbor, and his bride "Tod" were returning from their honeymoon on the same ship. We went to the large sitting room of their suite and found the couple on their knees on the floor which was completely covered with coins—coins, not bank notes—of the different countries they had visited. Nelson's grandfather, the original "John D." Rockefeller, had presented them with the trip with the understanding that they save every penny of change so as to give him an accurate accounting of what they had spent, and they were now in the process of balancing their enormous and miscellaneous currency. Such are the tribulations of the very rich.

CHAPTER VII

10 Gracie Square

OUR two mothers considered that our new duplex apartment at 10 Gracie Square, overlooking the East River, was way out in the country but were too tactful to say so. Shirley and Aunt Ruth liked both the location and the large handsome building, still sparsely occupied because of the Depression. It was flanked by two girls schools, Brearly and Miss Chapin's, which made Peggy think how convenient it would be if we had daughters, although she did not confide this to me until our first son Bill was born.

On weekends before our wedding we had picnic lunches up there together with Francis Lengyon, a delightful Englishman, who was our decorator, and who had done the distinguished designing of Grandmother's house at 1 East 71st Street. Our taste at the time was for classical English, Queen Anne, and Chippendale, and we were pleased with his proposal for a pine panel living room which had a fireplace, as did the library next to it. The library was all shelves for my overflowing collection of books with space reserved for a wall map which was to show our various travels.

While we were on our honeymoon the mothers, who had become allies, worked hard putting things in place, including the wedding presents. Mrs. Partridge had given us a Sully portrait of one of her ancestors which was hung over the fireplace in the living room and Moms arranged the Queen Anne pieces of furniture which we had picked out as her gift. Even the icebox was freshly stocked on the morning we returned.

The first days in a new home are memorable: we were continually delighted by the view of the river, and the Gracie Mansion (now the Mayor's residence), which was more spectacular than we remembered. Freddy Davies and his bride, who lived below us, came in for supper and when Bob Lovett, who was really responsible for our being there, dropped by for a drink, I suggested that we drive down together to the office next morning in my Mercedes SS. Exterior Street was at that time a stretch of about ten blocks, with almost no traffic and on the fairly smooth cobbles, as we talked automobiles, I got the car up to high speed before we slowed down to enter Third Avenue. He might have told me that a merger was impending that would make us "Brown Brothers & Harriman," but I don't remember that he did.

Back in the office I broadened my research in aviation. At an early luncheon with Ed Warner he said that in a nutshell the problems every builder was trying to solve was how to construct a plane that would carry more passengers than the Ford Tri-motor and be capable of operating at a profit without subsidy. He suggested that I visit the more enterprising builders nearby, Grumman on Long Island, Wright Aeronautical in Newark, New Jersey, Pratt & Whitney in Hartford; my boss, Mr. Brunie, approved and it was my idea that I would learn more if I could talk to the chief engineers who were working on the models of the future. I began at Wright Aeronautical in Newark, where I presented my credentials and had the good luck to meet the chief engineer, Ed Mead, a very capable character who had been closely associated with Fred Rentschler, one of the most

respected pioneers in commercial aviation. Mead was as interested in my new Duesenberg as I was in his engines, and this was
the beginning of what was for me a most instructive friendship.

Years ago with her usual frankness, Aunt Ruth had told Moms
that she would not take much interest in Shirley and me until
we were grown. "Then I'll show them what life is really like—
and expect to have a wonderful time doing it!" The time had
come. Although she was twenty-one years older, she and I now
shared a number of interests in common: gourmet cooking,
good wine and fast cars. She had long forgotten any reservations she may once have had about Peggy and I felt flattered
when she said to me, "Bill, it would be helpful if you and I could
lunch together every two weeks or so and discuss things." So
began our amusing, intimate companionship. We met in our
favorite restaurants, the Ritz, Delmonico's or the Pavillon, always began with caviar or pâté de foie gras, then veal or calves'
brain for the main course—both delicious at the Pavillon—
martinis and wine to stimulate rapport.

Aunt Ruth in her youth was handsome and with her high
coloring, her fine eyes and vivacity she was still attractive. Her
figure had filled out since the days when the tennis professional
kept her running; then she used to quench her thirst with
shandy-gaff. When I was old enough for the dinner parties at
Newport, champagne was her delight, and now martinis. She
invariably arrived at the restaurant ahead of me, selected our
table and was working on her second martini before I appeared.
This was done deliberately as I am usually punctual.

At the outset she was intent on finding how seriously interested I was in my work at the office—she referred to my frequent absences. What I told her about Mr. Brunie and, particularly, of Ed Warner's encouragement, seemed to quiet her
doubts. She began to speak of her activity, of how she had set up

"The Opportunity Shop," had bought the building for it and persuaded wealthy friends—and Grandmother—to donate furniture, china, rugs, draperies, anything they had no use for, good pieces that were sold for charity. She mentioned her interest in the New York Hospital. This was a serious side of which I was unaware. I knew she did all the ordering for Grandmother and that she was in charge of the servants at "Florham" (as many as 120 employed in the house, stables, gardens and farm), and of the smaller staffs at "Vinland," and at 1 East 71st Street. With such administrative ability I wondered if she would have preferred a business career instead of waiting on Grandma. Beneath what she was saying I felt a sense of frustration.

She had a masculine sense of humor and she made me laugh when, speaking of Prohibition, she said, "I bet you haven't any idea how much liquor is consumed at our house parties. When I saw that the Volstead Act was coming, I called in our wine dealer and ordered enough gin, spirits, wine and liquors to last until Repeal. That was fourteen years ago and the supply is still holding out."

She loved to talk about her father, Hamilton Twombly, and I asked what had long been in my mind—why had he built "Florham" on such a vast scale.

> "Oh, Bill, I wish you could have known him, as he was when your mother and I were growing up. He was so intelligent, a perfectionist in everything he undertook, and such a charmer—he was a beautiful dancer, and when he felt like it at one of the parties I've seen him do a buck and wing solo that made everyone cheer. He had already made millions before he married your grandmother! If you will look through the early pages of the guest book at "Florham" you'll see that his friends in New York, men like J. P.

Morgan, C. V. Whitney, and at Madison, Thomas Edison, were tops.

"It's hard to believe today, but Morris County, at the time he laid out "Florham" was the wealthiest community in the United States. More than one hundred millionaires had their country places there and several of them were father's intimates. They went in to their offices in New York in a private car and I used to meet him on his return and drive back in my four-in-hand. I'd love to have overheard the conversations in that car. Father would sometimes tell me one of their latest jokes, risqué and very funny.

"The reason why 'Florham' was by far the best of the Vanderbilt houses," she said, "was that first and last it was a labor of love. Father worked on every detail. Listen, Bill, to develop the grounds he chose Frederick Law Olmsted, the landscape designer who planned Central Park and for the house he picked the best architectural firm, McKim, Mead and White. He imported a herd of Guernseys and in 1904 they carried off all the prizes at the World's Fair at St. Louis, and he became the premier Guernsey breeder in the country. He was just as fastidious about the orchids (my mother's favorite)—there were ten greenhouses, with plants brought from everywhere—Venezuela, Colombia, and Mexico. Chrysanthemums were another specialty. And to supervise all this he lured Queen Victoria's gardener from Kew Gardens. Arthur Harrington was a supreme gardener. The Mikado of Japan sent over his headman to see why Father's varieties of chrysanthemums were so much better.

"All this wasn't for show or vanity. He had made his own fortune, my mother had brought him another. He was a director on some twenty boards. Now he decided to put a great deal of his energy and his love of the beautiful into creating an earthly paradise for his four children especially for his only son, Hamilton, who he hoped would love 'The Farm' as much as he did. But then my oldest sister, Alice, died at sixteen and when Hamilton was drowned the dream was shattered, and Father's heart was broken. Some time I'll show you a copy of the obituary which appeared in *The New York Times*. It will give you an idea of how he was regarded by his contemporaries."

Newlyweds, haphazardly or conscientiously, work out a design for harmony. We were carefree financially as my mother gave me a large allowance, and I still had a substantial part of my grandmother's birthday gift. We respected each other's preferences. Peggy maintained her love of art and between the births of young Bill and later our second son Bob she attended the Art Students League where she drew from live models— and realized she had a rather limited talent. I persevered at Brown Brothers & Harriman. The market staged a brief recovery in the early part of 1931, only to sag to deeper losses. I was shielded from the despair of so many of my elders on Wall Street, partly by my consuming interest in the promising development of aircraft, and chiefly because the fortune on which Grandmother, Aunt Ruth and Moms (and Peggy and I) depended was in gilt-edge bonds and commodities such as my grandfather's enormously productive investment in Louisiana sulphur.

We both loved the theatre and ballet and there were haunting and lovely lyrics which touched us and kept us humming: "I'll See You Again," by Noel Coward in the show, "Bittersweet," "I Love Louisa" and "Dancing in the Dark" by Howard Dietz in "The Band Wagon," the show which starred Fred

Astaire and his sister Adele, "Night and Day," to pick one of half a dozen by Cole Porter.

Our apartment became a meeting ground for Harvard friends, now married, Eddie and Barbara Weld, Cassie and John Mason Brown, Frances and Bill Wister, and our neighbors, Freddy and Diana Davies. And Peggy shared my admiration for those older men in the aviation world, like Ed Warner, whom we were beginning to entertain: the tall and handsome Clark Millikan, a professor at California Tech, who was a pioneer in rockets for the Navy, and the affable Ross McFarland, head of the Fatigue Laboratory at Harvard. My happiest reunion was with Bill Harding, a boyhood chum, now doing aviation research for Smith Barney; he and I were fond of each other and freely compared notes.

*   *   *

In summer we found our hearts' desire in Maine. Peggy had been taken to Mount Desert in infancy and I had loved Northeast Harbor since 1918. The island, eight miles in circumference and fourteen at its widest, is enhanced by a lovely range of high hills, small hidden lakes, a miniature fjord at Somes Sound, and everywhere by the salty view of offshore islands in the glistening sea. The Rockefellers are to be blessed for preserving the Acadia National Park, and the relations between the State-of-Mainers and the summer residents are at once good-natured and amusing. As the Walter Lippmanns' caretaker once put it, "Glad to see you come, and glad to see you go."

While we were on our honeymoon Douglas Burden's documentary film, "The Silent Enemy" had its opening on Broadway. The reviews were ecstatic but in essentials it was a silent film at a time when Hollywood had gone mad over sound and Jesse Lasky's failure to give the picture block-booking resulted

10 Gracie Square

Four Generations: Mrs. Twombly (holding Bob), myself, and Moms

Grandfather Twombly, as I never saw him.
From a portrait by G. Z. Munzig

Grandmother Twombly at the backgammon table in "Florham"

In my Miller Special

in a financial loss. One of the unsuspected dividends was that Shirley's participation determined his career. When Douglas Fairbanks came east Shirley called on him at the Sherry Netherlands and asked for a job. He was turned down but not deterred. He went to work with Walter Wanger, head of Paramount's Studio on Long Island, learning about sound. In 1929 Douglas's friend, Merian C. Cooper, a brilliant producer, called him to RKO in Hollywood. Shirley, who wanted to begin from the ground up, was appointed an Associate Producer and assigned to supervise the filming of the whales' migration to Baja Ca for a new "Moby Dick" (not produced). A second assignment was to work with a writer on an adaptation of Rider Haggard's "King Solomon's Mines," (which was never produced). By this time he had met and been fascinated by Bob Benchley; together they cooked up a comedy script for Charles Butterworth, Zazu Pitts and Benchley himself, using the by now discarded whaling footage—but Cooper didn't fancy that idea either. The effect of all this was to convert Shirley to a Californian. I believed the attraction was only temporary, but he describes how it became permanent.

"To add to the confusion, I was courting (in the old-fashioned way) a wonderful girl I had met on a blind date, Flobelle Fairbanks, the niece of Douglas Fairbanks. I had two friends at the studio besides my boss Merian Cooper, Ken Frank, who introduced me to Flobelle, and Dan O'Shea, who was head of the RKO Legal Department.

"One day I received a telephone call from my brother in New York. He told me that he and Victor Emmanuel, another car nut like himself, had ordered two Miller Special cars to be built in Los Angeles. He explained that Victor Emmanuel had gotten tired of doling out money and seeing no car and had cancelled his order. That left my brother holding the bag. He reminded me of what he had ordered: a car of sixteen cylinders, four-wheel drive, 500 horsepower, supercharged. He wanted me to get a lawyer and go to the factory to see what was going on. I explained the situation to Dan O'Shea and asked if he would help. A few days later Dan and I were on our way to look at the Miller Special. I don't know what Dan expected to see, but I visualized a small garage with a couple of greasy mechanics sweating over an engine block with holes in it. It took us quite awhile to find the address, but the factory—and it was a factory in every sense of the word— took up at least three-quarters of a city block. Inside we met Fred Offenhauser, a charming gentleman in a white coat who was in charge of the operation.

"The shop was filled with every kind of machine— lathes, drill presses, etc. At each machine was a mechanic working on a small shiny something. Later—much later— when the trip through the plant was drawing to a close, Dan and I got up enough courage to ask Offenhauser where the car was. He explained in a tolerant voice we had *seen* the car. All those shiny somethings when assembled would make one gorgeous Miller Special. As we left we asked how many people were on the payroll. The answer was twenty-five. We didn't talk much on the trip home. There really wasn't much to talk about. The conclusions were obvious. These men were artists. Money was no object, especially when it belonged to someone else. If you wanted the car badly enough, you had to pay up on their terms. It was hard explaining this to my brother. I think he understood. A lot of time and a lot of money later, the Miller Special was finally finished. The torpedo-shaped body was painted black. It had two rather uncomfortable bucket seats, a low windshield, and no top. The engine, which seemed to take up at least three-quarters of the length of the car, was a joy to behold. Whether it ran or not mattered little. It should have been in a museum.

"My romance with Flobelle was progressing, so I decided to take her for the first ride. It was summer. Large picture hats and diaphanous flower print dresses were in. There were very few houses on Cold Water Canyon Road in Los Angeles in those days. The grade was gentle and led to a beautiful view of the San Fernando Valley at the top. I decided to take her there.

"Flobelle was a sight to behold as she floated down the steps to Bill's black Miller Special chariot. The picture hat, the flower print dress, that beautiful blonde hair, and that face, that face—that wonderful face. The clothes were not exactly appropriate for the occasion, but who cared! I drove rather conservatively at first; I wanted to get the feel of the car. When we reached Cold Water Canyon I could not resist bearing down a little harder on the accelerator. The car leapt forward as a true thoroughbred should. Flobe was getting a bit edgy. She didn't seem to understand why we had to go so fast even when I explained to her in a loud voice that I had to test the car in order to give my brother a full report of its performance.

"I think we were going around eighty when it happened. There was a roar—the engine hood flew off and a geyser more spectacular than the one at Yellowstone National Park appeared from nowhere. I would have enjoyed the spectacle more had I not been so busy trying to stop the car. When I finally did, and took stock of the damage, I was speechless. Flobe, on the other hand, was not. She did everything but break off our engagement. Her picture hat

was ruined—her dress was ruined—her shoes were ruined
—her hair was a mess. I didn't look so good either, but that
was my problem.

"Several weeks later Mr. Offenhauser telephoned and
apologized for the accident. He said there was nothing
wrong with the car; the radiator needed adjusting.

"I didn't drive the Miller Special much after that. I was
too busy trying to get back in my future wife's good graces.
The car was eventually shipped to Mount Kisco. I never
heard from Mr. Offenhauser or my brother Bill why the
radiator needed adjusting, but several years later a bird
perched on my window ledge and told me when they
finished building the engine it was too big to fit into the
chassis, so they had to cut down the size of the radiator and
the cooling fan. Result: there was not enough water to cool
the engine.

"Well—it made beautiful geysers, and gave work to
twenty-five mechanics for a very long time."

I thanked Shirley for his help, but I was not reassured. When
I tested the Miller Special at Mt. Kisco I did so *alone*. The
steering seemed to me dubious for so heavy a car and the higher
the speed the more I distrusted the brakes. Peggy took a snap-
shot of me behind the wheel of my enormous black monster,
which had cost $35,000. Eventually I sold it back to Fred
Offenhauser for $600, the most costly disappointment of the
many cars I have owned.

*   *   *

The year, 1932, a desperate one in the calendar of finance,
was heartening for Peggy and myself. The guest room in our
apartment was now preempted by young Bill, our first son,

born a fortnight before New Year's, and his nurse. Then in the spring as the stock market sank ever lower, Herman Frasch Whiton, the vice-president of Union Sulphur, appointed me a director and I began to look forward to the monthly meetings. This was the most fortuitous of my grandfather's early investments. Herman Frasch had ingeniously invented the process of extracting sulphur from the salt domes in Louisiana by the use of superheated water but had failed to find a backer until he came to Mr. Twombly. They formed a partnership, fifty percent of the stock to Mr. Frasch; fifty percent to Grandfather. The first dividend paid in 1905 was for $800,000; they increased steadily, never missing a year after the death of Grandfather and the inventor, and during the Depression, the Twomblys' share in one year rose over three million. This simply staggered me. The inventor's grandson, Herman Whiton—we called him "Swede"—and I came to be firm friends; we worked together easily and one of my first duties was to visit the plant at Sulphur, Louisiana, as I made a practice of doing twice a year thereafter. I heard that in the office I was referred to as "the Crown Prince." No member of the family had been on the Board of Directors since Grandfather's death in 1910.

It was ironic that Robert Doherty who had long been in charge of the Twombly estate took a skeptical view of venture capital such as Union Sulphur. His only interest was in bonds; stocks were too speculative, particularly natural resources which presumably would run out in time. He must have had to blink occasionally at the dividends that came in from Grandfather's investment in sulphur, copper and gold, and he had died before my good luck when "Swede" Whiton and I struck oil in Louisiana as the sulphur after forty years did peter out.

Stirred by what Aunt Ruth had told me I borrowed her copy of Grandfather's obituary and began to fit the references, which were most respectful, into a picture of his swift success. A Bostonian with money back of him he graduated from Harvard, where he had been president of the A.D. in 1871. He spent the summer weekends in Newport and his capability and finesse seem to have impressed William H. Vanderbilt, the financier who had inherited ninety-nine percent of the "Commodore's" fortune, even before his confidence and his charm appealed to Vanderbilt's daughter Florence. They were married in 1877 and still in his early thirties Twombly was recognized as the right-hand man of his father-in-law in the railroad business, a director in time, of no less than fourteen roads. He became a trustee of the Guarantee Trust Company; chairman of Western Union during its formative period. He represented the New York Central and J. P. Morgan on the Chesapeake & Ohio board, and together with Morgan was one of the founders of the Metropolitan Opera.

Mr. Twombly was a stickler for details. For one thing, he could not bear to be late to an engagement. It is related of him that once, in the summer of 1905, to keep a dinner engagement at Newport, he chartered a special train while in Springfield, Massachusetts, made the hundred miles intervening between there and Boston in 108 minutes, and easily caught the early connection to Newport. My grandfather did not confine his ingenuity to railroads.

The *Times* said his investments in the Cerro de Pasco copper mine in Peru, a gold mine in Ecuador and Union Sulphur in Louisiana proved successful early in this century and that Mr. Twombly's donations to charity were large and anonymous, as for instance, the sending of some four thousand poor children from New York City to summer camps on the Hudson.

A surprising opportunity came my way that June. Hardwick Stires, head of the New York office of Scudder, Stevens & Clark, one of the Boston pioneers in investment trusts and mutual funds took me to lunch. I knew that he personally had made an early killing in Pratt & Whitney stock, and as we compared notes about aviation and the prospects for investment, I had the suspicion that he was thinking of asking me to carry on my research for his firm. I was right. Stires was a shrewd salesman; he pointed out certain advantages and I was not so naive to think that I and my file were his main objective. I might also be useful as a stepping stone to Aunt Ruth and her money. I knew it was a sound outfit with large assets and probably would be more venturesome in the field of my interest than Brown Brothers & Harriman. I accepted.

I was sorry to leave Mr. Brunie and Mr. Lovett whose encouragement had given me confidence. My file on aviation I took with me; I had compiled much of it at home, it contained the notes I had made about the plants I had visited, which would mean little to my replacement, besides I intended it to grow.

My new boss, Hardwick, was the second son of Bishop Stires whose fulsome often dramatic sermons I had listened to at St. Thomas's. The Sunday after the sinking of the *Titanic* the disaster was reviewed in many pulpits and the *New York Tribune* reported: "the Reverend Doctor Ernest Stires singled out for special mention the wealthy industrialist, Arthur Ryerson, praising, 'the quiet smile, the gentle determination, with which he put the dearest persons of all, the girls, the boy, even the maid, into the lifeboat and watched them row away to safety.' It is to be hoped that everyone in the devoted congregation— even the maid—was properly edified by these Christian sentiments. . . ."

Hardwick was a down-to-earth, a self-assured, compelling salesman (Aunt Ruth would eventually invest five million at Scudder's advice), and capable of fairness as he demonstrated when he set up Scudder-in-Canada without antagonizing, as too many executives have, the Canadians.

By mid-summer of 1932 the Market reached bottom. On September 3, 1929, the day the Bull Market ended, Industrials stood at 452; by July 8, 1932, Industrials had dropped to 58. The causes were the speculative orgy, heedless of warnings, that preceded the Crash and the misjudgments which prompted even the Secretary of the Treasury, Andrew J. Mellon, to sooth anxiety with the words, "There is no cause to worry. The high tide of prosperity will continue." The effects were brutal and long lasting, wiping out employment, devastating to the hopes of the middle-aged, and pitiable in the misery of the elderly. There were not a few among the young who became skeptical of the future of our economic system and thought they saw a better one in socialism.

With the election of President Franklin D. Roosevelt, another illusion, The Noble Experiment of Prohibition, came to an end. The minority of zealots, the W.C.T.U., the Prohibitionists, the wealthy idealists such as John D. Rockefeller, Jr. could have had no idea of what resistance to the Volstead Act would spawn: the rum-runner, the speakeasy, the home brew, the defiance of law were bad enough, what was worse was the opening of opportunity for the Al Capones and the Mafia, the ruthless defilers of our democracy, to gain their foothold.

When the invitations were received for Shirley's marriage to Flobelle Fairbanks, Aunt Ruth, Moms, Peggy and I planned to go west by train. Grandmother preferred to drive. This was Shirley's view of the family get-together:

"Getting married, the ceremony itself, whether it be in church, a house or a tired-looking room at City Hall, is shorter than the blink of an eye in one's life. What happens before the wedding and after are what one never forgets.

"Flobe and I were married in her mother's house in Hollywood, on April 25, 1935. The ceremony took place in the living room in front of the fireplace which was hidden by a lattice covered with gardenias and other fragrant white flowers that gave off an aroma even a top Madison Avenue advertising copywriter couldn't duplicate in words. We were married by a Catholic priest, Father McCoy, a wonderful man. Flobe and I would have liked being married in a church but she was a Catholic and I was an Episcopalian, and at the time, the Catholic Church took the attitude "never the twain shall meet"—in church, that is.

"Mrs. Fairbanks decided the best place to have the wedding was at the house, the living room walls would have to be painted and a new carpet, white, white, white, was essential. After weeks of fussing and fuming the decorating was finally completed. My Aunt Ruth was soon to arrive from New York and everything had to be ready by then. The beautiful white carpet was delivered and laid the day before she arrived. Dorothy, the colored maid, had been polishing the family tea set for a week. The whole house shone like a diamond. Mrs. Fairbanks, Aunt Ruth, Flobe and I were sitting by the fireplace carrying on what is known as nervous conversation when it happened. Dorothy appeared in the doorway dressed in her newly pressed black uniform carrying the newly polished family tea set which looked twice as big as she did. She got to the middle of the room, took one look at Aunt Ruth, dropped everything and ran. The carpet was never quite the same but we got to know each other in a hurry.

"When my grandmother Twombly announced to her

friends in New York she was motoring to Hollywood, California, for my wedding there was a near riot. They did everything possible to dissuade her. There weren't many commercial planes flying in 1935—Grandma wasn't very keen on trains, besides she was eighty-one, so driving was the only answer. Grandma's style of driving was a little out of the ordinary. She was accustomed to being driven in a maroon Rolls-Royce with two men on the box dressed in maroon livery to match the car. My mother and Aunt Ruth were also apprehensive about the trip but we all knew all too well when Grandma made up her mind about something that's the way it was going to be—and so it was.

"We were awaiting her arrival at 1725 Camino Palmero. That is, she was supposed to arrive, but we hadn't heard from her since she left New York, so we didn't know what to expect. It was late in the afternoon when her maroon Rolls-Royce drew up to the door. She walked into the living room fresh as a daisy and sat down. 'How was the trip?' my mother asked. 'Fine', she said. 'Did you have any difficulties?' 'No. Everyone told me to be careful so I told my chauffeur and the groom to remove their hats and put on caps when we reached the Mississippi River.' I looked out the window—there was the maroon Rolls-Royce with the chauffeur dressed in his maroon livery and the groom beside him also in maroon livery, both wearing caps. Things had changed a lot since the covered-wagon days, but determination never changes."

Shirley and Flobe spent their honeymoon in Honolulu where by coincidence his boss, Merian Cooper, was also honeymooning with the actress, Dorothy Jordan. The two couples naturally got together and it was then that Shirley learned that Jock

Whitney, who had heavily invested in RKO, was pulling out, which might explain why a young man with reputed Vanderbilt millions was so cordially received. He also learned that Cooper was returning to RKO as an independent producer to work on two pictures, "The Last Days of Pompeii" and Rider Haggard's "She," starring Helen Gahagan Douglas, of which Shirley was to be the Associate Producer. It was all as exciting as it was frustrating and in the end he decided to set up his own commercial motion picture company known as "Tradefilm." His talent for photography would assert itself thereafter.

CHAPTER VIII

The Raceway and the Zeppelin

IN the 1930s there was an accelerating interest in airline stocks following the leadership of a handful of men like Juan Trippe who had a profound effect both on the development of commercial aviation and the speed-up in the manufacture of military planes.

The Congressional investigation of the airline industry carried out by Senator Hugo Black of Alabama revealed the interlocking directorates by which aircraft manufacturing companies controlled the airlines. Under the Black-McKeller Act of 1934 this was outlawed and the way was cleared for capable executives such as C. R. Smith, the Texan who headed American Airlines; Fred Rentschler, the chief engineer who deserted Wright Aeronautical, founded Pratt & Whitney, and ultimately United Airlines; Howard Hughes, the young millionaire and extraordinarily capable pilot who backed TWA and demanded ever faster and more powerful twin-engine planes. He bought Lockheed Electras for TWA which he piloted around the globe through fog and rain, completing the New York to Paris leg in half the time it took Lindbergh. Equally aggressive were Robert Gross and his brother Courtlandt who were friends of mine and who, as the heads of Lockheed, were destined to play a major role in commercial and military aviation. I was on their Board for ten years.

Robert Gross inherited a considerable fortune from his father and, as a partner of Lee, Higginson & Co., did extremely well during the up-phase of the stock market. He was an imaginative man; aviation appealed to him more than banking and in 1932 for only $40,000 he purchased Lockheed Aircraft which had gone into bankruptcy. I had great respect for both brothers and when Bob invited Shirley and me to join them on the ground floor we hesitated—actually we may not have missed a very great opportunity because Lockheed, after the war, experienced some pretty rocky days. Courtie Gross once told me that the twenty years during which he devoted a twelve-hour day to Lockheed produced rather mediocre capital gains. His house was about twelve miles from the factory and he remarked that if he had thrown the car keys out of the window anywhere along the route and bought a reasonable amount of real estate where they fell, his capital gains would be five times as great. Of course there was the little matter of preserving America and the part that Lockheed played in that.

In my second year at Scudder, President Roosevelt, impelled by the Black investigation, suddenly cancelled the government contracts for carrying the mail, a subsidy on which every airline depended. When United Airline stock dropped to $3.00 a share I bought a sensible amount and advised Scudder to do the same —which they did. The President's quick decision in January, 1934, was a disaster. The only alternative was to have the mail carried by the Air Force which it was ill-equipped to do in what happened to be a winter of continual snow and ice. "After fifty-seven accidents and twelve deaths in seventy-eight days," as Carl Solberg summarized, "the commercial airlines were back carrying the mail," and Postmaster General Farley was relieved of further lambasting.

Now the search was on for a dependable, profitable passenger plane. The all-metal, low-wing 247, which Boeing introduced in 1933, Solberg calls "the first modern airliner,"—retractable landing gear, 180 m.p.h. cruising speed (40 m.p.h. faster than the Ford trimotor) and monocoque fuselage. Meanwhile Donald Douglas, a Naval Academy dropout, had decided that California offered the most favorable flying conditions and lower labor cost and at Santa Monica the Douglas Aircraft Company entered the competition with a twin-engine design, powered by Wright Cyclones. The DC-1 had room for only twelve passengers; when the DC-2, with seats for fourteen became imminent, C. R. Smith ordered twenty for American Airlines but what he really wanted was a wider plane with a capacity for twenty-one seats. This was the DC-3, "the plane that changed the world," and the first that could make a profit carrying passengers only. Solberg says it cut flying time across the country to fifteen hours flying east, seventeen hours flying west. Two years before American got its DC-3 Smith testified before Congress that his company lost $758,000; two years after, American made its first profit.

It gave me a great lift when Joseph P. Ripley, the senior director of United Airlines, in lining up a new Board, asked me to become a director. There was nothing I would have liked better. At twenty-nine I was the youngest and least experienced; the lively and attractive Sumner Sewall, who came aboard at the same time, was a veteran pilot of World War I and on his way to becoming Governor of Maine. At that time United was one of "the Big Three," the others being American and TWA, and my election gave me carte blanche to visit any airplane factory and from then on I kept in close touch with Boeing, Douglas and Lockheed. Lockheed had put together an exceptional team, led by Kelly Johnson, original and brilliant, who designed the Constellation, by far the fastest, four-engine transport of the day, in utmost secrecy for Howard Hughes, who owned TWA, as the purchaser. When war broke out the Constellation was pressed into military service, and proved to be a stupendous achievement. In addition they had Paul Hibbard, chief engineer, Cyril Chappelet, the businessman, and Charlie Barker, an uncanny treasurer.

Bobby Gross and his younger brother Courtland, my classmate at Harvard, were superb salesmen. They had a unique method which with an air of hesitation they applied to each new plane: after running it down almost apologetically to the prospective buyer they would say, "But I'm sure you'd prefer to buy from Boeing (or Douglas)." This soft sell usually had the desired effect, the prospect was tantalized and insisted on seeing the Lockheed model. Courtland was the ideal deputy. In 1938 he flew to London and persuaded the British government to order 750 Hudson bombers, the military adaptation of the Lodestar, which was by far the largest single sale to the Allies before hostilities.

*   *   *

I was working hard at my new job, intensely interested in the evolution of flying. Our second son Robert was born January 17, 1934, and Peggy devoted herself to our two youngsters spending what time she could spare at the Art Students League. Weekends in the spring and fall we drove the boys out to the big house at Mt. Kisco which Moms had turned over to us. The alacrity with which she moved her things into the apartment below ours at 10 Gracie Square revealed that at heart she was a New Yorker. Summers we spent in a rented cottage on Mount Desert—it was all we could do to get Moms up for one long weekend—and we bought a lobster boat in which to fish and go for picnics on the islands.

We enjoyed having guests for weekends in Mt. Kisco, especially when the weather was warm enough for tennis and drinks beside the pool. They included the John Pells, Douglas Dillons, "Swede" Whiton, the Langbourne Williams, Frank Russells, Philip Hofers, Ed Warners, Hanson Baldwins, John Mason Browns, Dick Myers, and Imrie de Vegh, a Hungarian economist.

John Mason Brown was unique. He was a scintillating drama critic, a supreme lecturer in the prewar years, a born mimic, and an altogether delightful friend; he and his wife Cassie came to us often and the party was always happier for his wit. When John was commissioned in the Navy and went overseas as an aide to Admiral Stark, his writing acquired strength and depth. I like to recall what distinguished careers our other friends were about to enter: "Swede" Whiton as president of Union Sulphur, Douglas Dillon, Under-Secretary of State and later Ambassador to France, Philip Hofer, head of the Houghton Library at Harvard. Hanson Baldwin was to be widely respected as the military correspondent for *The New York Times*, Frank Russell became vice-president of National Aviation, Langbourne Williams, president of Freeport Sulphur; Alajalov, a designer of fascinating covers for *The New Yorker*.

I realized it was time to build up an ample wine cellar and was guided by Frank Schoonmaker who installed a choice one with airconditioning in the lower part of the barn. 1928 and 1929 were marvelous years for both Bordeaux and Burgundy, which were selling for about forty dollars a case! The next year of comparable vintage was 1961 when the best wines had risen to six hundred dollars a case.

My appetite for books was as keen as ever. My preference was for history as lively as *The Epic of America* by James Truslow Adams and *Only Yesterday* by Frederick Lewis Allen. In biog-

John Mason Brown at Mt. Kisco

Young Bill and Bob in their model cars at Mt. Kisco

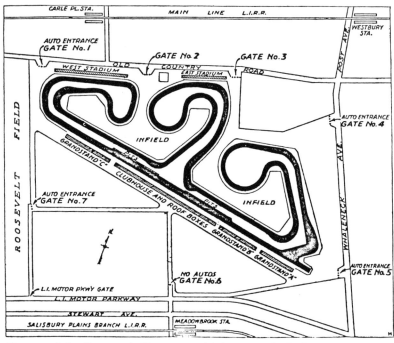

Course of the Roosevelt Raceway with its many hairpin turns

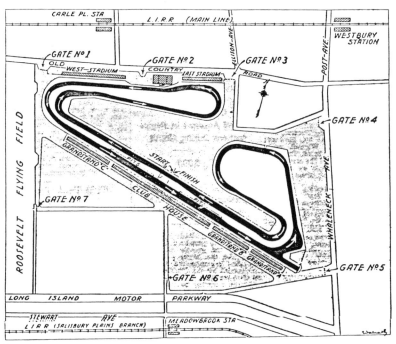

Roosevelt Raceway, when rebuilt

The Duesenberg J limousine which I owned from 1931 to 1939

Peggy and I with Noel Coward, on shipboard en route to Japan, 1935

Ready for a drive in Peking, myself and Cecil Lyon on the box, Peggy and Elsie Lyon within, the inscrutable Chang in the background

raphy I enjoyed *The Story of San Michele* by Axel Munthe and *British Agent* by R. H. Bruce Lockhart who had been in St. Petersburg at the beginning of the Russian Revolution. The year 1935 was particularly fruitful with *North to the Orient* by Anne Morrow Lindbergh; *Life with Father*, by Clarence Day; *Seven Pillars of Wisdom* by T. E. Lawrence; *Rats, Lice and History* by Hans Zinsser, and *R. E. Lee* by Douglas Southall Freeman. Peggy and I took two of these, Anne Lindbergh and Clarence Day, with us on our trip to the Orient.

We both had an insatiable desire to see the world, to visit those countries which were still terra incognita on the map in our library and it was part of my understanding with Scudder that I should have latitude of a month or so away from the office. In 1934, I took Peggy on her first visit to Egypt (no fooling about in an iron rowboat this time) and the following spring we headed for Japan and China on a slow Canadian ship. Noel Coward was aboard; we introduced ourselves and took almost every meal with him. One could not have asked for a more entertaining companion. I wondered later, after reading his autobiography, *Present Indicative*, if he hadn't been writing part of it on the ship. What he did write for us before we parted was this poem about the endless games the three of us played in which we tried to stump each other with the names of celebrities, *and what they did*.

Souvenir
by Noel Coward
In memory of a charming trip
On board a dull but noble ship
In memory of endless games
And scores of unrelated names
Including that of Doctor Wence
Who first discovered Flatulence

Also the famous Elmer Hale
Who pitched a ball eight times for Yale
Without forgetting Witzenback
That hero of the Harvard Track
Nor Mrs. Hiram J. MacFarr,
Who wandered, nude, through Iowa
Under these clarion trumpet's din
Sometimes a lesser name crept in
Such as Napoleon Bonaparte
Or even Plato or Mozart
But men of such obscure repute
Were seldom passed without dispute
So we returned with great relief
To Senator Augustus Spief
To Ida Chubb and Wendell Green
(The first to cauterize the spleen)
To Ethan Beck and General Bight
And Mabel MacNamara Wright
To Doctor Bowes, the insect man
Who perished in Afghanistan
Without a thought for Otto Kahn
Or Drian or Reynaldo Hahn.

In Tokyo we were guests of Ambassador Joseph Grew, dean of our diplomatic corps and a charming host. At a formal dinner we were introduced to several Japanese, the most attractive, Jiro Shirasu of the Foreign Office who looked us up whenever he came to America and after the war was seriously considered as their ambassador in Washington. We visited Nikko and Kyoto where the ancient temples, which I had seen hurriedly before, were most interesting, and Nara, with its Giant Buddha and the friendly deer park.

My great friend, Cecil Lyon, had resigned from the brokerage business to enter our Foreign Service for which he was perfectly adapted. After his marriage to Ambassador Grew's daughter, Elsie, he was appointed our third Secretary in Peking and they had urged us to make a leisurely visit, so we crossed the inland sea to enjoy that wonderful old city in the lingering days of the ancient regime. The embassies, as I have said, were guarded since the Boxer Rebellion and in the Foreign Quarter there seemed hardly any anxiety of trouble to come. He and I played tennis and I watched him play polo on his string of Mongolian ponies. He was team captain and high scorer. (He was also kicked by a pony and afterwards required an anti-tetanus shot.) They took us to the theatre where there was no scenery other than what is suggested by gestures of the actors (this motion to indicate mountains, that the rivers, etc.). Elsie, a natural linguist, spoke Chinese fluently and translated for us. Tea was served throughout the performance by ushers in the aisle and should a spectator wish a hot towel it was tossed to him by a man on stage, without distracting the performance.

Cecil has kept a diary throughout his entire diplomatic career, and these four quotations from it will give the true flavor of our entertainment:

> April 14, 1935, Sunday
> "On a picnic to Jaques' Temple, Shih Tzu Wu (Sleeping Lion Temple) in the Western Hills with the Cadogans. Bill and Peggy loved it. The Minister's sister, Lady Sophie Scott, who has just arrived on a visit came with us. She is a perfectly delightful 'Huntin'' character, and I never realized so many words ended in 'ing' until I heard her talk, for she completely amputates all 'g's thus making them conspicuous by their absence. Her favorite sport is 'deer

stalkin',' and as for 'fishin', shootin' and ridin',' well they are only comparable to dancin.'

April 18, Thursday

"...Flew over the [Great] Wall this afternoon. The Burdens enjoyed it enormously, but Elsie, whose first flight it was, was scarcely as enthusiastic. In fact as we touched earth she exclaimed, and I might add it was about her only indication of life during the entire hour and a quarter we were aloft, 'That's my last trip in an aeroplane!' I hope she'll change however, for it's a noble sport and in spite of being a bit rough to-day it was grand flight; better than my last one for we went right over the Ming Tombs. Incidentally these are being repaired as part of the program to make Peiping a tourist center.

April 20, Saturday

"We'd planned a grand week-end expedition to Tan Cheh Ssu and Chieh Tai Ssu, but unfortunately Peggy Burden was taken ill yesterday, not seriously, and so she couldn't go, so Elsie dropped out with her. However Bill, Lady Sophie Scott, Walter Graham (Sir Alexander's new P.S.), Patricia and Cynthia Cadogan all came for lunch at two thirty and in a howling dust storm we started off. It was pretty awful, especially going through the filthy coaling village of Men Ta Kuo, all the inhabitants of which look like residents of Inferno, but after we had got up above the dust into the mountains it was lovely and clear. We arrived at Tan Cheh Ssu, which is a lovely old buddhist temple, at about half past six. The boys, whom we had sent ahead in the morning, had rooms fixed for us in a removed court. One room for women, one for men, with our own camp beds, linen, and later in the evening a per-

fectly served five course meal out under the stars. Camping
in China is done most comfortably in a method of which I
thoroughly approve. One has all the atmosphere, but none
of the discomforts—at least practically none, for Chau,
ever inefficient, had not sent enough Scotch and soda, or
any cocktails. It was a grand moonlight night and when
the practically full moon climbed up over the cloud banks
and then burst forth onto the glorious tiled roofs of the
temple it was of an Arabian Nights splendor.

April 21, Sunday
". . . Advice to China excursionists: Always take an
English huntin' lady with you. Lady Sophie was the supreme companion. She not only was amusing, the personi-
fication of energy, but without doubt is the best equipped
human being I've ever known in my life. Not one of the
men had a mirror to shave in this morning, Lady Sophie
produced a superb big one; arrived at the second temple
for lunch, hot, weary and dusty, Lady Sophie produced a
minute washing kit, including not only a towel but Lavender Soap, Yardley's at that!

"Incidentally to-day is Easter, but we spent it entirely
in a Pagan setting."

*   *   *

William von Meister was a huge German, six-foot seven
inches, 250 pounds, and getting fatter. His mother was American, his father a Prussian aristocrat and his godfather, the
Kaiser. Willy was a little older than I, his wife, Countess Scherr-
Thoss, was a remote cousin of mine and what brought us together was our addiction to automobiles and flying. He was
efficient, fluent in English and German and had his finger in

many pies: he was working in the New York office of AGFA, the German equivalent of Eastman Kodak, and acting on the side as the agent for the V-12 cylinder Maybach car with five-speed, semi-automatic transmission. He tried in vain to sell me one but as I demonstrated—to his horror—it had nothing like the marvelous acceleration of my Mercedes. Willy introduced me to the wine of the tiny but beautiful vineyards of the Rheingau, the Rheinpfalz and the Moselle, and as we dined, he would expatiate on the plans now developing for a lighter-than-air dirigible line between New York and Europe, to be operated with German-built Zeppelins. The American Zeppelin Transport Company was being reactivated under the presidency of Edward P. Farley, head of the American Reliance Steamship line; Willy was vice-president, and I was in line for the skeleton board of directors.

A more down-to-earth project of mine was the construction of a road race course on Roosevelt Field, Long Island. I had been recruited as one of the backers by Robert Thack, lobbyist for Pan American Airways in Washington, and his friend, Howard Marshall, owner of the Washington Redskins, the "promoter" who would show us how to attract the gate. The track was to be built of bluestone held together with tar (macadam), designed in the shape of a pretzel by the "expert," George H. Robertson, whose chief credential was that he had won one of the old Vanderbilt cup races in 1908. The course had many straightaways for high speed on the outside and loops which would enable the cars to show their "cornering ability" in the inside. For the spectator there was an east stadium and a west (admission $4.50), a long grandstand, clubhouse, and roof boxes (reserved seats $7.00 to $27.50) and general admission to the infield at $2.75. We figured on an attendance of 75,000 and that the fastest cars would lap our track at 120 m.p.h., with bursts of over 150 m.p.h. My cousin, young George Vanderbilt, was persuaded to invest a few thousand in a huge silver cup, designed by Cartier, for the winner.

In our innocence we did not realize that while European road races attracted a very large attendance, admission was charged for very few of them except for small, deluxe stands. Nor could we understand why for our first race in the early summer of 1936 we were unable to enlist any of the top Mercedes-Benz or Auto Union racing teams. We did get the very dashing Bugatti driver Jean Pierre Wimille of France and the inimitable Tazio Nuvolari of Italy with his sixteen-cylinder Alfa Romeo Special. They were our stars and there was a dubious second-rate group of European and American drivers to whom we had to give subsidies just to have their cars on the track.

George Robertson who had laid out the track was confident that the fastest cars would lap the track at 120 m.p.h. and that on the straightaway they would climb to 150 m.p.h. The race consisted of 75 laps around the four-mile course making a total of 300 miles and in every lap there were fifteen straightaways and sixteen turns of varying sharpness which were banked only one percent. As it actually turned out, the fastest lap in practice was run at 69.9 m.p.h., and in the race itself the winner Nuvolari averaged only 65.9 m.p.h. over the 300 miles, a sharp disappointment to the spectators, and even more to the organizers. The first prize was $20,000 and ten lesser prizes for a total of $60,000. Fifty-nine cars were entered (three of which bore the name "Miller!"), and I cannot say how many finished. I think what went wrong was that Robertson grossly overestimated the speed at which any car could negotiate the mildly banked curves. It is my recollection that each of the organizers lost about $100,000.

After such a disappointing performance there had to be improvement before next year's race. We found a real expert to redesign the track and eliminate most of the slow-speed turns, and electric timing devices were installed so that we could honestly inform the "customers" how close the leaders were coming to the desirable 180 m.p.h.

It was Willy von Meister who introduced us to Dr. Hugo Eckener, the Captain of the *Graf Zeppelin* in whose hands that giant airship made 600 flights, mostly to South America, transporting more than 13,000 passengers without casualty. As Carl Solberg says in *Conquest of the Skies,* the *Graf* record put Germany ahead in long-range air transport, which was why the steamship people like Ed Farley wanted to get into the American end of the trans-Atlantic airship service as they foresaw their business drying up in competition with air travel in the not too distant future.

In mid summer Peggy and I decided to go to Germany with the hope of achieving two results: to quiet the German fear that their best drivers would be molested by thousands of Jews from New York City if they appeared on our track, and, secondly, to inspect the *Graf Zeppelin.*

It was when we crossed the German border that I first became aware of Hitler's strict regime. We were being driven by our usually calm chauffeur Joseph in my Mercedes and were questioned by some tough-looking Nazis about the purpose of our visit. I made the fatal mistake of talking to them in my badly broken German, explaining that we were about to visit the Zeppelin Works in Friedrichshafen. I thought in my naive way that this would eliminate suspicion. Quite the reverse, for they assumed that my knowledge of Dr. Eckener and the Zeppelin was camouflage and that we were probably American spies. It was sometime before we were released and when at last on the road Joseph made it quite clear that I should shut up and stop talking about Zeppelins in my broken German.

In Berlin we got in touch with an ardent Nazi, Dr. Herbert Scholz, a handsome Teutonic hulk with flashing blond hair and chiseled features, very impressive in his black SS uniform. We had met him and his beautiful wife, Thyssin's daughter, when he was the German Consul in Boston. Later he was promoted to Second Secretary in the German Embassy in Washington, and had now come over for the Olympic Games. We had no desire to see the Olympics (where Hitler was so infuriated by the four gold medals won by the American black sprinter, Jesse Owens), but after a good talk with Scholz we left with his reassurance that we could count on having some of their ablest drivers in 1937.

We stayed in a small hotel on Lake Constance where we were met by four of the top officers of the *Graf*. We invited them and their wives to dine with us and ordered cocktails which the men may have tasted before in New York but not their wives. The latter seemed delighted by these apparently harmless drinks. (Remember P. G. Wodehouse's description of the mint julip— "It puts its baby hand in yours and the next thing you hear is the judge saying, '£5 and costs.' "). After a couple of martinis and the German wines that followed the good ladies were looping; not so Peggy and I for at the thought of flying over the Alps and the great valleys of Switzerland, as we had been invited to do the next day, the prospect was rather sobering. Peggy was sleepless and about 2 a.m. she awoke me to ask, "Bill, tell me what you think might *possibly* go wrong during our flight?" I pacified her as best I could. Finally, the dawn came, a beautiful one, and Peggy was convinced that she would go.

We drove out to the hangar where the elderly Captain Eckener greeted us. I must say the *Graf* looked perfectly enormous.

For a moment Peggy hung back as if irresolute, then she put her hand in mine and we went aboard. We entered the gondola, nearly 100 feet long, and 20 feet wide, and were escorted to the passenger lounge, the entire area carpeted and curtained in Burgundy red. The windows on either side were tilted so that the passengers could look out as they flew. A ground crew of a hundred men held the two main handling ropes and walked the huge ship out of its hangar. Luckily there was no wind. When the ropes and ballast were dropped the great ship rose slowly, majestically, to her cruising height, and she seemed so stable that we began to relax.

The passenger lounge of the Zeppelin was far larger than I had imagined, large enough to hold a piano; bedrooms for twenty, and a smoker's room. Smoking, being the ultimate fire hazard, was forbidden in any room but this one. Peggy began to relax as we sailed away smoothly, dipping down over the Swiss lakes low enough to see sailboats in detail, then soaring to the heights of the mountain peaks. We flew so near to Mont Blanc that one could have thrown a stone at it. The Zeppelin had great maneuverability for such an enormous vehicle, and it was piloted in and around the mountains with the greatest of skill. Having Dr. Hugo Eckener in command made the flight all the more memorable.

I had a chance to visit the bridge and watch Eckener himself at the wheel, and the surprisingly simple array of instruments he used. Later I walked down the rather slippery cat-walk in the interior of the ship, observing the huge ballonets filled with hydrogen, coming finally to the noisy, oily engine gondola where the five powerful Maybach engines were pounding away. We returned at last to Friedrichshafen, not only alive but elated —though I must admit that Peggy laughed with relief to have her feet again on terra firma.

It was common knowledge that Dr. Eckener was not a Nazi and that he resented the idea of having the swastika painted on his great ships. This of course got him into trouble with Goebbels, and when the new Zeppelin, the *Hindenburg*, larger and more spacious than the *Graf*, made its maiden voyage to New York, Captain Lehmann was in charge but with Eckener beside him in the command gondola.

While he was in New York, Dr. Eckener took a late supper with us in our apartment; he was a fascinating conversationalist whose courage and simplicity stood out. He told us of his earlier flights and of the supreme importance of meteorology in navigating such a huge airship over the seas where one had to run before the high winds and avoid the sudden storms.

It was Willy von Meister's idea that a number of VIPs should be invited for an all-day cruise on the *Hindenburg* as a way of encouraging those who might help to finance the American Zeppelin Transport Company. It was a mixed and distinguished group which gathered at the Yale Club before midnight: three admirals, a general, government officials, leaders in aviation, such as Eddie Rickenbacker, the German Ambassador, Winthrop Aldrich, the chairman of the Chase Bank, Nelson Rockefeller, members of the press and of course Willy and myself. (A member of Nelson's family telephoned in some agitation to ask if I thought the trip would be safe, and I replied "Perfectly safe.")

We took off before sunrise in a DC-3 on a shuttle trip to Lakehurst, and the alcohol we had consumed did not lessen our enthusiasm. The *Hindenburg* was enormous, 804 feet long and a maximum diameter of 135 feet. She had seventy small private cabins in the big gondola, an ornate lounge with an aluminum baby grand piano, a spacious dining room, and two observation decks which gave the passengers opportunity to move around and observe the scenery from the large windows. On this trip to Boston and return we flew at a low altitude at a cruising speed of seventy-five m.p.h. We departed at 8:30 a.m., wound through the Housatonic Valley and on north, and one had the impression of being on a large Atlantic liner on a completely placid sea. Shortly after noon we were served a sumptuous meal, cold salmon, tenderloin steak, iced California melons, and the finest wines. Again I walked down the long slippery cat-walk to observe the Daimler-Benz diesel engines of 1200 horsepower, the noise and vibration were terrific, and the German mechanics, although their overalls were oil-soaked, seemed to be the essence of efficiency. The so-called "Millionaires Flight" ended calmly at 5:17 p.m. when we were moored to the mast at Lakehurst.

Flying diminished my interest in the Roosevelt Raceway. There were thirty-six cars entered in the race that took place on July 3, 1937, and they did achieve a higher speed and a more exciting finish. But the gate fell far short of meeting the expenses and Hitler's menacing figure and the war clouds gathering in Europe did not embolden us to try again.

The American Zeppelin Transport Company had many meetings but accomplished little. One of our objectives was to purchase the non-flammable helium gas of which the United States government had control on the sensible theory that a helium-filled airship would be far safer than a hydrogen-filled airship. With this end in view I called on Secretary of the Interior Harold Ickes, accompanied by Dr. Eckener and Willy; was courteously received and turned down flat. "Helium," said the Secretary, "is war material and not for sale."

The *Hindenburg* was not long for this world for on her second trans-Atlantic flight to America (Dr. Eckener was not aboard) just as she was being secured to the mast at Lakehurst, the stern

of the great ship burst into flames and the whole structure collapsed. Sixty-two persons survived, thirty-five perished. It was
thought that leaking hydrogen had been ignited by static electricity as the rope touched ground. This was the doom; the sister ship under construction was flown once by Eckener and then
broken up to salvage the metal at Goering's order.

Our third son Hamilton was born on May 17, 1937, but I did
not realize how absorbed I had become in the family and my
affairs until in 1938 I became a member of the Council on Foreign Relations, nominated by Langborne Williams and Hanson Baldwin. At the fortnightly meetings we were addressed by
a speaker, usually a diplomat, an economist of international
reputation, someone of authority in Washington, whose "off
the record" remarks were challenging and ominous. I listened
avidly, perceiving as I had not a year earlier, what a powerful
threat Hitler was to Europe's stability. Among the older members I was impressed by Russell Leffingwell, the Morgan partner, and Allen Dulles who became a close friend. I had begun
to cut my wisdom teeth.

Washington and Rio

OUR Guest Book at Mt. Kisco was begun in June, 1936, and was more personal than the stiff, stylish one at "Florham," ours being embellished with photographs, verses, jokes and endearments instead of the copperplate signatures. It opens with the family, Moms, Peggy and myself, young Bill photographed in his miniature Bugatti (made by Bugatti, and powered by electricity), and Bobby in a toy model propelled by pedals. That autumn I studied the "Florham" Guest Book, 206 heavy white pages, gilt-edged, bound in leather, Vanderbilt maroon, which had stood for forty years on the huge mahogany table in the marble-floored hall. It was a catalogue of Grandfather's circle, financiers, some distinguished diplomats, such as Ambassadors Henry White and Whitelaw Reed, men he personally admired like Henry Fairfield Osborne, Robert Bacon, and William Woodward, the banker and horseman, very few foreigners and, of course, a number of relatives, the Webbs, the Sloanes, the Hammonds, and Shepards, all Vanderbilt-connected.

I turned back to the housewarming of October 6, 1896; Grandfather was forty-seven and Grandmother, at forty-two, a more vivacious and charming woman than I ever knew. At their very elaborate houseparties guests could do as they chose: riding, tennis, golf, backgammon, and bridge in the spring; the drag-hunt, the horseshow and cards and dancing in the autumn. Every overnight guest was expected to sign the great book.

"The weekends did very well for the footmen," so James Rarity recalled. "Each of us had two or three gentlemen to valet and would get from $5 to $20 from each. You were lucky if you drew Hiram Manville who always gave $50." Rarity remembers John Rogers saying to the elegant Frederick, "Everything always seems to go off so well in this house. I wish someone would *just drop a plate*!" Rye was the favorite whiskey. Mr. Coster Wilmerding took a good glass of rye upstairs at night and his empty flask was always full when he left.

The entertainment was much like that in the great country houses of Edwardian England except that dalliance was not encouraged and Donon's menus, I am sure, were far superior. Guests such as the Duchess of Marlborough or General Pershing added a special lustre, as did Thomas Edison when he came to lunch. A hypochondriac like the financier, Charles Hayden, confided to Aunt Ruth that on his next visit he expected the medicine chest in his room to be stocked with the fifty items he had at home. He gave her a list but Grandmother laughed at the suggestion. And Sir Noel Charles, Commander of the Cunard Fleet and Captain of the *Aquitania*, remarked plaintively to Frederick, the butler, that "By Gad, 'Florham' is longer than any of my ships!"

One of Grandmother's favorite guests, Margaret Laurance, late in life, wrote her bread-and-butter letter in verses which capture the flavor of the traditional houseparties:

The Guest Book

This a book that tells a story
Written in signatures for fifty years.

We, who turn a disk, to listen
To recorded music, turn instead a page.
We find recalled to memory
The record of some cherished date,
Of friends, and finest hospitality.

We hear once more the sound
Of gravel crunching from high skipping hoofs
Of gangling pole chains—Then
The coach horn's note as once again
Ruth or Mr. Twombly tooled the brake.
In driving aprons and long buttoned coats.
The ping of tennis balls in spring—
Here in the hall masses of color
Its Azalea time!
While Roman emperors with marble eyes
Are sentinels in line.

Next comes the drive to church at Madison.
The smell of Brewster leather in the wagonette
The cut steel buckles on a pinching shoe,
The family prayer books; the backbreaking pew.
The men that stayed at home to smoke cigars
Reading the Sunday papers; while Mammas
Wore ostrich plumes and little spotted veils.
Cards were forbidden as a Sunday sport
But always cold champagne at dinner
And old port.

Passed is that time—
And yet some things stand out one never can forget.
That lovely look of pride
Which Mr. Twombly always gave his wife.
Their devotion, and her graciousness
I'll remember all my life—

Each season passes, and once more
We see the silver gleam on damask
While clocks strike eight.
And silent footmen show us to our chairs
Gibson is at the organ—"Götterdämmerung
Or Liebestod thrill through the house
While Josie Cutting quite unlike our Harold
Has forgotten cards in music—
The book goes on recording names
So many are the same!
Florham is still as beautiful as then
And we as grateful to be asked again.
   With love and appreciation to the Twombly family
   Margaret Laurance

In the entries of the 1920s were some of those to whom I had been introduced—Henry and Ruth du Pont, the creators of "Winterthur," Harold ("Mike") Vanderbilt, Chairman of the Board of the New York Central, John Nicholas Brown, the brainy millionaire of Providence, Rhode Island, Marshall Field, the publisher and Henry S. Morgan, who almost kicked me off *The Corsair* at Red Top, for coming aboard with tar on my sneakers.

After her debut Aunt Ruth became the hostess of two of the annual houseparties, and among her guests I tried to identify her serious suitor. An old friend of Ruth's told me that my grandparents had planned that she should marry Childs Frick, but neither of the couple was interested and when Ruth fell in love with the stranger she ran into opposition. Ruth was defiant and had secretly set a date for their elopement which happened to be the very week her younger brother Hamilton, a councillor at the Groton Summer Camp, was drowned in Squam Lake.

There had to be a postponement and Grandmother, growing suspicious, threatened that "If you marry him, you give up 'Florham' and all it stands for." Aunt Ruth capitulated and came into part of her inheritance; she never wanted to marry anyone else and remained under the thumb of Grandma.

My reverie was a form of self-evaluation brought about by the uncertainty of the times. I was coming to the end of my tether at Scudder's; my research had paid off—I knew more than most brokers about aviation; I had been offered the vice-presidency of the National Aviation Corp.—I liked the name— a "captive" corporation of G. M.- P. Murphy & Co., which made it clear that my appointment was contingent upon their receiving a substantial investment from my family. I was tempted to take it—it would be a relief to get out from under Hardwick Stires—and it was a recognition of my specialized knowledge. Now in my early thirties I was ambitious to live up to my grandfather Twombly. So many husbands before me had used the Vanderbilt inheritance as a comfortable pillow.

My grandmother was in good health and might live for another twenty years in the style and with the staff Grandfather had chosen. Frederick, the butler, would be loyal, and Donon, her chef supreme, who had resisted the offers of other envious guests beside that of Mrs. Harold Vanderbilt, would never leave her. (Actually he remained forty-one years in our service.) They were the two mainstays at "Florham," and probably after Grandmother died I should have to decide the fate of the great mansion and its 900 acres. It had become an anachronism. I doubted if either of our boys would wish to be saddled with its taxes and upkeep. Peggy was expecting our third child —hoping, I felt sure, for a daughter. When Hamilton, our third son, was born on May 17th, 1937, I realized that whatever my inheritance, I should have to plan for their futures—and that of my grandchildren—and, incidentally, solve the future of "Florham."

Robert Doherty, who was in charge of the Twombly Estate, felt it his duty to protect the $75 million left by Mr. Twombly and see that it did not diminish as it passed to Moms and Aunt Ruth, and eventually to Shirley and me. He did not envision its increase. But I could countermand his caution: my presence in Scudder Stevens had led Aunt Ruth to invest several millions in stocks they recommended and my vice-presidency in National Aviation resulted in a Twombly brokerage account there. I had already become a director of the South American Development Company, Grandfather's gold mine in Ecuador, managed by my cousin, William A. Kissam, which had yielded big dividends for over thirty years, but was now thinning out.

In the farm at "Florham" changes had taken place. The stables which once held 100 hackneys now contained a score of carriage and riding horses. The dairy herd of 400 Guernsey cows which in 1924 produced over a million gallons of milk and cream—at a profit—was reduced to fourscore sufficient to provide for the family and neighbors. The greenhouses, famous for their orchids and chrysanthemums and fruit, still fulfilled Grandmother's needs at her three residences.

*   *   *

Ever since our marriage only a single painting had decorated the walls of our apartment at 10 Gracie Square, Sully's portrait of one of Peggy's Livingston ancestors, long deceased. It did not occur to either of us that we might enjoy something more lively until in 1937 I was asked to join the Junior Advisory Committee of The Museum of Modern Art.

The Museum which opened in the autumn of 1929 was conceived by very wealthy patrons whose plans were in no way deterred by the collapse of the Stock Market. Foremost among them were Abby Aldrich Rockefeller, the wife of John D., Jr., Miss Lizzie P. Bliss and Mrs. Cornelius J. Sullivan. Mrs. Rockefeller, who was the best executive of the trio, had already assembled her unique collection of American Primitives, now a showpiece in Colonial Williamsburg, but was no less ardent in her appreciation of contemporary painting. In the winter of 1928–1929 she and Miss Bliss visited Egypt and on the ship home had a fortuitous meeting with Mrs. Sullivan; they exchanged ideas about the desirability of opening a museum in New York devoted to what was then considered by many to be outrageously advanced paintings and sculpture.

Miss Bliss had been collecting ever since the unorthodox "Armory Show" of 1913 and under the guidance of the American painter, Arthur B. Davies, had bought two Redons, two Degas and a landscape by Renoir to which, as time went on, she added Cézannes, Seurats, Matisses, Picassos and Toulouse-Lautrecs of exceptional quality.

Mrs. Sullivan had studied at the Slade School of Art in London under Roger Fry and had taught at the Pratt Institute. After her marriage she and her husband together acquired a selection of Braque, Modigliani, Cézanne, Picasso and van Gogh.

Mrs. Rockefeller, at the time her husband was in the thick of restoring Williamsburg, had amassed "with her own money," so to speak, an admirable collection of modern prints. "The Ladies," as they were affectionately referred to by the trustees and staff, willingly loaned the choice of their collections for the initial exhibitions which attracted hoards of viewers—70,000 in the first ten weeks.

"The Ladies" wasted no time. In May, 1929, Mrs. Rockefeller invited A. Conger Goodyear of Buffalo to become the first

president of the new museum; he was wealthy, an able orga-
nizer and his own collection of Maillol, van Gogh, Renoir,
Seurat and others, included the very favorites of Miss Bliss and
Mrs. Sullivan. For a brief period he had been president of the
Albright Gallery in Buffalo where he had affronted fellow trustees by purchasing a "pink period" Picasso for $5,000, and they
wanted him out of office. Mrs. Rockefeller realized that the best
time to "collect" collectors was when they had had a row with
their home institute.

Their second talented ally was the famous Paul Sachs who
had retired from the family firm of Goldman Sachs to teach fine
arts at Harvard. He was younger than "the Ladies"—at fifty-
one an inspiring scholar who was attracting brilliant pupils
such as Lincoln Kirstein, John Walker, and Edward M. War-
burg, all of the class of 1930. It was said that Sachs was responsible for training an entire generation of museum curators.

Sach's preeminent "find" was Alfred Hamilton Barr, Jr.
who had taken his doctorate at Harvard and was teaching the
history of art at Wellesley. When Sachs approached him Barr's
response was prophetic: "The fact that you are even considering me as a possible participant in this great scheme has set my
mind teeming with ideas and plans—That is something I could
give my life to—unstintingly." Never were truer words spoken.

At first sight Alfred was not impressive. He was wispy and
had the evangelical air of a clergyman—his father and two
uncles were clergymen—but one soon realized that his dedication, his evangelism were wholly devoted to art. He was that
paradoxical mixture of a shy scholar and an inspired showman.

Peggy and I really came to know him that afternoon in the
late summer of 1938, after our return from Germany, when we
invited him and Monroe Wheeler to drive out and have supper
with us at "Uplands." We had just installed a new high fidelity

phonograph with powerful outdoor amplifiers of which we were proud so we dined on the terrace, our Austrian chef outdid himself and the Montrachet 1935 just right.

There was a full moon and by its light Stravinsky's Le Sacre du Printemps seemed marvelous. Afterwards Alfred absorbed us in a fascinating discussion of contemporary painting and sculpture until someone discovered how late it had become.

Peggy suggested that it would be more comfortable for them to spend the night with us and drive in in the morning.

To our surprise Alfred demurred: "You know, Bill, it's unfortunate but I can't sleep anywhere except in my own bed."

This was literally true: he suffered from insomnia and was going through one of his periodic phases. However it was so late that we persuaded him to try our guest room, and he admitted at breakfast it wasn't so bad.

Some friendships open a new vista. What Paul Sachs did for Alfred he in turn did for me: Barr so stimulated my appreciation of modern art that it became a lifelong enjoyment.

The Junior Advisory Committee, to which I was invited, and composed mostly of young enthusiasts, was organized in 1930 by the architect George Howe, of Philadelphia, who served as the first chairman and was succeeded by Nelson Rockefeller. We were a seed bed: with funds of our own—never more than $5,000—we purchased additions to the collection at ridiculously low prices, such as, for instance, the three Mondrians we bought for $1,500. Our scouting was of course approved by the trustees and in time, the more energetic juniors, such as Monroe Wheeler and the knowledgeable Katherine Warren and Eliza Bliss Parkinson moved up to the board of trustees. Our meetings were attended by Alfred Barr and his talks to us were lively and memorable; the Committee elected me their chairman in 1940, and I became a trustee in 1943.

Peggy and I both came under Alfred's magnetism, I perhaps more eagerly because I had never heard anyone speak of the arts with such illumination. He revealed the beauty in contemporary painting and sculpture and one caught fire from his appreciation. Peggy on the other hand ever since her girlhood had been imbued with her father's preference for the nineteenth-century Italians, and it was more of a wrench for her to come to like modern paintings.

Most young collectors are unsure of their taste and Alfred was most encouraging. He took us with him to important exhibitions of the dealers and at first we had a hard time making up our minds. At Knoedler's there was a Matisse, "Pont de St. Michel," which appealed to me strongly. I have always loved Paris and I went back to study this painting again and again, took an option on it, and asked if we might hang it in our apartment to see if we wished to live with it. This was the first canvass we agreed that we wanted, and I bought it in 1941 for $4,000 which seemed to Moms, Grandma, and Aunt Ruth absurdly extravagant. Years later Knoedler's said we "stole" it.

There were many times when we did not agree: Peggy had little patience with Picasso. "That picture," she said, "is so terrible I won't have it in the house." Marsden Hartley's painting "The Portland Light," a wonderful study in blue and white aswirl with waves, provoked her. "The lighthouse is crooked," she said. "Yes," I argued, "but it ought to be," and people who see it today over the fireplace in our living room at Northeast Harbor feel the surge and strength with which it is painted. I could have bought a painting of Pollock's for $800, but Peggy resisted. I suppose what I should have done was to buy and put what I liked in storage. Since we have always done things together I wanted her approval.

*   *   *

As Hitler's ever-encroaching demands ridiculed the "peace in our time," which Chamberlain thought he had secured at Munich the normal good nature of our guests at Mt. Kisco broke out into arguments pressed by those who believed in America first and who quoted Walter Lippmann's early prophecy that "This is not our war." That question hung fire but it forced every man of military age to consider what he would do if it indeed became "our war."

Our friendship with Walter and Helen Lippmann began on the tennis courts in Maine. They had bought Admiral Byrd's "camp" at Southwest Harbor, where they spent July and August, and were always looking for players for their very good court. We were introduced by Jane Wilmerding, a good friend of ours, who was Walter's ward. Her mother, an actress, was always traveling, so she made Walter Jane's legal guardian, much to the satisfaction of both. Helen and Walter played tennis well into their seventies. They gave tennis lunches every Wednesday, inviting friends who would take turns playing doubles after lunch. We went often, and came to know them both very well.

Walter was very modest for a man of his reputation, and was constantly asking people for their views on world affairs, and would listen—an endearing quality. I disagreed with him on almost every subject, but we had good-natured arguments and mutual respect. Helen was an excellent hostess and conversation starter, with a sense of humor which could be sharp at times. She was Irish by inheritance and shared my dislike of most English people—preferring the French, whose language she spoke so fluently that she would often translate for Walter on their trips abroad.

How fast a fatal decision was approaching in Europe I did not realize until Peggy and I were leaving Mt. Desert at the end of August, 1939. We had a farewell dinner party with the Lipp-manns at their camp during which Walter and I got into one of our arguments; he was doubtful that if war came it would in-volve us. I disagreed—I said it was bound to come and the only question was how soon. The next day on our drive to Mt. Kis-co, we were listening to the radio and were stunned by the an-nouncement that Hitler had invaded Poland. While we were still conjecturing came the reaction: Britain and France de-clared war on Germany.

We stopped off at Stockbridge to have lunch with old friends Alma and "Tic" Morgan. They had not heard the news and Tic thought we ought to line up immediately with Britain and France; I said we were far from ready.

That autumn as Poland was overrun by the Blitzkrieg, America began to look to its defenses. Classmates of mine were pulling strings for commissions and because of my known interest in aviation I was urged, almost begged, to get into Na-val Aviation. But I hesitated not sure that my eyes were good enough or that I'd be effective in combat.

One of the first of my contemporaries to be called to Wash-ington was Nelson Rockefeller, whom President Roosevelt ap-pointed Coordinator of Inter-American Affairs. Nelson took with him my boyhood chum, Bill Harding, to be his adviser on aviation. In January 1941, Bill telephoned me to say that Nel-son was seriously concerned about the threat which the Axis airlines in South America posed to Allied shipping and, if Hit-ler swept Europe, to our own defense. He had told the President of his fear and had received FDR's approval to do whatever was necessary to oust the German Condor and the Italian Lati lines from their bases in Brazil, Argentina, and wherever they had made inroads. Bill asked if I could drop everything and prepare a report on their penetration, the extent to which their planes were already revealing the position of allied ships to the U-boats in Southern waters, and the danger this would be to us should France and England capitulate. I had done some investigation and was confident that I could get a detailed account to him in two months' time. If what I wrote was approved, it was probable that I might be asked to come to Washington. Peggy was eager for me to go ahead. She argued that my years of studying aviation would be of value to the government, her confidence overcame my uncertainty and I called Bill back to say I'd do it.

"See if you can get your report to Nelson by early April, Bill," he added, "this government is unlike anything you could ever imagine. It is all done by writing letters: you go in advance to the man you have in mind to make sure he is ready for what you are going to ask. And you make sure of the contents of the letter he will send you in reply." I did not at the time understand what the hell he was talking about. But I would learn.

I worked full-out on my report through February and March and I must say it surprised me to discover how deeply the Germans had entrenched themselves commercially and militarily. There were 900,000 Germans residing in Brazil, many of them in top jobs! My emphasis on the deadly accuracy of the radio communication between the Axis planes and the U-boats, and the sinkings which had already resulted had to be taken seriously. I sent my report to Nelson and awaited results. A week later he was on the phone, said that the President had read my report and agreed that the situation was threatening. "Bill," Nelson said, "how about coming down and working on the program?"

I still was not confident; I had never administered anything. But Peggy insisted that I was underestimating myself, and she pushed me into it.

Peggy and I left for Washington in early June 1941. Luckily, for that summer we were able to sublet Archie and Ada Mac-Leish's charming house in Georgetown. It was a little boite with a big sitting room–dining room on the ground floor, and an equally big double bedroom above. And to add to its charm there was a delightful little garden at the back. It was really like a second honeymoon, for our boys, Bill, Bobby and Hamilton, for the time being remained at Mt. Kisco. We loved the cool and quiet of the summer evenings, outside the Capital, and we had a cheerful competent black to do the cooking. In this friendly setting I entered government service for what turned out to be seven years, an experience which completely changed my life.

Nelson complimented me on what I had written, said that the Axis airlines must be expelled, and to give Bill Harding and me the necessary clout in carrying out our sub rosa program, we were appointed joint vice-presidents of the Defense Supplies Corporation, a subsidiary of the Reconstruction Finance Corporation, and installed in a suite of offices in a new building, rather above our station in the bureaucracy.

Bill had been working out details and proposed that I make our first try in Bolivia but I insisted that we tackle the biggest, Brazil, a country I knew and a people I liked, and we agreed. Any attempt to eliminate the Axis airlines, many of whose pilots were Luftwaffe officers in training, must be predicated on our readiness to provide American planes and pilots as soon as the Condor-Lati planes were displaced. Nelson secured the President's permission to requisition 20 DC-3s or Lockheed Lodestars, which were as scarce as hen's teeth, and for their purchase and the thirty or more pilots we were given an appropriation of eight million. Experienced pilots were in short supply and to find them I turned to Reed Chambers, our third ranking ace in World War I and a good judge of men. The obvious source were the commercial airlines and one of our first volunteers was Ernest K. Gann, the novelist-to-be, who was then flying for American. Gann, in his autobiography, *Soldiers of Fortune*, vividly describes the hazards of a flight to Rio via Central America, down the west coast to Lima, Peru, and thence across the forbidding Andes to Rio. He made four such flights successfully in the autumn of 1941. Confident that pilots were available I prepared for Rio.

Juan Trippe, whose airmail contracts amounted to a virtual monopoly in South America, regarded our mission as an intrusion and he became even more suspicious when he heard that we had designs on two of his fleet of flying boats, the famous Yankee Clippers, which we needed to replace the Savoia-Marchetti landplanes and the four-motor Focke-Wulfs that had been making the long over-water flights from Italy. We carried no weight with Trippe but when Will Clayton, the Under-Secretary of Commerce and Deputy Director of the Defense Supplies said to him quietly, "We must have these planes, Mr. Trippe," he had no alternative. Bill and I presented the letter of authorization and accused him of interference. "I have never interfered with any government undertaking" Trippe declared. "Yes, you have!" we said. And, for the first and only time, I saw Juan Trippe weep in frustration.

Peggy, knowing that we should have to find a new home in September, had been scouting for prospects in Georgetown. The house that most appealed to her was the residence of Grant Mason, who was in the process of getting a divorce. It was comfortable and capacious with a garden and almost an acre of land at the back, ideal for a playground for our boys. She made a bid for it and left instructions with my secretary in New York to cable us if it was accepted. Planning what she would do to the

Mason house probably distracted her anxiety about our three-day journey to Rio. Before her Zeppelin trip over the Alps and even the short crossing of the English Channel she was terrified of flying as many women were at the time.

I had signed up Frank Russell whom I had come to admire during my work at National Aviation; he would be helpful in whatever opposition we were likely to encounter in Rio. His bluestocking wife, Dorothy Milburn, the daughter of Devereux Milburn had done quite a bit of flying and her presence together with liberal doses of smelling salts and cognac sustained Peggy. We flew from Miami to Trinidad in a Sikorsky S42 landplane, and the long jump from Panama to Belém to Rio in a DC-3. By the time we reached Belém we were all longing for a good night's rest but were kept awake by the band playing endless sambas in the sleazy hotel. Planes flew low in those days. We passed through a number of turbulent tropical thunderstorms and were struck by lightning several times—a frightening but not a dangerous experience as we were traveling in an all metal airplane which dissipates electrical charges. The harbor of Rio is miraculously beautiful and the Copacabana Hotel, whose rooms open on the beach, is the best in the southern hemisphere. It was with sighs of relief that we bathed, dressed in light clothes and relaxed at supper with a good wine.

The next morning Frank Russell and I presented ourselves at the American Embassy with letters of introduction to Ambassador Jefferson Caffery. We had received some fuzzy and superficial briefing from the State Department and it was our innocent supposition that we would approach the Brazilian government, offer them an American-Brazilian operated air service, superior in operation to what Condor-Lati could afford, and be received with open arms.

Caffery was the archtype of the career diplomat, tall, good

looking, with a cool reserved manner and a wealthy wife. It did not occur to us that he would resent our being trusted with a mission that in his eyes should properly have come through regular channels to him. He was frostily polite, listened to our hopeful program and commented dryly that the Brazilian government was confident that Hitler would win the war. He then presented us to the members of his staff, and excused himself.

Since Caffery had not offered us any office space in the Chancery we were on our own. Luckily the first week of our arrival we met a Brazilian couple who have become lifelong friends, Paulo Sampaio, a dashing Brazilian Naval aviator, a member of the Caterpillar Club (pilots who had saved their lives by bailing out in a parachute), and his wife Gilda, rich, exceptionally pretty, with a svelte figure. They had a charming house on Copacabana Beach and another up in the cooler hills sixty miles from Rio. Gilda danced the most beautiful samba I ever saw and I must add that Peggy and Dot were much sought after in the late night dancing as we were introduced to Brazilian society. It was through Paulo that we met the presidents and operating heads of the non-German airlines in Brazil to whom we proposed a merger of our planes and theirs to replace Condor. They appeared politely agreeable to the idea but Brazilians are slow to act, particularly so at a time when Hitler was winning and when they were unsure if we would enter the war.

As for the Brazilian government it would not move at all; it had no intention of offending the Germans with whom they had valuable commercial ties. So we were stymied. (Although we did not know it, the tide had begun to turn on June 22d when Hitler invaded the Soviet Union. From that day Brazilian intelligence predicted it would be his downfall.)

But we did not give up. As our stay lengthened Caffery took pity on us and offered us an office—a pleasant verandah where we could reconsider as we encountered more resistance. This time it came from Jay Rice, head of the Latin-American division of Pan American who had probably been told by Trippe to make things difficult.

Pan American and its partner, Pan American Grace, maintained the fiction that only their pilots could cope with the special conditions in South America. They objected to the communications system installed in our aircraft. Our planes were equipped for voice-radio (standard in the Army Air Corps and domestic airlines). Pan American on the other hand had been using radio-telegraph, which they maintained was the only safe way to communicate because of the language problem. (This too proved to be no problem eventually.)

The Nazi and Fascist lines bought their gasoline from American or British owned companies. We put our case to the local managers of Standard who refused to act until they received instructions from New York. Why should they offend valuable customers for vaguely patriotic reasons?

It was a stubborn situation with quite a bit of pleasure along the way. We had been joined by Peggy's best friend, the enchanting Susie Scott from Philadelphia. She had begun the long flight to Rio with the same trepidation as Peggy, but the Pan American pilots made much of her at every stop. She was unprepared for the surpassing beauty of Rio's harbor and was as much drawn to Paulo Sampaio and his lovely Gilda as we were; together we made plans to have them visit us as they did later that autumn at "Florham" and in Washington.

Among the fabulously wealthy Brazilians was a wild man, Darké Behring de Mattos who was eager to give us a good time, and who, incidently, taught us to dance the samba. Darké was about thirty-six, short, chunky, strong as an ox. He had inherited cattle and coffee plantations as well as the profitable cocoa firm of Behring & Co. He owned a beautiful island in Rio bay and took us there for a picnic in his speed boat. On our next party he showed off one of his favorite ploys which was to pass a Rio streetcar that has stopped to take aboard passengers, but passing it *on the wrong side*. He did this at high speed, blowing his horn furiously, gambling that the people would disperse, and that no traffic would be coming toward him head on. Frank and I pled with him to slow down but he won on both counts. After this he invited us to fly with him to one of his estates and the girls said "Never!" Years later he killed himself stunting at a low altitude. Bemelmans should have written a novel about him.

Our mission had been rebuffed at every turn and I felt it was time to return. Peggy alone could count on an achievement: shortly before our departure a cable stated that her bid for the large ramshackled house in Georgetown had been accepted. It was the place she had set her heart on and the thought of it cheered her during the long flight back.

Toward the end Ambassador Caffery seemed to warm up to the necessity of what we were after. We learned that before we appeared he had registered protests against the German radio stations, suspected of being in touch with the U-boats, and at his renewed pressure they were shut down. We decided to give a farewell party in his honor—and what a party it was!

We hired a small restaurant, engaged an excellent samba orchestra, ordered a splendid Brazilian meal, set up a well-stocked bar, and invited some sixty of our Brazilian and American friends including the entire Embassy staff. The dancing lasted until the small hours of the morning. At the end of the party Caffery was propped up against a wall, thoroughly stoned, smiling blandly but hardly articulate.

During the waning hours we noticed that the proprietress of

the restaurant—a tall buxom woman, probably of Germanic origin—was laboriously putting down columns of figures on a long, becoming ever longer, sheet of paper. It kept unrolling before her until it reached the floor, rather like the "broad tape" from the news ticker in a brokerage house. We peeked over her shoulder—the paper snake was The Bill, a vast compilation of fact and fiction which we immediately christened "the great Brazilian novel."

We paid the enormous "conta"—it was worth it—and went cheerfully home as the dawn was breaking, driven by our friendly Naval Attaché Lieutenant (later Rear Admiral) Harry Brownlee Temple. En route we passed the well-known statue of Pasteur, "Brownie" stopped the car, we all piled out and bowed solemnly to the great man, chanting in unison in our best Brazilian "Homenagem a Dr. Pasteur."

One morning later we—Peggy, Susie, Dot, Frank and I— were due to take Pan American's flight to Washington which like all Pan American departures required the passengers to be at the airport at 4 a.m. They did not fly at night, so they wanted us to be in the air by dawn in order to make use of every daylight hour. We were seen off by our Brazilian friends who festooned the girls with orchids, sang Brazilian songs, danced the samba, and gave us the Brazilian special sense of "saudade" for the lovely city we were leaving.

On the way to the airport I had complained to Jay Rice, the Pan American manager, that it was ridiculous for the company to require passengers to be at the airport *two* hours before take-off. He explained patiently that sometimes passengers forgot their passports and time had to be allowed for them to retrieve them. I grandly said: "If people forget their passports they *deserve* to be left behind."

As we passed through the Brazilian immigration Peggy dis-

covered that she had left her passport behind in the hotel (the
first and last time she ever did it in our fifty-one years of
marriage—so far!). Paulo Sampaio made a mad drive to the
Copacabana in grand prix fashion, and returned barely in time,
waving the passport triumphantly. For *once* PAA was justified.

Back in Washington I told Nelson and Bill Harding that
the Brazilian government and the Brazilian airlines were fully
aware of our concern but hesitated to make the break. Adolf
Berle, the Assistant Secretary of State for South America, had
evidently received word from Ambassador Caffery and he decided to apply his power of persuasion.

Berle grandly summoned the export manager of Standard
Oil of New Jersey who handled the Brazilian market to his
impressive office in the "civil war" atmosphere of the "Old
State" building, and asked us to be present. The hard-boiled
executive, whose whole career had been concentrated on mak-
ing more money for the Rockefellers, was not fazed by the State
Department, the large American flag behind the desk, nor by
Berle himself, much less by Burden and Harding.

Berle began with a legal presentation of the case, shifted to a
passionate appeal to patriotism and finally, that having failed,
to threats that the massive power of the U.S. government might
be involved. None of these approaches worked. The oil man
flatly refused to reduce, much less stop, gasoline sales to the
Germans and Italians.

Berle was furious, Bill and I were not surprised. But the
diplomacy, the politeness were at an end. We talked to Nelson,
his father, John D. Jr., talked to the Standard Oil executives
and by force from the top the problem was solved. The Brazilian Standard Oil subsidiary shut off the gasoline supply of
Condor and Lati and they ceased operations in December 1941.
The British oil companies followed suit.

*   *   *

Georgetown during the war years became a picturesque and overcrowded oasis. Founded in the early eighteenth century as a separately incorporated village with shady, tree-lined streets, and a few handsome brick houses in the Federal style scattered among the tiny, unpretentious wooden dwellings, Georgetown from the first rejoiced in its gardens, which provided a cool retreat from the Capital's "foggy bottom." From the street one could hardly imagine the beauty that bloomed behind the unprepossessing yellow shingle exterior of our house at 1224 30th Street, which was to be our home for six years.

Georgetown doorways were painted with every imaginative tint; it was what lay within and behind that was refreshing: our living room, where our new Matisse was much admired, and the dining room were spacious enough for large parties. The latter opened out on the garden which was of three levels: the first, a dining—or drinking—terrace, very convenient for an overflow; above that by a couple of steps, a large walled garden glorious in April when the tulips, jonquils, the magnolia and flowering cherry trees were in bloom, and back, a few steps higher, a good sized vegetable garden, the greenhouse and to the left a playhouse with a single room, 50′ by 30′, full of electric trains, and underneath it, a three-car garage. It was a happy establishment when the boys arrived, and only a twenty-minute walk from my office in the new R.F.C. building.

Looking after us was an English butler, Alfred Day, who was proud of his early service in Buckingham Palace, very good with the children and un-English in his recognition of our intimate friends who, as he opened the door, might say with a smile, "Well, Day, at least I know somebody who's here." He mixed a deceptively strong Swedish punch which we always serve at our New Year's party.

Washington in the autumn of 1941 was attracting men of ability from every state in the Union, some summoned, some cruising to see where they might be of use, some veterans of World War I to sign up as "retreads," some charlatans. And in the Indian summer when the heat downtown rose over 100° the medley of strangers and new office holders at sunset would crowd into Georgetown for cocktails, ladies and their escorts perspiring profusely, all the ice melted, the drinks warm, no place to sit and the din resounding from garden to garden. It was an American "black hole of Calcutta" and when the last guest had left, the exhausted hostess counted her scalps. But rules were observed: those going on to dinner parties left early and even at black-tie dinners at the embassies guests were expected to be punctual to the minute, and to depart at or before 10:00 p.m.

As cool weather came I remember standing in our open doorway on a balmy Sunday afternoon. Tom Finletter, who was working in the State Department came down the street with a worried look on his face—he and his wife Gretchen lived next door to us. Peggy called "Tom what are you doing on a Sunday afternoon?" "Going to the State Department," he said in his clipped manner of speech, "Bill, if you haven't heard, the radio says the Japanese have been bombing Pearl Harbor! Since early morning, Honolulu time."

CHAPTER X

Jesse Jones and Will Clayton

PEARL HARBOR was a shocking humiliation to the leaders of our armed forces, from the President down, and the disaster that generated a national resurgence which would make us the leader of the free world. The remonstrance of America First was stilled; the speed-up of our equipment: tanks in Detroit, planes in Texas and Dayton, and on the Pacific Coast ships in Oakland, was matched by the intensified training of our manpower. Washington was the nerve center and the ablest men in every branch of government were at their desks fourteen hours a day, or more.

The removal of the Axis airlines and their personnel throughout South America went on during December but the extent of the Nazi infiltration and the menace of their planes, especially the four-motor, ocean-going Focke-Wulfs, were little appreciated and I felt it would complete Bill Harding's and my mission if I filled out my initial report to Nelson Rockefeller with the additional details I had acquired in Brazil and from other sources in the South. I was convinced that our postwar passenger traffic by plane to Latin America would be six to seven times larger than it had been in 1940 and that such a vast increase would necessarily involve several international airlines, and should not be confined to a single "chosen instrument" such as

Pan American. This inevitably put me on collision course with Juan Trippe.

My report, with many maps, photographs, and the comparative tables of statistics, grew to be a book of 245 pages and I felt gratified when Hamilton Armstrong, editor of *Foreign Affairs*, proposed that it be printed under the auspices of the Council on Foreign Relations. It took me the better part of a year to get the material in perspective, and to check the proofs. Trippe did his utmost to prevent its publication but Armstrong would not give him the time of day. It appeared early in 1943, entitled *The Struggle for Airways in Latin America* by William A. M. Burden, Special Aviation Assistant to the Secretary of Commerce, and it was dedicated to Peggy ''whose encouragement and help made this book possible.'' True words, for without her push would it ever have been written?

It was while I was writing that I received a telegram from Shirley in Los Angeles that Moms, who was visiting him, was ill with a recurrence of her tuberculosis and the probability of a collapsed lung. I was given a No. 1 (White House) priority, which meant that I could not be bumped off, and flew to California. Moms was seriously though not critically ill and it was a week before I felt it safe to leave her. Shirley was busier than I had ever seen him. His company, Tradefilm, had been given an order for fifteen training films for the Navy and as other orders were expected from the Army he had increased his staff from 4 to 30, and set up an animation department headed by one of Disney's best men.

While I was in Los Angeles I received a telephone call from Will Clayton saying that he wanted to talk to me about a new position and hoped I could return at once. I was on fire to know what he had in mind and appeared in his office the following morning.

He told me that he would like me to become Aviation Assistant to Jesse Jones, the Secretary of Commerce, with responsibility for the Civil Aeronautics Administration, the Weather Bureau and the Coast and Geodetic Survey. He said that it would give me plenty of scope and added that, although he could not guarantee it, there was a high probability that I would eventually be appointed Assistant Secretary. I was delighted: it meant that I would continue to serve him with vastly extended authority.

I discovered later how this came about: there had been a protracted debate between Secretary Jesse Jones and Under Secretary Wayne Chatfield Taylor, an old friend of mine, whether, after the resignation of the former Assistant Secretary, Robert Hinckley, his post should be filled or whether it would be easier to leave it vacant. Jesse Jones was in favor of letting things ride —as he usually was. And I don't doubt that the retiring Hinckley advised him to do just that. However, Chatfield-Taylor and Clayton, being more far-sighted, believed that if Commerce did not have an energetic Assistant Secretary to promote its priority in civil aviation, it might well lose that authority to the newly created Department of Transportation, a possibility that they regarded with horror. "Who is qualified for the job?" asked Jones. "Burden," said Clayton. (My appointment came over the ticker tape a couple of days later when I was lunching at India House in New York.) I told Peggy immediately, then telephoned Bill Harding, who had left Commerce for a Captain's Commission in the Air Transport Command. "Congratulations, or what have you," he said. "Bill, are you going to move into Hinckley's forty-foot long office?" "Yes," I said, "and with a brand-new blue carpet."

The post offered me by far the greatest opportunity I had ever had. Little did I realize the pitfalls of civil service or the stubbornness of bureaucrats when faced with directions from one they considered a "political" appointee who would only be in office for a limited period.

My predecessor, Assistant Secretary Hinckley, had been determined to continue the Civilian Pilot Training Program, keeping the base operators who were doing the training despite the probability of mobilization. This was one of the first hot potatoes I had to handle. The program was directed by the inefficient Charles Stanton (who could not be fired); it would involve 239,000 candidates (1941–1943) and, as I soon discovered, only about thirty percent of the instructors were efficient. Evidently I had to by-pass Stanton with the best man I could find.

I began by talking to my old friend, Bob Lovett, then Assistant Secretary of the Army in charge of the Army Air Corps, and to Artemus L. Gates, Assistant Secretary of the Navy for Air, as to whether they really wanted all these partially trained pilots. Both Lovett and Gates said they most certainly did.

Bob said that the Army Air Corps would continue to back the Civilian Pilot Training Program *providing* that I could find a topnotch administrator to run it. Neither the Air Corps nor the Navy had any confidence in the political and inefficient manner in which the Program had been handled by Hinckley and Stanton, the Administrator of Civil Aeronautics. Then I asked what they thought of Robert McLean Stewart, whom I had in mind. They had both known him on Wall Street, far better than I, and they approved. "He'll get the job done," said Bob.

In my search I had turned to Joe Ripley, head of Harriman and Ripley. He had proposed me for the United Airlines Board of Directors; we had become close friends and I trusted his judgment.

"I think," Joe said, "I have just the man for you. 'Mac'

Stewart has all the ability if you can stand his personality which is not easy to do. He charges ahead like a bulldozer, regardless of the feelings of his colleagues or his adversaries (a very accurate description it turned out to be) but he does get results. Moreover, he is bored to death with Wall Street and is dying to get into the war."

Robert McLean Stewart of Scotch blood was born in Quebec, educated in Canada and in England, and had a distinguished World War I career in the famous Canadian Black Watch. He worked from 1918 to 1927 for the Canadian Government as assistant secretary in the department for the civil re-establishment of soldiers, an experience most helpful to him in blasting (*not* wending) his way through the maze of wartime government in Washington.

From 1927 until 1942 he was in investment banking with the National City Company. With the collapse of that jerry-built empire of Charley Mitchell, Stewart began looking for a war job. When I first met him he was forty-seven and at the height of his physical and mental powers which were considerable. Six feet three and powerfully built, he must have weighed at least 210 pounds. He had a strong beaked nose, flashing blue eyes, high coloring, black hair and an assured air of command. Peggy's word for him was "tempestuous."

In his youth "Mac" had been an enthusiastic amateur actor of considerable ability. Once I learned how much of an actor he was, I paid less attention to his towering rages, assumptions of injured dignity, etc., which had periodically disturbed my approach to problems. But "Mac" had a high order of intelligence, primarily pragmatic; he liked to allow his powerful mind to roam in the fields of philosophy. He never suffered from excessive modesty. Certainly I underestimated the hostility which in less than a month developed between Stanton and himself.

The Weather Bureau, my second responsibility, was in the hands of F. W. Reichelderfer, a long-time appointee, extremely competent, and in almost every case his recommendations received my approval. He was a bear for research, we liked each other and all went well in that department.

The Coast and Geodetic Survey, especially their mapping, was useful to the Navy in its increasingly successful hunt for the U-boats. Otherwise it followed routine under the direction of Admiral Colbert. Two of my three agencies were a civil servant's dream and made their routine reports to me, and gave me no trouble.

The exception, of course, was "Mac" Stewart's accelerated program for the training of civilian pilots. One of his requests was for sixteen million dollars for the purchase of planes for pilot training. The size and urgency of this annoyed Jesse Jones, who could not understand why it was necessary, but Stewart was right for it gave Commerce complete control of the program, which it had lacked before, and the money was forthcoming.

In the increasingly anxious months of 1942 I began to observe my two bosses, big men, each of whom had made great fortunes in Houston, Texas, devoted public servants and as different as night from day. Jesse Jones, Secretary of Commerce, was born in Tennessee and moved to Houston in 1898 when he was twenty-four. He made money fast in banking and building and when he was twenty-seven became an original stockholder of the Humble Oil Company (oil in 1901 was selling at $3 a barrel), which became a very profitable investment. By 1913 he had his fortune; that year he accepted the chairmanship of the Houston Harbor Board and thereafter devoted a major part of his time and energy to public service. He became a close friend of Woodrow Wilson; he was the chief fund-raiser for the Democratic conventions which nominated Davis and Al

Smith and when FDR appointed Jones Chairman of the Reconstruction Finance Corporation he was in a position to make a prolonged and powerful contribution. No one ever opposed Jesse Jones successfully on the R.F.C. board.

His working habits were formidable: he worked incredibly long hours and, like Will Clayton, always came to the office on Sunday mornings. He preferred the telephone to writing letters; when he wrote a letter he insisted it be kept to a single page, a meticulousness that plagued his assistants. He never appeared hurried or excited. As a Southern banker he was suspicious of Wall Street, yet he attracted to the R.F.C. five-figure executives, groomed them on low government salaries and returned them to finance at the war's end. His method with FDR—a disorderly administrator—was fascinating. He acceded to such demands as seemed wise or safe but when Roosevelt wanted something that Jones considered wrong or clearly unwise, he listened, withheld argument and then contrived an escape by inconspicuous inaction.

His relaxations were bridge, poker and good bourbon; his Washington favorites were Senator Carter Glass, Secretary of State Cordell Hull, Vice President Garner, all Southerners. From 1940 to 1945 Jones was chairman of the R.F.C. and overall director of the Federal Housing Administration, Home Owners Loan Corporation and the Export-Import Bank.

I can almost hear Mr. Jones speaking in this paragraph from Bascom N. Timmons's authorized biography, *Jesse H. Jones, The Man and The Statesman*:

> "It is sometimes taught that one of the most essential elements of success is the ability to say 'No.' But I want to tell you from the fullness of my practical experience, of far greater importance is the ability to say 'Yes' and back it

up. The 'No' sayer and the 'Don't' sayer never get very far. It takes vision, faith and courage, to say 'Yes.' By saying 'No,' you forego the possibility of gain, whatever the proposition may be. You may save yourself trouble and losses, but there can be no profit if you say 'No.'

"The fellow who is able to analyze everything and tell you why it should not be done never gets any real practice in doing. It is the affirmative one, the positive man and the one who tries again and again after each failure, who gets practice enough to succeed. It is necessary to say and act 'Yes' more times than you say 'No' and at the right times. I would not say there is no place in our life and language for 'Don't', but I do say the word 'can't' should be abolished. Too many timid people stumble over it. There is a way to everything worth doing, if we can find it."

Will H. Clayton, or "Mr. Will" as everyone called him, was the first really distinguished American I had ever worked with. I am sure I made little impression on him at first; as a specialist I had been called into a large, soon to become enormous, government organization. Probably he listened to what Nelson Rockefeller and Robert Lovett said about me and waited for results.

From the moment I saw "Mr. Will" I was awed. At sixty-one he was a lean, strikingly handsome figure, six feet two inches tall, with iron gray hair turning white. His was a kind face, lined by experience, with confidence and warmth in his smile. Everyone who had worked for him soon appreciated that he had the ability to command but command gently. And in whatever he said or did there was a personal Southern courtesy, a quality rare in the world of 1941, and even rarer today.

He was born in 1880 on a cotton farm near Tupelo, Mississippi, and he was self-made. His first job when he was twelve was at the courthouse in Jackson, Mississippi, where he learned shorthand and taught himself to type. At sixteen he went to New York to work for the American Cotton Company. At the request of his Sunday schoolteacher he took the pledge and never smoked or drank until at the close of his life. From New York he wrote the family, "It takes a lot of courage and grit to live up here . . . and work day and night without a single pleasure in a whole month or a single hour to read a book."

His exercise was a daily three-mile walk over the Brooklyn Bridge, but as success came to him in the cotton business, he took dancing lessons in New York, read widely in the evenings, and treated himself to a play a week. He married Sue Vaughan at twenty-two and with his brother-in-law Frank Anderson formed a partnership in Houston, Texas, with the capital of $9,000. There were many long established cotton merchandisers in the north and east, such as George H. McFadden & Bros. of Philadelphia and Steven M. Weld and Co. of New York, but Anderson-Clayton grew to be an empire and topped them all.

"If you have a problem," "Mr. Will" used to say, "get off by yourself and think it out. But be sure to think it out to the end, not just part way." And I know that whenever I came to give him a report he would not let me leave the room until a decision had been arrived at. Like my Peggy, "Mr. Will" had a natural love of people of all ages (which is perhaps why he and Peggy were so fond of each other).

During the four years in which I was intimately in touch with him, I never heard him criticize any member of his staff, and he certainly took the blame for the mistakes made by others. He kept "farmers' hours," rising each morning about six and walking the three miles from his home near the Shoreham Hotel to his office in the Lafayette Building. This meant that he was usually at work an hour ahead of any of us and at the end of a long day he walked home.

In sharp contrast to Jesse Jones he was a teetotaler. His eye never roved toward attractive women, but I did notice that his Southern charm—and there was plenty of it—was more available to beautiful women like Peggy than it was to the intellectual. "Miss Sue" as he always called his wife was as tiny and temperamental as he was big and courteous, and she had him absolutely under her thumb. We were to see more of them later and my admiration never diminished. He had, as some rare persons do, an air of nobility about him.

Early in the defense preparation Jones brought Will Clayton to Washington as Assistant Secretary of Commerce and Director of the Defense Supplies Corporation with authority to produce, buy and store critical strategic material. In this "Mr. Will" was a moving force, as he was in the building of war plants. It is a measure of our nation's resourcefulness that by the end of the war our war plants had the capacity of manufacturing fifty percent of the nation's aluminum, ninety percent of its magnesium metal, seventy-one percent of aircraft and aircraft engines and ninety percent of synthetic rubber.

*   *   *

In 1943 we proposed to the Russians that there be a preliminary discussion in Washington about the exchange of civil air rights looking toward postwar flights from New York to Moscow and vice versa. The Russian delegation was led by General Rudenko, undoubtedly a fine combat officer but as a diplomat he was brutal, lacking in tact and in no way cooperative.

Before we sat down at our first meeting, Averell Harriman, who was soon to be our Ambassador in Moscow, advised me wisely, "Don't give them anything unless you get as much or more in return." But the Russians had no intention of giving. What they really wanted was to extract the maximum amount of information from us about our techniques in operating civil airlines—instrument flying navigation, blind landing aids, airport operations, etc. In all of these areas we were very superior to the USSR and whatever they could extract from us was to use the British phrase "money for jam." My assistant, Charles Stanton, Administrator of Civil Aeronautics, led the discussion for our side and cannily recognized what the Russians were after. On his advice we rapidly turned off the spigot of technical information and just as rapidly the talks slowed down and quickly came to an end. Following the State Department's guidance we drew up the usual press release stating that the discussions had been "fruitful" and called it a day.

When the talks ended it was de rigueur under Soviet protocol that the Russians give us a party at the Soviet Embassy, as they did. I had heard about the Russian practice of trying to drink Western diplomats under the table by repeated toasts of ninety proof vodka, two against one—two Russians alternately offering "bottoms up" toasts against one American.

The American delegation, or at least the Harvard-trained portion of it (Under-Secretary of State Joseph Grew and myself), had hard heads and took reasonable precaution. We drank large quantities of olive oil in advance—a supposedly sovereign method of lining the stomach with a liquid that slowed the absorption of alcohol. We were also very cautious in avoiding the two Russians for one American in toasts. However, as the evening wore on, our caution was somewhat diminished and we left the Embassy in a considerable degree of disorder. We were not, fortunately, disgraced; no American passed out. No state secrets were disclosed on either side.

Rigid gasoline rationing was in effect and I owned a little two cylinder air-cooled Crosley which did some fifty miles per gallon thus making the most of the five gallons of gasoline per month that were allotted to every American citizen *regardless* of the size of his car. I stepped into this tiny vehicle in a lordly fashion and invited Under Secretary Grew to sit beside me, then I started off with a jerk in low gear completely oblivious of the fact that we were parked one foot behind a Cadillac.

Result—a horrendous crash. I was thrown against the windshield wiper and cut a great gash in my forehead with accompanying copious emissions of blood. Grew had braced himself and escaped unscathed. I drove him home and then proceeded to my doctor's office in the middle of the night and woke him up to stem the crimson tide. As he bandaged my brow he naturally inquired how the accident had happened. He found it difficult to believe but took my word for it and no harsh words were spoken.

The next morning Joe Grew and I met at the State Department. Naturally we were both suffering from hangovers. But Grew proved himself a true Harvard man when he said: "You know, Bill, I think this sort of thing is good for a fellow every once in a while. It relieves the tensions." And how right he was!

The time had now come for us to invite the Russians back.

It was June and Peggy had already taken the children up to Maine. I was a bachelor and free to make my own arrangements. Our large and beautiful Georgetown garden was in full bloom with azaleas and looked both superb and romantic.

I decided that we would have a mixed rather than a stag party and I scoured Washington for the most beautiful girls I could find, among them Margaret Griggs who had been Ambassador Caffery's hostess in Rio and a half a dozen others. They all looked superb in their lovely dresses as only the most

My swearing-in ceremony as Assistant Secretary of Commerce with Jesse Jones, Peggy, Moms, Bob and young Bill

Will and Sue Clayton in their garden in Houston

With my pilot license

Flobe, Shirley and myself

attractive American girls can look. The Russians were smitten by their beauty but being Russians and rather direct in their relations with women came to the conclusion that, since none of them were there with their husbands, they were probably ladies of the evening invited for one purpose. The American girls were also naturally intrigued by the dashing Russians.

Both the Washington belles and the Russian officers arrived more or less on time. We moved promptly into the garden (a little hot I must say) where a delicious dinner was served by our old butler Day. Hardly had the caviar and vodka been put on the table when General Rudenko leaped to his feet to make a speech—with of course, being Russian, a toast.

The speech, translated by the handsome translator, turned out to be a) very long and b)a diatribe against the capitalist system and all its work. I suppose Rudenko had been instructed to do this by higher authorities. Soviets, in government and in wartime, hardly ever act from impulse or if they do, are likely to end up in the Lubyanka.

The speech went over like a lead balloon and I felt compelled to reply without gloves, making it very clear that we Americans were very pleased with the capitalist system and were quite confident that it would far outperform the Soviet version of communism over the years ahead—and so it has.

Then we all sat down and began dinner. Thanks to the beneficent influence of excellent food and wine, pretty girls, handsome or at least interesting officers (the element of curiosity was strong in the girls too: hardly any of them had seen a real live Soviet officer at close range), a lovely garden and liberal toasts —this time in the American manner—things began to warm up in a delightful and effective way. The garden was a very large one with plenty of conveniently distributed bushes.

After dinner the officers started pursuing the girls into the shrubbery with obviously amatory intent. Perhaps a few approached their objective but for the most part all that happened were squeals of feminine rage. The Soviets reluctantly backed off. Even they realized they were in a private house. So the party closed late but in a somewhat orderly fashion. I thanked all the girls by telephone the next morning. They deserved it, and they professed to have enjoyed the experience.

I have never forgotten the evening. It was a remarkable example of Soviet schizophrenia—attack the capitalist system and then attempt to avail yourself of its fairest fruits. There were two subsequent attempts to resume these talks and dates were set but the Russians failed to appear.

*   *   *

My appointment as Assistant Secretary of Commerce for Air came through in September 1943 and Moms, Bill, Bobby and Peggy were present when I was sworn in by Secretary Jesse Jones. My office was running smoothly. The routine and the training of civilian pilots were now competently administered by "Mac" Stewart who had become my most trusted assistant. He was in the best sense a bulldozer, and once I saw through his bluster we worked together with mutual affection.

As the war in Africa, Russia and Europe began to turn against Hitler, the State Department rose from its lethargy to plan for an exchange of landing rights between the United States and the many other nations which wished to collaborate with us when peace came. This called for an international conference, the first I had ever attended and in the preparation for it Adolf Berle would speak for the State Department and I for Commerce. Fifty nations were invited to send delegates to an aviation conference in Chicago in November. I asked Berle, who outranked me, why Chicago? "If we hold it in Chicago," he said, "Congress will be more likely to endorse our recommendation."

Adolf was a very brilliant man and in time he became a close friend, but at this stage he did not wish—or accept—advice from anyone.

I found that there were two contending proposals held by those who would represent the United States in Chicago: one group favored a multilateral treaty to which every nation must comply; the others favored a bilateral exchange, differing in detail as local conditions required. Berle made a major effort as far as the British were concerned, but all came to naught with the change in British government and the appointment of Lord Swinton at the last minute as Minister of Civil Aviation.

As a result we had to have a conference within a conference with the British, French, Dutch and one or two others. Swinton was a tough nut to crack but he gave in at the end. Meanwhile, while the major aviation powers reached a meeting of the minds, the several delegates of the smaller nations sat fuming. As each day passed they grew more angry and impatient. Chicago in raw weather is not the most attractive place in the world, and after one has visited the Art Museum and the Field Museum, the Stevens Hotel, where we all congregated, was a not particularly stimulating resort. The delegates worked off some of their irritation by devising a conference emblem: they had a Stevens Hotel towel made up for each delegate with the words: "No! No! 1000 Times No!"

The one abstinence was the Soviet Union. Their delegates had actually reached Anchorage in Alaska when they were recalled, which I have always believed was the Kremlin's decision to begin the Cold War.

And I had my personal problem; Peggy remained in Washington, momentarily expecting the arrival of our fourth child and I had a plane standing by to fly her to the Presbyterian Hospital in New York. When Ordway, our fourth son, was delivered in late November, 1944, he became known as our "Conference Baby."

As time wore on this became a conference in confusion; as the end approached Berle felt that we needed an inspirational speech to bring us to our feet after so many weeks of bickering and he persuaded Mayor LaGuardia of New York to speak to us at our closing session—and LaGuardia was infallible. But at the banquet which followed, attended by all 500 delegates, a representative of the aircraft industry, who shall be nameless, was foistered upon us, supposedly because he was amusing. But the weather was foul, his plane was four hours late so the dinner was ruined, and when at last he arrived he was so drunk that he was inarticulate and had to be cut short.

The one and only accomplishment of our six weeks was the unanimous vote that we should meet in Montreal in 1946 to establish a permanent civil aviation organization. But even this objective was confused, for as we were packing the word circulated that President FDR had fired Adolf Berle, which of course threw doubt on what the American attitude would be when we came to Montreal. This hapless maneuver was the work of Juan Trippe who had somehow convinced FDR that the proceedings in Chicago would not be good for American interests—(by which of course he meant would not be good for his Pan American charter). The pill was sugar-coated for Berle as the President simultaneously offered him the Ambassadorship in Brazil where, as it proved, Adolf, who spoke excellent Portuguese was well received and very successful. But to the homegoing delegates the effect was confusing.

I headed the American delegation two years later in Montreal and very early at that meeting I spoke vigorously in support of bilateral agreements suitable for each of the two parties involved, and my talk had a rousing reception. The Soviet Union again did not attend. Actually the New York–Moscow run was not inaugurated until 1968.

An impasse of a different kind took me to California. The Hughes Aircraft Company, despite the genius and immense wealth of its owner Howard Hughes, had shown very little expertise in aircraft production but because of the very close relationship between Hughes (a Texan above all Texans) and Jesse Jones, it received a contract for what came to be known as "The Spruce Goose," and an appropriation of 16 million.

This was to be a flying boat, large enough to transport a company of infantry and equipment. But the use of metal was denied (aluminum being so scarce) and Hughes went ahead to build it of wood. The project might have cost the government hundreds of millions but it was critically reviewed by the National Advisory Committee for Aeronautics (of which I was a member) and there was agreement that such a monster, even with eight motors, was dubious. But Hughes was not deterred.

Secretary Jones would have been happy to abandon the project and President Roosevelt, I suspect, had long forgotten about it. So, in the classical Washington tradition, a committee was formed to which the buck was passed—Ed Warner, Vice Chairman of the Civil Aeronautics Board, and myself, Assistant Secretary of Commerce for Air. We were to advise Secretary Jones whether the RFC should continue to finance the "Goose."

We were both naive about Washington politics and to the extent of Hughes' political power in Texas. We flew out to California on American, surveyed the giant, talked to Hughes and his engineers and concluded that from the technical point of view the undertaking was not feasible, and should never have been started—much less continued. Hughes himself piloted the monster briefly on its only flight.

President Roosevelt ungraciously fired Jesse Jones early in

1945 and when the latter returned to Houston Will Clayton soon followed. Henry Wallace became the new Secretary of Commerce and it was not a job he much wanted. Wallace was an odd mixture, an agronomist, very practical in matters of the soil, an idealist whose wishful thinking led him astray. As the Secretary of Agriculture he was highly regarded; Harvard awarded him an honorary degree and FDR favored him for the vice-presidency, an elevation the Democratic National Committee opposed. Before the 1944 election Roosevelt realized that the Party would not accept Wallace but Henry himself was intoxicated with the dream. It was Arthur Krock who leaked the news that Harry Truman would be Roosevelt's running mate but Wallace did not accept the disqualification; he did not share the suspicion of Stalin as the Soviets imposed their satellite government in Poland, and in the two years I served under him Wallace's thoughts were mainly on his political future.

While I was in the Department of Commerce I made my first flight across the Atlantic in one of Pan American flying boats taking the Southern route with a stop in the Azores for refueling. Then in February, 1946, I was one of a group from Washington including Postmaster General Bob Hannegan and two of the ablest Congressmen, Lea and Cannon, who inaugurated the first passenger flight of TWA's *Constellation* from New York to Shannon where we were held up for more than twenty-four hours by engine trouble before continuing on to Paris. An editorial in *Air Transport* for February 1946 had this to say:

Bonnet for Mrs. Burden

"... We were there at Orly airport when the TWA *Constellation* arrived with its distinguished passengers and Capt. Harold Blackburn and other crew members. A few days later we saw them off and noted that Bill Burden was carrying a hat box—a Paris bonnet for Mrs. Burden.

"That epitomizes air transport to us for several reasons. First, we never have known Mr. Burden very well; we had to go to Paris to cotton to the gentleman and that Paris hat had a lot to do with it. Fast transport does that for people and if it did that for Bill and us, it follows that it will for Americans in relationships with the French and the British, the Russians and every other nationality. Second, the hat for Mrs. Burden proves how airlines, if they are allowed freedom to haul traffic in and out of a country, will bring needed foreign cash to entrepreneurs, designers and workers which in many cases wouldn't be spent otherwise. When Max Hymans, director of civil aviation for France and Bill Burden's counterpart who was at Orly to meet and see the *Constellation* off, takes a quick trip to the United States on one of the 13 ships of the same model and make which Air France has ordered, he will find something which we at home are especially good at and bring it back to France with him. People in America will learn how to pronounce his name (Immance, with the accent on the last syllable) and he will learn more of how the CAB and CAA function so he can do his job better for Air France and French civil aviation in general. Those are just two advantages to air transport 1) getting to know people better, understand them and their problems and thus to respect them and 2) the opportunity it gives people to buy more things which particular nations are expert in. Let the imagination play a bit and there can be hundreds of other advantages which the bonnet box we saw Bill Burden carrying will call to mind."

CHAPTER XI

Eniwetok

I N 1944 Secretary of War Stimson sent John Marquand to the Pacific to observe the morale of the men in service. It was a wise commission for Marquand was at the peak of his career and from this experience he wrote one of his best novels, *Point of No Return*, the hero of which, George Gray, rebels at the thought of returning to the limitations of his former job. Many men shared that feeling; I know that in the future I intended to be my own boss.

Given my heritage and my thirteen years on Wall Street it was predictable that I would return to finance and continue to extend my knowledge of aviation. When my grandfather Hamilton Twombly died in 1910 he left all his worldly goods—he was a multi-millionaire—to his wife. His estate was reported to be in the neighborhood of 75 million at a time when there was *no inheritance tax*. My grandmother entrusted the estate to her watchdog, Mr. Doherty, and ultimately bestowed fifteen million on each of her two surviving daughters.

But as time passed Grandfather's gold mine in South America would thin out, and the inheritance tax was rising to be the inescapable divider. It seemed to me imperative to set up a New York limited partnership, engaged in investing its own capital, and to do so I needed a partner *and the capital*. I thought immediately of "Mac" Stewart who had gone back to his financial connections after VJ Day. For thirty months in the Department of Commerce we worked together with understanding; I was not put off by his bluster and I admired his ability to cut red tape and get things done.

At a quiet luncheon I disclosed my plan and invited him to be my partner. "Mac" jumped at the opportunity. He was shortly elected a director of Union Sulphur and of Grandfather's South American mines, and went down to familiarize himself with the properties which had been so immensely profitable in the past. Out of this came his brilliant proposal that since the Portovelo Gold mine in Ecuador was due to run out in a few years, what we should do was to "high grade" the mine and take all the ore out in two years, with a profit he estimated at $2,500,000. Grandmother and Aunt Ruth agreed to this, and further, that the proceeds should form the initial capital for an investment firm established under the name of William A. M. Burden & Co. The initial partners would be Shirley and I and R. M. Stewart, Moms and Aunt Ruth limited partners. While the negotiations were in progress, Shirley, in California, would remonstrate, "Bill, why do you keep pestering those kind women who have been so generous to us?" But eventually he understood.

So it was done, and from the outset the returns were encouraging. Over the years practically all of the Burden capital has found its way into that investment company which now numbers seven working partners. "Mac" and I teamed successfully for a quarter of a century and I was fortunate to recruit Robert R. Barker, who had also served with me in Commerce and he too became a partner. Dear Bob was one of the first to perceive the enormous potential in the computer. Our original capital has now appreciated to $126 million while providing the living expenses of all those involved. I like to think that Hamilton Twombly would have approved.

In Washington I had been so immersed in my job that I had little time for anything else. On our return to New York we settled into our apartment at 10 Gracie Square (our winter home) and into a more relaxed and diversified life. Harvard had happily appointed me to the Visiting Committee of the University Library and I was asked to serve as Chairman of the Committee for Aviation Research at the Business School, which recalled me to Cambridge for stimulating, unhurried visits.

Peggy was much more cautious than I when it came to buying a picture and we missed a number of good ones such as the marvelous Modigliani "Nude." She went so far as to get Johnny Walker, Director of the National Gallery, to say that he would not consider the Modigliani. Twenty years later he confessed to me that he'd said this to keep on the right side of Peggy, and that actually he thought it was superb. I haven't forgiven him yet.

Actually I believe such disagreement is quite usual. Some rich collectors in Los Angeles apparently have a solution to this problem. The couple hang the pictures they both like—the more conventional—in their house; the husband, more avant-garde than his mate, hangs the pictures he likes but his wife cannot stand, in his office; and those that are so avant-garde they wish to dispose of, are eagerly appropriated by the children.

Our older sons had been studying at St. Albans in Washington; now they were in boarding school, Bill at Milton Academy, which he liked and where he made lasting friends, Bobby at Groton where he found the religious atmosphere fostered by the Rector rather stuffy. They came back to us for holidays at Mt. Kisco and were much looked up to by the younger pair,

Hamilton, who was born in 1937, and Ordway, our "Conference Baby." It was during the summer at Northeast Harbor that the six of us were affectionately drawn together. The harbor is one of the most beautiful on the Maine coast and in our renovated lobster boat, piloted by our skipper, "Captain" Stanley, we went fishing or to watch the races and on cloudless days to picnic on one of the outer islands. He was elderly, had stories to tell, and in his picturesque way taught the boys the lore of the sea.

In late September of 1947, a fire in the town dump fanned by a force ten gale almost devastated Bar Harbor. We had just moved into a house at the entrance to Northeast Harbor which Wallace Harrison had redesigned with spacious windows opening on the sea. Peggy and I were in Philadelphia when the caretaker telephoned that the flames were so close a fire trench had been dug—then fortunately the wind shifted and the fire was driven back on itself.

For well over half a century we have had an insatiable love for Mt. Desert with its rocky heights, the hidden, green ponds, the bright blue of the sea or when the fog conceals the fleet in the harbor. We loved its informality, the lunch parties with the Lippmanns, a picnic lunch at the Finletter's cove with Tom stirring his hash-brown potatoes, drinks in the late afternoon with Jim and June Byrne, our next door neighbors. I had grown up with the Rockefeller boys but it was not until I was courting Peggy that I began to know them individually—with Nelson, politics and art, David, art and business, with Laurance, aviation and conservation, and with John and Blanchette just fun.

About May, 1950 I heard rumors that Tom Finletter was to replace Stuart Symington who had been Secretary of the Air Force since 1947 when that third branch of our Service was detached from the Army. I was surprised that he would take this position under Louis Johnson, an unattractive character who, relying on our monopoly of the atomic bomb, was intent on cutting 13 billion from the defense budget. After the Russians exploded their first atomic weapon Johnson's slashing reductions were shown to be absurd, the more so when the Korean War broke out in June. President Truman faced this new crisis by appointing General George C. Marshall Secretary of Defense; Johnson was gone, and the Pentagon came to life. Before Tom went down to his post, he told me that I ought to think seriously of returning to Washington.

This time there would be no hesitation if a definite offer was made. Our older boys were in boarding school and for the younger, the schools in Washington were better than those in New York. I could trust "Mac" Stewart to keep the Burden Company on the tracks while I was away. In August I lunched with Tom and his Under Secretary, John McCone, in Washington, and was offered the choice of two jobs: 1) Assistant to the Secretary for Research and Development, or 2) Assistant in charge of the development of the new bases which would give "longer legs" for the SAC B-52's with their atomic bombs.

I eagerly chose the first. For over twenty years I had followed the research and development of the major aircraft companies from a financial point of view, though without access to classified information. In 1949 I served as President of the Institute of the Aeronautical Sciences (later re-christened the American Institute of Aeronautics and Astronautics, Inc.) which had given me some insight. I felt I knew where we should be headed and the right questions to ask.

Later in August Tom dramatically picked up Peggy and me at the Bar Harbor (Trenton), Maine, airport in his Air Force Constellation. The longest runway at that time was 4,060 feet

Peggy and I with the four boys at Northeast Harbor
(Courtesy of Toni Frissell)

Peggy and I with her mother, Mrs. Partridge, young Bill,
Will and Wendy

and our takeoff was a close shave (thereafter Tom realized it would be less conspicuous and safer if he used Dow Field in Bangor). Peggy slept like a baby on the Constellation's couch while I questioned Tom and George Brownell, who had previously served as Bob Lovett's assistant, about the attitude of the Air Force officers. Would they accept me, knowing I was not a scientist and had never fired a gun?

"If you can do anything to help them solve their problems, they'll be your friends for life," said George, and how right he was. With those cheerful words I became Assistant to the Secretary of the Air Force, the first ever appointed for Research and Development.

*   *   *

It was typical of the general apprehension of atomic bombing at this time that I asked Admiral Lewis Strauss if he thought it would be safer for my family if I rented a house in Chevy Chase, Maryland, rather than in Georgetown which was four miles closer to the Pentagon. Lewis laughed, "Bill," he said, "you must have a higher opinion of the Russians' accuracy than I do."

During the war I had, of course, paid occasional visits to the Pentagon, that magnificent structure known as "McCloy's folly," since he had driven through its construction. But this time as I got out of my car to climb the imposing steps of the "River entrance" there was an amusing coincidence: a three-quarter-ton Ford truck drove up with the words "Air Coordinating Committee" emblazoned on its side. Well, six years earlier Bob Lovett, Di Gates and I held monthly meetings to speed up the transition of civilian pilots into the Army and Navy. We accomplished quite a bit, we had a single secretary, and we called ourselves jokingly the "Air Coordinating Committee."

I regarded this as a good omen. (When I inquired about the new committee I learned it had a staff of two hundred to take care of the paper work!)

I was ushered into a very handsome office, adjacent to Tom's, with an appropriate anteroom, a large desk and a pretty, blond, and highly efficient secretary, Miss Frances Taylor. Government secretaries assigned to relatively high officials, work incredible hours without complaint and are intensely loyal to their boss. I had two excellent ones in Commerce, Mrs. Turner and Mrs. Paris, and now the attractive, capable Miss Taylor. Anyone of the three could have commanded better pay and much shorter hours in New York but in the Capital they were dealing with more fascinating material and felt closer to the seat of power.

Within a few minutes in came Finletter's aide, an Air Force Colonel, to discuss the necessary "clearance." Why someone who had been trusted by the Government for years must be reclassified before being trusted by the Pentagon is an Alice in Wonderland dilemma which I cannot go into because it, too, is classified. However I can describe the four levels of classified material:

1) "Confidential"—which really meant nothing at all. Most information so classified could have been printed in the newspapers, and often was.

2) "Secret"—which sounded impressive but had been degraded by overuse. In 1912 in the old State Department building, according to the late Ambassador William Phillips, documents marked "Secret" were placed in a basket hung on the outside of the office door for hand delivery.

3) "Top secret"—which really meant something. Most of the important information I dealt with was so classified.

4) "Eyes only"—this, in military parlance, meant that it should only be read by the man to whom it was addressed and then destroyed by him.

I should add that there were separate classifications covering secret atomic matter, the necessity for which was better appreciated after the British agents, Burgess, Maclean and Philby had fled to the Soviet Union.

Clearance required an in-depth investigation by the FBI running to several weeks. This perhaps was justified if years had elapsed between one's government jobs, to make sure one had not become an alcoholic, homosexual or a friend of the Russians in the interim.

What I really needed at this time—though I did not immediately realize it—was a thoroughly competent scientific assistant who was expert in the areas which were vital to the USAF, and those in which it was weakest. The hindrance in my knowing was the "iron curtain" which separated the work of the Atomic Energy Commission on atomic warhead design from the study by the Air Force of delivery systems for atomic weapons, either by airplane or *particularly* by guided missiles, i.e., rockets.

I was beginning to find my way into this maze when Secretary Finletter was called up on the Hill to testify before the Senate Committee on Defense Appropriations and to give a review of the Air Force R & D program. I would be at his right and speak when my turn came.

I well remembered from my past performance in Commerce how nervous I became under questioning and how could I speak with authority at this early stage? But luck plays an important part in all our lives. As I was preparing for that dreaded ordeal, my office crammed with Air Force generals, colonels, and majors, each endeavoring to cram me with details of his pet projects, who should drop in but my old friend, Garrison Norton. He quickly saw that the situation was out of control and that I needed help.

Garry had had years of experience in aviation. He had qualified as a Naval Aviator, USNR, and had served as a flight instructor at the Naval Air Station, Pensacola. As Chief of the Plant Facilities Branch of the Bureau of Aeronautics, he had risen to the rank of Captain and had served in the European Theatre, whence he was called from Naval duty to become Assistant Secretary of State. His chief responsibilities were post-war negotiations in the field of international aviation, shipping and telecommunication. That duty fulfilled, Garry was on the point of leaving Washington to rejoin his partners in the New York accounting firm of Arthur Young & Co. when I prevailed on him to stay as my assistant, and beginning with the Hearings on the Hill I was increasingly grateful for his sound advice.

The "state of the art" was a favorite military R & D expression which was applied to almost anything in process.

Before I joined the Air Force the big "flying crane" helicopter was given to Hughes and, years after my departure, was finally allowed to die on the vine. The atomic powered airplane, a much more expensive project was snarled up in interservice rivalry (and ultimately came to nothing). The problem of developing a long-range unmanned weapon which would carry an atomic bomb (warhead) to key targets in the USSR, as much as 500 miles distant, was in the air. What Garry and I objected to was the habit of attacking any problem one step at a time instead of leapfrogging the intermediate stages and going directly from the manned airplane (B-52 plus the KC-135 tanker) to the guided ballistic missile. That was just what the Russians did, and did successfully. In contrast to such prolonged experiments was Admiral Rickover's brilliant development of the moving, submerged submarine discharging missiles with a range of 2,000 miles or more.

I was absorbed and fascinated in getting an immediate overview of the Research and Development and felt impatient when we had to renew our testimony before Congressional committees. Fortunately we did not have to contend with an executive like Charlie Wilson of General Motors, Eisenhower's first Secretary of Defense, who stated publicly that "Research is what you do when you don't know what you are doing."

It soon became necessary for Garry and me to visit various R&D projects many of which were in Los Angeles. On our flight we were accompanied by Lieutenant Colonel Theodore F. Walkowicz, an Air Force officer, with a penetrating mind, the amiable Don Putt who looked at things from a military point of view, and my loyal aide, Lieutenant Colonel Vincent ("Vince") Ford, an ardent Catholic, injured in a glider accident and unable to keep his flying status. "Vince" knew the Pentagon backward and forward, just what ropes to pull, and was devoted to me. A good military aide can make all the difference. We learned a lot about the immense program and about the chief engineers and scientists in charge. But the question in my mind was whether the Air Force with its new-found affluence might be trying to carry out too many projects with insufficient discrimination in their planning. For instance, I could not understand why we were not concentrating on rocket propulsion, above all, to create intercontinental ballistic missiles to replace the conventional heavy bomber. Perhaps it was natural for the Air Force to be in favor of the manned bomber, remembering the magnificent organization of SAC which had become almost a religion. But the truth was that we were not only hesitant but backward in the rocket development.

In the last stage of the war there was a mad race between the Russians and ourselves to seize the ablest of the German scientists at Peenemünde. Each of the two services got about half; the Russians put theirs to work almost immediately on rocketry whereas the Army squirreled away our half of the scientists in the isolated Army base at Huntsville, Alabama. When I visited Huntsville, it was under the command of General Medaris, a very military type. Naturally I wanted to spend my time talking to the German scientists, particularly Wernher von Braun, who was working on rocket construction, and his no. 2 man Dornberger. General Medaris dismissed the idea. "Why do you want to waste your time with these Krauts?" and when we sat down at a table for dinner I was surrounded by only high-ranking Army brass.

For the Germans the construction of an intercontinental ballistic missile—or even a moon rocket—was child's play. Von Braun actually proposed to power the first moon rocket, the Saturn, with *eight* rocket motors. The Air Force and the Army took the dimmest possible view of this idea. They argued that *eight* rocket motors could not possibly work at the same time. "Don't worry," said von Braun, "the eight cylinders on your Cadillac work very well and my eight rocket motor will work well too."

I was presented with a thick mimeographed document of some 150 pages stamped NSC (National Security Council). "This," said the Colonel who gave it to me, "is the law of the Medes and the Persians for Air Force Research and Development, and for that matter the United States." This rather scruffy looking document gave positive answers to such reasonable questions as: 1) If World War III is about to take place, will the Russians make the first strike? 2) Should the major U.S. strategic weapon be SAC (manned bombers), long-range guided missiles, or submarine launched missiles, the two latter as yet in a very early stage of development. This was only the first of a whole series of other major NSC Policy Papers, and I was submitted to an endless series of briefings by Air Force officers. At first I took these briefings as the gospel. Later I came to realize that a number of them, particularly those on the atomic powering of airplanes were so-called "snow jobs," i.e. sales pitches, based more on the wishes of the Air Force than on fact. But of course there had to be an answer, a series of decisions for the whole vast expenditures on the U.S. defense establishment at that time, some sixty billions a year, depended on what the NSC said about our relative strength compared with that of the Russians.

The tests of our thermonuclear weapon were conducted on the Eniwetok atoll with success and despite unexpected interruptions during the three years 1950–1952. Its code name was "Greenhouse" and it was under the command of General E. R. ("Pete") Quesada of the Air Force who had distinguished himself in World War II and who had the perfect temperament for such an assignment. Quesada briefed the heads of the three services and members of the Atomic Energy Commission in Washington before any of the devices were actually detonated and as I listened to the many very human and logistic problems he had to cope with I decided I must question him further and hear again the fascinating details.

In Florida in 1980, at a friendly reunion Quesada gave me this vivid recollection of the whole operation, which was taken down by my secretary.

"The very first problem," he said, "was to convert the atoll strewn with the debris of war, into a clean outdoor laboratory, a task the Corps of Engineers did most efficiently. We had a fleet of ten or a dozen freighters to carry out the building material and instruments, and since it is a truism that you usually lose or misplace half of what you ship, we assembled our equipment in a warehouse on the dock at San Francisco according to carefully organized tables—what we should need at once and what should remain aboard ship until it was called for. You see we didn't have enough room on the islands to store much; for example, we couldn't store cement; we had to have the cement arrive at the rate we would use it. That applied to almost everything so the logistics problem was a very severe one, requiring an incredible amount of minute planning."

"It must have taken months," I said.

"Oh, months—remember the whole thing lasted three years.

"Eniwetok was eight by ten miles in diameter with a lovely lagoon in the center and two large islands where we built the quarters for our people, and a smaller one where we had our animal colony and the two dozen attendants. All told we had a population of 10,000 people living on the atoll and aboard ship.

" 'Greenhouse,' the code name, had a dual purpose: the first, was weapons improvement, to what degree was the weapon being tested more efficient than other devices; the second was the weapon's effect, that is, what happens to houses, to miniature factories (only sections of them, of course), and to live beings when the device goes off. The medical people were very concerned about the effects of ionizing radiation, and they had a biomedical program, using three types of animals: dogs, because their respiratory system is similar to man's; pigs because their skin surface is similar to man's; mice because of their very rapid

General Elwood Quesada

Fireball of the world's first thermonuclear explosion, Eniwetok
Proving Grounds, November 1, 1952 (local time)
(Photograph supplied by United States Atomic Energy Commission)

response. One of the requirements was that all the animals to be exposed had to have three generations on the atoll behind them.

"Just to give you an idea of how the animals were used," Quesada explained, "we had big cylinders and after the pigs were anesthetized they were placed in these cylinders which were located at a precise point under a very complex timing device: a window would be opened, a second before the device went off, then closed at a prescribed time, and of course portions of the pigs' skin would be radiated, either by ionizing radiation or thermal radiation. The animals were then killed, and the portions that the scientists used to examine, particularly the bones, were preserved as the effect on the marrow was very important.

"But the dogs presented a problem. We had to bring them out there two years ahead of the test if we were to test those of the third generation."

I interrupted. "Why did they need to be of the third generation?"

"So that they would be acclimated to the island and the effects could not be traced to any change in their environment," Quesada explained.

"At that time there was a very strong anti-vivisectionist movement in Chicago run by Fred Astaire's sister Adele. So we had to move quietly. We sent to Kentucky and bought a pack of hounds—coon dogs, and they started breeding. About nine months passed before we discovered that they were not increasing at the rate we had anticipated, and it was only then we learned that this breed only come into heat once a year instead of twice as most dogs do.

"Somebody goofed, and we had to send back for a different breed, and a greater quantity of dog food for the two packs. Out they came in big boxes marked: RUSH, PRIORITY ONE, DOG FOOD, LT. GEN. E. R. QUESADA. U.S. AIR FORCE, ENIWETOK. RUSH, DOG FOOD, printed all over the damn things. I'll bet every guy who lifted those things up with a dolly wrote home to his congressman.

"This occurred exactly at the time that the Chinese were knocking the hell out of MacArthur at the Yalu River, and all of a sudden there were dozens of letters to many members of Congress exclaiming: Men are dying and Quesada is shouting for dog food! All of a sudden in came a message from the War Department, the most harsh reprimand of an official nature I have ever received. I wondered what the hell is this all about? What have we done? And only then did I find out about the hounds and their breeding habit. I said, Oh, my God! But this is silly, so I sat down and in my answer I described the miscalculation in the productivity of our dogs. I made it jocular and humorous, but I explained the scientific reason. Three days later I got another message. All the letters of complaint were being forwarded to me, and I should answer them in the same vein."

"Tell me again," I said to Quesada, "about what happened in the Quarry."

"Well," he said, "the story of the dogs, that miscalculation, was humorous. This was not. It is an incredible coincidence.

"We had a very large construction program, requiring a great deal of concrete. When you are mixing concrete you need aggregate and we quarried all our aggregate from the coral reef. To reduce the number of people on the island, we had many of them working on three shifts. The quarry worked around the clock, and one evening the night shift found that there were no lights. The foreman was furious, madder than hell. 'How can I make my quota if I haven't got any lights?' He got hold of the electrician and blasted him out. 'Damn it, get some lights down there so we can make our quota.' So the electrician threw the big master switch, and when he did so he electrocuted the man on the prior shift who was still down in the quarry splicing a cable that a bulldozer had severed—the bottom of the quarry was obviously wet—and he was killed instantly."

"Who do you suppose he was? He was the executioner at the Nuremburg Trials, the Army sergeant who was in charge of the pulleys, the trap door, the hanging of the Nazis condemned at Nuremburg. When the Trials were over he came back to the U.S. along with everyone else, and the Army wanted to get him away from the public gaze. He was a marked man, and they asked if I would take him out to Eniwetok. I said of course I would be willing; nobody there knew him, my chief of staff and I were the only ones who knew his past, and he was the guy who was electrocuted. It was a fantastic coincidence."

"In your Washington briefing," I said, "you spoke quite a lot about Al Graves, the chief scientist."

"Yes," said Quesada, "Alvin Graves was in command of the scientific task force, and a marvelous guy. If it wasn't for his personality things would not have gone as smoothly as they did. I was the commander and the staff did the planning. I had an Air Force Commander and a good one in Bob Lee. We had an Army Commander in charge of the Corps of Engineers, and a Navy Task Force, and the most important was Doctor Al Graves who was in charge of the scientists. The trouble was not with him, the trouble was with the people in the scientific community who felt animosity toward Edward Teller, which I didn't share and a lot of other people didn't share. They knew that Edward Teller was the man most responsible for pushing through the thermonuclear device. The minority I speak of thought we ought not to develop such a weapon.

"For a time the elements threatened to blot out our experiment. As we were getting near the test, very close to test time, a typhoon began raising hell throughout the entire Pacific. Waves were measured up to fifty-four feet. We could see its side effect on Eniwetok; we were right in its path, and we got instructions from Admiral Radford's headquarters that we were to abandon the island. Well, I was my own boss. The Department of Defense could have ordered me but not Radford, and so I had no intention of abandoning the island. My God, here we had worked for two and a half years, all the instrumentation worth hundreds of millions was in place. So we worked out a system that if the typhoon came within so many miles, we would assemble on the beaches; if it approached within so many more miles, we would get in our boats, assemble in the boats in the atoll; and then if it was on us we would go out to sea. Well, we didn't even have to assemble on the beaches. It skirted us by about ten miles, the center was about ten miles off."

"That was pretty damn close," I said.

"Yes," Quesada replied, "the highest point on the island was only about seven feet, and I got a lot of pressure to abandon our work. When proof is positive then I will, but not until then; and in the end everybody was glad. The critical period lasted about twenty-four hours."

Garry and I flew out to Eniwetok ten days before the final detonation took place and were enormously impressed by the precise, calculated teamwork and the prevailing conviction that the test had to be made. True there was that splinter group of scientists who believed with Dr. J. Robert Oppenheimer that if we did not produce a thermonuclear bomb the Russians would not feel compelled to do so. This was wishful thinking and proved to be fallacious.

There were four definite stages in the development:

1). On January 31, 1950, President Truman directed the AEC to proceed with the preparation of the hydrogen bomb.

2). The prototype of Teller's device, tested on Eniwetok was too big to be a practical weapon. It was not a true thermonuclear weapon, but in the experiment an *essential principle was proved*.

3). Early in 1952 Secretary Finletter said, "Let it be known that the Air Force is prepared to produce a hydrogen bomb."

4). In November, 1952, we exploded our hydrogen bomb, and nine months later, in August, 1953, the Russians exploded theirs. Had it not been for our speed-up, the Russians might have been the first to do so. It is undeniable that they had been proceeding on their own initiative.

There remains the question why Dr. J. Robert Oppenheimer, the genius at Los Alamos, opposed so far as he could, the inevitable next step?

To understand Dr. Oppenheimer's position as the "King" of American physicists in the early fifties and to appreciate the adoration—it is not too strong a word—with which most of the young physicists regarded him, one must realize that in the late 1920s and early 1930s, it was he who trained them at both the California Institute of Technology in Pasadena and the University of California at Berkeley. As the Alsop brothers said in their article, "We Accuse,"

> "He was the center. If the vast majority of American physicists today quite genuinely venerate Robert Oppenheimer it is because he trained so many of them, and because the rest rightly regard him as the man who took the lead in 'naturalizing' the New Physics in this country."

I do not believe that Oppenheimer was intentionally disloyal and certainly not a Russian spy. The Gordon Gray hearings were in my opinion aimed at the wrong things. What Oppenheimer did wrong, and it was very wrong, was to give misleading information as to the probable time of a successful H-bomb development. He must have known better. I believe he gave these misleading technical opinions because he was against the H-bomb on moral grounds. For this he should have been promptly discharged as an adviser—which he ultimately was. The real question about Oppenheimer, from my point of view, was that he gave false or certainly misleading information to the AEC, to his government about the possibility of creating *rapidly* a thermonuclear weapon when he must have known it was technically possible. He felt that if we built the thermonuclear weapon first, it would encourage the Russians to do the same, thereby accelerating the "arms race." He could not believe that the Russians would go all-out to build the thermonuclear weapon first—which is actually what they tried to do.

After the Russians had exploded their atomic bomb in August 1949, the fateful question of the next step could not be evaded. Dr. Glenn T. Seabury wrote Oppenheimer, "Although

I deplore the prospect of our country putting a tremendous effort (into the H-bomb program), I must confess that I have been unable to come to the conclusion that we should not." Oppenheimer, Vannevar Bush and James B. Conant all had their misgivings, as Oppenheimer clearly states in this signal letter to Conant:

> "What concerns me is really not the technical problem. I am not sure the miserable thing (i.e. the H-Bomb) will work, nor that it can be gotten to a target except by oxcart. It seems likely to me even further to worsen the *unbalance of our present war plans. What does worry me is that this thing appears to have caught the imagination, both of the Congressional and the military people, as the answer to the problem posed by (the Soviet atomic test)*. It would be folly to oppose the exploration of this weapon. We have always known it had to be done; and it does have to be done, although it appears to be singularly proof against any form of experimental approach. *But that we become committed to it as the way to save the country and save the peace, appears to me full of dangers*."

In Washington I had met and been strongly impressed by Edward Teller. Teller sharply rejected Oppenheimer's attitude at Los Alamos. Teller wanted the H-bomb pursued on the Manhattan Project scale immediately and he was furious that there was no crash program on the H-bomb right after the Russian atomic explosion. When President Truman announced his decision to build the H-bomb at all costs on January 31, 1950, Teller should have been the key man to do this work at Los Alamos. But he claimed that his efforts there were being hampered and asked for a second laboratory, which was set up for him at Livermore, California. The effect of the President's decision and the existence of the second laboratory were to force

Norris Bradbury, the reluctant director of Los Alamos, and an ardent admirer of Oppenheimer to get to work seriously on the H-bomb, which he previously did not want to do. Most of the serious development of the H-bomb was accomplished at Los Alamos, but it would never have been done with such speed had it not been for the threatening competition of the second laboratory.

Looking back at my three years as Assistant Secretary of the Air Force for Research and Development, I can say without modesty that the encouragement I gave to Edward Teller was my signal contribution. As Hans Bethe wrote in April 1950: "So we come finally to one reason, and only one, that can justify our building the H-bomb: namely, to deter the Russians from using it against us, if only for fear of our retaliation." A pretty good reason I think.

I had immensely enjoyed my work under Secretary Finletter and as the Presidential campaign began to warm up, I told him that I felt the time had come for me to resign, and that I wished to raise funds for the election of General Eisenhower. Tom, who was a lifelong Democrat, thanked me for what I had done and we returned to New York.

CHAPTER XII

The Museum of Modern Art

DURING those postwar years in Washington I was utterly absorbed in my assignment and reasonably competent; I had an indispensable assistant in Garrison Norton and, what is so essential in government, a superior in Tom Finletter, who had confidence in me and supported me wholeheartedly. With the exception of John McCone, who left in a huff in 1951, I worked on cordial terms with the other top officials with whom I was involved; with Roswell Gilpatric, who succeeded McCone as Under Secretary; with Bob Lovett, the Secretary of Defense; Archie Alexander, Assistant Under Secretary of the Army, whom I had known since boyhood, and who had married the lovely Jean Sears, and with John Nicholas Brown, Assistant Secretary of the Navy for Air.

We saw a great deal of the Browns who were living in the Lincoln house of Georgetown, which backed up upon our garden. Ann Brown was very intelligent, amusing and likeable; we enjoyed the parties she gave for the Navy brass, and our sons liked each other, our Bob rooming with their son Carter at Groton. John was five years ahead of me at Harvard, we both belonged to the A.D. and now became fast friends.

After General Eisenhower's nomination in August I began raising funds for Ike's election. Garry Norton stayed on and was soon appointed Assistant Secretary of the Navy for Research and Development where he played a conspicuous part in the completion of "Poseidon," the atomic headed missile launched from underwater by our atomic submarines.

As with all of us in Defense I returned to civilian life bearing in mind the staggering cost—and the threat—of atomic weapons. Today the R&D budget of the United States has risen to be larger than the total budget of medium sized nations. Only we and the U.S.S.R. can afford such expenditures. During the 1960–1970 period our development of Polaris, Minuteman, the ABM have cost an average of over 3 billion each. Is there any alternative so long as the suspicion and hostility in the Kremlin remains?

On my visits to Mount Desert I often saw Nelson Rockefeller for whom Wallace Harrison had built a spectacular house on the rocks at Seal Harbor. We had a bond in common in our devotion to the Museum of Modern Art of which he had been president since 1946 and one day he said, "Bill, now that I'm heading into New York politics I simply won't have the necessary time to preside over the Museum. I wish you'd let me propose you for the job. There are many members of the Board who would be pleased if you'd accept." Changes had occurred during my time in Washington, René d'Harnoncourt, Nelson's protégé had been added to the staff in 1944; as one of the trustees said, "It was very cleverly done, Nelson got him in just to be around and get the sense of the place while the staff came to appreciate him." It proved to be a brilliant move for he and Alfred Barr worked together like a charm; each complemented the other, Alfred, the supreme innovator and connoisseur, René, so imaginative in installing and lighting the exhibitions. In time René became the Director and Alfred the roving Curator, a partnership which made the Museum preeminent and whose standard was emulated throughout the art world. They became bosom friends. To collaborate with them was inviting and after talking things over with Peggy who I knew would be much involved I decided to accept. My partners, "Mac" Stewart and Bob Barker, were keeping the William A. M. Burden Company on a steady course; the Museum would be a diverting responsibility.

Physically and temperamentally, Alfred Barr and René d'Harnoncourt were a contrast; Alfred thin, weighing 120 pounds at most, quiet and so intense, the shy scholar, but insatiable acquisitioner; René, a colossal six feet five, 230 pounds, given to reminiscing about his beloved Vienna which he could not be stopped talking about as he was stone deaf. It was René's planning of an exhibition which made him famous. In our show "Indian Arts of the U.S." he presented to the Trustees, two months before the show was to be installed, scale models of the three floors of the Museum with *each object* to be shown in its place. He began by making a scale drawing showing where everything would be, its lighting precisely conceived, the background painted in their final colors. And in our show he displayed more than a thousand objects with a dramatic effect. In René's words—"Installation is a very exciting subject and it requires humility, who comes first, the installator or the guy who is being installed? A museum director shouldn't add to a work of art, he must not prostitute the whole thing and finally make a peep show of it." As Eliza Parkinson put it, "René didn't want to get along without Alfred and Al couldn't function without René." In their careers they became wonderfully cooperative.

At our meetings Alfred in his impatient way often nagged at René, tried to cut him down, was rude and disagreeable; but René would never resent it. With his tranquil disposition he could handle the prima donnas, not only those on the staff but among the Trustees. He had a way of keeping the situation from ever getting out of hand, and most problems dissolved before his deliberate, sympathetic manner of dealing with them.

I used to meet him once a week during the fall, winter and spring in my office for an hour or two to discuss administrative problems of the Museum. I was very busy in this period, anxious to get to the root of the matter rapidly—and I invariably told him so. Invariably, René would open the conversation with a long rambling, usually amusing story of his old life in Vienna. He had an unlimited store of these, and they were delightful but not when you were trying to get to your next appointment. Once René started it was impossible to stop him, as he refused to wear a hearing aid, and seemed completely impervious to signals of one's impatience; and in time I learned to hold my horses as the stories sometimes had a bearing on a problem we had to solve.

*   *   *

In the spring of 1954 Peggy and I spent a few weeks in Paris and saw quite a lot of Douglas Dillon, our Ambassador, and his delightful wife Phyllis. He told me of his plan for a "Salut à la France," in which we would send to Paris our finest selection of 19th and 20th century French paintings together with a couple of Broadway hits and our most popular musical comedy. He asked if I would head up the project. He was confident he could persuade President Eisenhower to be the Honorary Chairman.

I said I would have to duck the theatrical side of it but I was sure the staff at the Museum of Modern Art would jump at the artistic idea. Doug arranged a meeting with the President, who happily approved, and I said I thought it would be possible to open the show within a year. We christened the exhibition "De

Alfred Barr, Jr., Rene d'Harnoncourt and myself on the roof of the Museum in 1953

Peggy and I with Emily and Garry Norton at Exhibition of De David à
Toulouse-Lautrec in Paris, 1955

Mr. and Mrs. Alexis Leger at their wedding in Washington;
taken by young Bill

With Mrs. Lyndon Johnson at Museum 1964

David à Toulouse-Lautrec" and the French, surprised and delighted, offered us the Orangerie in Paris as the most appropriate place for it. My staff were bursting with enthusiasm.

Not so the timid mice in State and our Cultural attaché in Paris who feared the display would dramatize the degree to which "rich Americans had robbed France of her cultural heritage."

It is not an easy matter to select fifty-five oils and forty-five drawings from museums and private collectors, insure, pack and ship the priceless lot abroad in ten months. But we did it; only twelve had been bought by museums directly, the balance by individuals for their homes or eventually bequeathed to museums. We persuaded the living collectors that we—"the Modern"—would be responsible for the shipping, the hanging and the security and that they could look forward to a dinner at the American Embassy, a reception at the Elysée Palace, visits to French private collections—and the delight of Paris in the spring.

One would like to list the entire dazzling catalogue but these will suggest the quality:

> David's masterly portrait, "Napoléon dans son Cabinet"
> Daumier's "L'Homme à la Corde"
> Gauguin's "Les Vieilles Filles d'Arles"
> Daumier's "Un wagon de troisième classe"
> Corot's "L'Italienne"
> Cézanne's "Garçon au Gilet Rouge"
> Degas' "Danseuses ajustant leurs chaussons"
> Degas' "M. Degas père écoutant Pagans s'accompagnant à la guitare"
> Toulouse-Lautrec's "Au Moulin Rouge"
> Monet's "La Seine à Bougival"

Cézanne's "Les Grandes Baigneuses"
Cézanne's "Nature morte"
Renoir's "Au Cirque Fernando"
Renoir's "Nu-Etude pour 'Les Baigneuses' "
Seurat's "Etude définitive pour 'Dimanche d'été
    à la Grande Jatte' "
Van Gogh's "L'Arlésienne (Mme Ginoux)"
Seurat's "Etude pour 'La Parade' "
Van Gogh's "La Nuit Etoilée"

The exhibition was on view for ten and a half weeks. (There were 178,535 paid admissions and some 10,000 individuals or groups received complimentary tickets.) Except for the communist papers which either ignored or panned the exhibition the French press was cordial and forthright. Two points were stressed: first, criticism of the short-sighted policy of French officials who had failed to recognize the merit of the 19th and 20th century French masters, and acquire them for the Louvre; secondly, that American collectors began acquiring the Impressionists before most French collectors had awakened to their artistic significance.

The tone of the appreciation is heard in quotations from these reviews:

> "One of our leading critics said the other day to the organizer of the exhibition: 'How were you able to take such marvellous things away from us?' and with that brusque joviality which is not the least part of the charm of our Yankee friends, he replied: 'We didn't have to take them away from you. It was you who offered them to us, and who still continue to do so.' This is quite true, for we have missed the boat twice. The first time was when these works were unknown and could have been had for a song, the

second time was when they had already become famous but when we did not dare to pay the required price. . . ."

(The masterpieces at the Orangerie show are worth at least ten times what they were in 1955.)

"We should consider these masterpieces as our most influential ambassadors. Our politics, our economy, even our more or less morose literature are not always admired abroad. On the other hand no one dreams of disputing that France is the only country in the world which from the fifteenth to the twentieth century can show an uninterrupted line of painters of the first rank."

"Many of the American private collectors regard themselves as only the *stewards* of their treasures; *they open their collections to the public.* . . ."

"The taste of these American collectors has led them towards exceptional works. Nothing at the Orangerie is banal or expected. Almost all of these paintings show the masters in an unaccustomed light. And this is one reason for the enormous attraction that this exhibition holds for us. . . ."

Naturally Alfred Barr and René came to Paris at this time and Alfred took Peggy and me to the principal dealers in modern art and then on fascinating trips to the Brancusi studio and the Braque studio. He knew both artists well. Brancusi's studio was a delight because he had many of his original works on display, two or three versions of the "Bird in Space," and the famous bust of Mlle. Pogany. He was a tiny man, like a gnome with a long white beard; he spoke no English but was very friendly. His studio was a mess because he was the only modern artist who did not have a mistress to keep things in order. We should have bought many Brancusis but we only acquired the "Bird in Space" and not directly from the artist.

Braque was everything Brancusi was not. He was an extremely tall and handsome man, impeccably dressed and well supplied with mistresses. Peggy was much taken with his "Series of Black Birds" but didn't have nerve enough to buy one although they were very cheap.

She was definitely against buying pictures which were disagreeable and Barr confided to me that all of the series were of the Black Bird of Death, but fortunately she did not realize that. We also saw a magnificent self-portrait of Picasso for $8,000, probably worth $500,000 today, but she did not like that either.

We finally settled on a marvelous Delauney of the Eiffel Tower which hangs in our dining room in 820 Fifth Avenue. All in all it was a wonderful experience to see these artists with Alfred. He continued to advise us on pictures up to the time of his fatal illness.

Occasionally, but very occasionally, I bought a picture that Peggy did not approve of and put it in storage. She actually relented about hanging the marvelous Bacon portrait of Velasquez, which impulsively I gave to my nephew, Carter Burden, for a wedding present. (It cost $10,000—present value $500,000.) I also bought a famous Picasso "Flayed Bull" which I still own, but Peggy will not let me hang it. Such are the tribulations of two devoted collectors with different tastes.

On our return from France Peggy and I found ourselves enmeshed in family and museum affairs. Young Bill had married Leslie Hamilton in his junior year at Harvard and their first child, our grandchild William A. M. Burden IV, was the subject of affectionate attention. And what was inevitable and quite pressing after the Paris triumph, Peggy found herself committed to the opening of new exhibitions, the cocktail parties and the dinners for visiting artists at which the wife of the president must be the hostess.

*   *   *

My grandmother, looking as slim and autocratic as ever, passed by her eightieth year in 1934, nor was there anything special ten years later while we were in Washington. But in 1949 when on a drive the limousine skidded and she was flung to the floor with internal injuries. She became an invalid and died in 1952 at the age of ninety-eight. "Florham" was stilled.

My years in government limited the opportunity for a continual intimacy with Aunt Ruth. On my brief visits to "Florham" our affection for each other momentarily revived but it was not until Peggy and I returned to New York that Aunt Ruth and I resumed our luncheons together, and they were not as light-hearted or confiding as they had been. She did not share my devotion to Modern Art, she seemed only mildly interested in my deep concern about air power and our relations with the Soviet Union. I felt more than ever that her administrative ability had been selfishly appropriated by my grandmother and it saddened me that despite Aunt Ruth's efforts to conceal it her dependence on alcohol helped her forget what might have been. I knew of no way to reach her or to prevent it.

Aunt Ruth with a traveling companion went to Paris in the early spring of 1954 and in April a cable warned me that she was desperately ill with cirrhosis of the liver and to come at once. I telephoned to Shirley and with Moms we flew over the following day but when we reached the Ritz she had lost consciousness, and she died under sedation.

In our family that had suffered such early deaths—grandfather Twombly, his eldest daughter Alice at the age of sixteen, and his only son Hamilton, then my father—Aunt Ruth's self-destruction seemed to me pitiful. I remembered how vital she had been; her buoyancy when she took me beside her on her triumphant sleighride through Central Park, how happily she planned the building of the Playhouse and how mercilessly she drove herself in her tennis lessons with the pro—to keep her weight down. It was she who taught me to drive her car and showed her pride when I was elected to the A.D. Now "Florham," to which she contributed such vivacity, was lifeless. Moms agreed that I must close it; the furniture was auctioned by Parke Bernet and the heart of the estate and the gardens were adapted to the use of Fairleigh Dickinson University.

*   *   *

One of the most interesting explorations that I took part in while I was President of the Museum was the three-week trip to the Soviet Union that René d'Harnoncourt, Alfred Barr and I made in May, 1956.

We believed that it would be a real coup for the Museum to organize a loan exhibit of Russian pictures from the early nineteenth century to the present. There were really few contemporary Russian pictures of any quality, for the Soviet government did not approve of abstract art any more than had the Nazis before them. What little contemporary, abstract painting was done within the Soviet Union was done sub rosa and obviously very derivative since the young artists were not allowed to travel abroad and had little source of inspiration as to what was going on in the rest of the world.

Public exhibitions of abstract painting were strictly forbidden and what few abstract pictures young Russians did paint were hidden and sold on the black market, usually to ballet dancers who were among the few Russians of an artistic bent who had any money. They, of course, had to secrete their purchases: hanging them would have been dangerous in the extreme, as the KGB would have gone after both painter and owner.

However, there were a number of Russian painters of the past from the early nineteenth century to 1914 who were really first class—artists who painted Russian landscapes and dachas in the style of the Italian Corots; enormous battle scenes, some of them certainly as good as David, including a number of interesting paintings of the conquest of Siberia—a fascinating phase of Russian life little talked about, especially by the Soviets; and some unknown painters in the late nineteenth century who painted in the French Impressionist style.

We would have sent a collection of contemporary American paintings in exchange for the Russian paintings had the Soviets wanted them and in fact they became one of the arresting features in the American Exhibition in Moscow in 1959. The atmosphere for such a cultural exchange between the U.S.S.R. and the U.S. was much more favorable then than now. The Soviet Ambassador appeared to favor our project and we were most encouraged by my classmate and close friend, Charles E. ("Chip") Bohlen, then our Ambassador in Moscow who was keen to have it done.

We obtained our visas without trouble and René, Alfred and I—a congenial group if there ever was one—set off for Moscow full of hope. We traveled by Scandinavian Airlines, at that time one of the most pleasant airlines in the world; it had an excellent safety record (always important to me), fantastically good food and blond, beautiful stewardesses, perfectly trained in the art of unobtrusive and perfect service. If one has to be awakened after sitting all night in a chair, it is far better to be aroused by a truly beautiful woman—and we were!

But no sooner had we landed at the new giant Moscow air-port—some forty miles from the city—than we ran into trouble. Alfred was a compulsive birdwatcher. He never traveled any-where without a huge pair of binoculars with which to track down his prey. Birds are a notorious nuisance around airports, the cause of several bad accidents; one of the worst at Logan Airport in Boston where gulls were sucked into the intake of the jet engines of a Lockheed Electra, with the loss of sixty-six passengers.

I had warned Alfred before our departure that he should *not* take his binoculars. I explained that I had just resigned as Assis-tant to the Secretary of the U.S. Air Force for Research and Development and was privy to most Air Force secrets, that the Russians were probably aware of this and that our art visit to Moscow coincided with a big Soviet aircraft show at which their latest military models would be exhibited and at which General Twining, Chief of Staff of the U.S. Air Force, and other high ranking officers would be present.

Therefore, it was highly undesirable that a member of our party should be roaming around airports peering through high-pow-ered binoculars. Barr, who was both innocent (he had visited the U.S.S.R. before and highly approved of their government) and stubborn, paid no attention to my suggestions. I suppose I should have made them orders. I did point out that if anyone was going to end up in the notorious Lubyanka Prison it would be I—not Barr or d'Harnoncourt—but that made no impres-sion on either—René had been converted to a bird fancier by Alfred and was too deaf to hear me anyway.

We had hardly cleared the Customs when a couple of military types who had been observing Barr's bird-watching activities descended on us in menacing fashion to find out what *that man* was doing. Fortunately Alfred, who spoke no Russian, or any other foreign language as far as I was able to find out, was able to fudge his replies and we were admitted. However, we were followed, watched and I suppose listened in on for the rest of our trip in a much more intensive manner than any ordinary art group would have been.

Having overcome this first hurdle, we were driven at a snail's pace to our hotel in Moscow, the National. This dismal building may have been erected in Tsarist times; it was dark brown, filthy, and with a cuisine which the hungriest castaway would have scorned. All Russian hotels obey the rule imposed by the secret police (KGB). The traveler on arrival is obliged to turn over his passport to the concièrge with the promise that it will be returned on the day of departure. I never felt comfortable in the U.S.S.R. without my passport, however, that is the law. Another unpleasant custom is that the hotel employee in charge of each floor—usually a formidable woman with all the earmarks of a KGB operative—confiscates one's room key every time one departs and returns it grudgingly when one comes back. In addition, of course, one suspects that one's room is electronically bugged—a practice the Russians adopted long before the United States did. Finally, my suite, which had a sitting room attached, permitted no view whatever—the single window confronted a blank stone wall a few feet away, hardly a pleasant atmosphere in which to spend almost two weeks.

After sampling everything on the limited, well-thumbed menu, we came to the conclusion that a meal must be preceded by a large aperitif of vodka, always served lukewarm in dirty glasses. Soviet wines were varied but uniformly undrinkable. Life could be sustained on caviar of rather mediocre quality; even the fiercely nationalistic Soviets admitted that Iranian caviar was vastly superior to their own. The only delicious Russian caviar I had in Moscow was at the one reception we attended at the Kremlin. After the caviar the next edible item at the National was Chicken Pojarsky stuffed with butter and not at all bad. However, repeating this dish twice a day was, to put it mildly, monotonous.

What we should have done of course was to have gotten letters of introduction to as many Western ambassadors as possible. They all had good chefs and were dying for visitors as a change to entertaining each other. The Russians seldom engaged in social pleasantries unless they had something very specific to gain.

We devoted our first days in Moscow to visiting the principal museums, getting to know the curators of those collections in which we were interested and making tentative selections of the pictures we wanted to borrow. Almost without exception we found the directors and curators competent—usually quite young and very enthusiastic about our ideas for the show. The curators of later Russian art were however frustrated because, since the government officially disapproved of modern Russian painting, the fine Kandinskys, Malevichs, etc. were not even shown and never lent abroad. They, the modern curators, therefore had practically no opportunity to visit Europe or the United States in contrast to the curators of say the nineteenth century great Rembrandt collection in the Hermitage at Leningrad who had many opportunities to visit Western Europe with "their" pictures.

Moscow, except for the Kremlin, is far from being a beautiful city or even an interesting one. I remember "Chip" Bohlen remarking: "Leningrad, yes. That is a beautiful and fascinating city—half European, half Russian—but what is there to see in this rather dismal Moscow with its dismal climate, its bleak uninteresting buildings and the depressing atmosphere which goes with a police state."

However, we did have a couple of occasions which definitely enlivened our visit. We were in Moscow on the Queen of England's birthday, May 31, and as I happened to know the British Ambassador—William Hayter—rather well from Washington days we were invited to the Embassy reception in the Queen's honor.

"Chip" Bohlen strongly urged that we should go, for "all the big boys" were going to be there and it would be our only chance to see them. So we did go and, as billed, the "big boys" were there: Khrushchev bowing, smiling, fascinating and also throwing his weight around, Bulganin dull and nervous, his colorless face adorned by a ragged goatee. The party was like most embassy parties—several hundred people jammed into a small garden on a hot day with lukewarm drinks and poor service.

However, in addition to the "big boys" there was present the U.S. Air Force delegation headed by General Twining, in Moscow for the Soviet military air show, and this prompted the Soviets to send their most important Air Force generals and, far more interesting, to me, some of their outstanding air designers including the famous Andrei Nicolayevich Tupolev at that time sixty-eight years old.

I began a most animated conversation with him in English on the long-range plans for the Russian Air Force though it soon became clear that his English was very faulty. We then shifted to French and got on splendidly. I am sorry to say—for he was quite extraordinary—that when it became clear to the KGB men present that I was extracting some valuable information, they closed in on us and interrupted further conversation much to my sorrow. A great opportunity missed but as my granddaughter Wendy puts it: "You can't win them all."

Our trip to Leningrad was far more pleasant than our stay in gloomy Moscow. It was originally named St. Petersburg, built by the energetic and imaginative Peter the Great and the administrative capital of Russia until 1918, a distinctly European city with beautiful buildings. It was badly damaged during the 900-day siege by the Germans in World War II but had been partly rebuilt by the time we were there. The reconstruction of Peter's elaborate palace—Peterhof (Petrodvorets), about twenty miles from the center of town, which was called a little Versailles and which contained several rooms completely walled with malachite and amber and many elaborate fountains—must have been a tremendous job in itself.

A large part of Leningrad is interlaced with charming canals, so much so it is often referred to as "the Venice of the North." The whole city built in the eighteenth century by a Western oriented Tsar retains a strongly Western atmosphere as compared to the strongly Byzantine atmosphere of Moscow. We stayed at the Astoria, a distinctly French eighteenth-century style hotel, somewhat faded but still presentable, which must have been quite elegant when in its prime. The food was mediocre but quite a lot better than in the horrible National in Moscow. The whole atmosphere of the place, though still definitely U.S.S.R., was more cheerful than Moscow. In the evening the Astoria was enlivened by a crowd of not unattractive youths who had a passion for dancing and danced to a noisy jazz orchestra.

Apparently jazz records were practically unavailable in Russia at that time and the young folk—at considerable risk since it was against the law—listened at home to whatever foreign stations a) played jazz and b) were powerful enough to get through the Russian jamming. The jamming, plus the fact that the sale of foreign newspapers, magazines and books was prohibited, did a pretty effective job of cutting off the mass of the Russian populace from any knowledge of what was going on abroad. The Russian papers, one of which was published in English, consisted almost entirely of government "hand outs" which pictures the U.S.S.R. as an earthly paradise surrounded by oppressed capitalist populations living under miserable conditions, armed to the teeth and dying to get at the throat of "Mother Russia."

*   *   *

A few Russians were allowed to travel abroad (under strict supervision), particularly ballet troupes which provided good publicity for the U.S.S.R. except when a famous dancer such as Nureyev tried to defect at the Paris Airport (Orly) in 1961 and succeeded because the French gendarmes dragged him from the clutches of the KGB men who were trying to force him into the Russian Aeroflot airplane, waiting to carry him back to "Mother Russia." He has lived happily in Europe and the United States ever since, dancing with the famous though much older English Margot Fonteyn as his partner.

I have always had a particular interest in Nureyev because of an amusing incident in which he and my brother Shirley were involved. Shirley's wife "Flobe" was generally regarded as a patron of the arts and when Nureyev and Fonteyn were dancing in Los Angeles someone suggested that she give a reception for them after the performance in her large and luxurious house in Beverly Hills. She accepted with alacrity.

Large amounts of caviar were purchased and several bottles of the finest vodka. It turned out that the program consisted of a short solo by Nureyev followed by a long program involving the whole company including Fonteyn but *not* Nureyev. The program was not over until after midnight and Shirley, "Flobe," Fonteyn and the other guests hurried back to the reception.

They were horrified to find Nureyev passed out on the living room sofa. He had arrived at the house two hours before and had occupied himself, eating *all* the caviar—some two kilos—and washing it down with two bottles of vodka. Obviously he was in no shape to mingle with the guests. Oh, these Russians!

Russian scientists were also encouraged to travel abroad—under proper KGB supervision of course—for it was essential that they keep up to date on developments in Western science which, in several areas, was far ahead of their own. Occasionally some of them succeeded in defecting but a few were killed by their friendly Russian guardians in the process. The Soviets usually made sure that the scientists left behind in Russia their wives and children who would effectively serve as hostages. This tended to keep defections down.

Although every attempt was always made not to let Russian travelers tell their fellow Russians what they had seen, it is hard to believe that they did not tell *something*. Some intelligent Russians must have had the idea that the outside world was not exactly as described in the two most important "official" Soviet newspapers *Izvetzia* (The Spark) and *Pravda* (ironically The Truth).

As the next generation of Russians grow up, I imagine they will demand—and get—more information about the outside world. Already (1982) more foreign newspapers and magazines are on sale in Moscow and Leningrad, jamming of radio communications was at least briefly reduced and some—though little—additional foreign travel allowed.

As I have said the city was infinitely more charming, the weather better and I had gotten over my cold which I had had in Moscow. What a difference these things made! We were introduced to the Directors and the appropriate Curators of the great Hermitage and the newer Russian Museum, and we devoured the art collections. In 1935 Peggy and I had seen the Hermitage but seeing the paintings now through the eyes of Alfred and René—and the Soviet curators—was something else again.

Alfred was the author of two definitive books, one on Picasso (1948) and the other on Matisse (1951) which he wrote when in "exile" in 1944 and demoted to Advisory Director by Stephen Clark, the difficult and autocratic president of the Museum from 1941 to 1944.

Moscow and Leningrad bookshops were flooded with copies of the "Picasso," for Alfred with his communist sympathy and his famous "Dove of Peace" was highly approved of by the Presidium. However, there was not a single copy of his book on Matisse in *all* of Russia as far as we could ascertain.

The Curator of "modern" Western art in the Hermitage was a charming highly intellectual woman of about forty, bilingual in French and English (important as Alfred spoke no foreign language).

The Russian museums as a result of having expropriated the magnificent private collections of rich merchants had some of the finest Matisses of the best period—1910–1920.

She and Alfred almost immediately engaged in a discussion of the *exact* dates of some of the finest paintings of Matisse in his great period—was this particular masterpiece painted in the spring of 1917 or the fall of 1918? Alfred, who had a very short temper, quickly became annoyed. "You will find all that information on page 512 of my book on Matisse," he said. The lady Curator was horrified. Not only did she not have a copy of his book on Matisse but she did not even know it existed. The all-powerful Soviet government evidently did not "approve" of Matisse as they had not allowed a single copy of Alfred's masterpiece on Matisse behind the Iron Curtain.

It was all very embarrassing to the Russian Curator. I do not know how many years it took her to get a copy of Alfred's book, but I am sure it took a long time. This also gave her an opportunity to bemoan her fate as a curator of modern art of not being allowed to visit Western Europe or the United States while the curators of Rembrandt and other famous sixteenth and seventeenth century artists were allowed to travel freely. Apparently the private rooms of the Hermitage were not "bugged" or the lady did not care, for she certainly talked very freely.

There were myriads of other wonders in the Hermitage which were not in our immediate field of interest: dozens of great Rembrandts, and of course their enormous and very rare collection of Scythian gold of which they are continuously finding new treasure troves.

Having ransacked the Hermitage (formerly the Winter Palace of the Tsars) from our point of view, we transferred our investigation to the Russian Museum which at that time was devoted to Russian painters of the nineteenth and early twentieth centuries, including canvasses commemorating Russian military triumphs of the conquest of Siberia—a foreign country to them at that time whose conquest was not unlike the American conquest of the West.

Few Americans realize that the U.S.S.R. was constituted by acquiring the territories of many non-Russian nationalities. Neither the Ukranians nor the Siberians, the Mongolians or the Usbecks were really Russians. They were absorbed by force of arms. Some day they may break apart again!

We knew that despite the rather mediocre pictures hung in the great halls of the Russian Museum (formerly the palace of the Grand Duke Michael, built between 1819 and 1825 by Carlo Rossi and adapted in 1895 to its use as a museum), there were dozens of fascinating "modern" Russian painters of the more or less abstract schools—Kandinsky, Malewich, etc.—which were not hung because they were condemned by the censors in the Kremlin.

Alfred was determined to see these "forbidden pictures" as were we all, for they would have formed an important part of our proposed show in the United States. We knew that they were stored in the reserves or stacks of this huge museum but we couldn't get at them. The Russians are experts at procrastination; they were reasonably polite, they didn't say no but neither would they say yes. Finally, after a week in Leningrad and two days before our fixed departure, the Director relented and said we might visit the reserves the following morning. Filled with anticipation we climbed up the long flight of stairs leading to the door of the forbidden storage area. I turned to look behind when what should I see but twenty or thirty young men and women clambering behind us.

"Who are they?" I asked the Director in French, for I had been assured that this was a very special and secret visit just for us. "Oh," he answered nonchalantly, "they are junior curators of the museum who have never been allowed to see these pictures either!"

For hours we inspected dozens of late nineteenth and early twentieth century masterpieces, many of them not known to either Alfred or René despite the fact that Alfred had visited Moscow in the 1920s—but I suppose these pictures were not on display then either.

Having made a list of the pictures in the Russian Museum and the Hermitage that we would like to have for our proposed exhibition in New York, we prepared to return to Moscow and then back home. Before leaving René and I did have time to visit the fascinating Leningrad Institute of Ethnography and

Anthropology established by Peter I in 1718–1725. This eccentric monarch had two hobbies: first the collection of all abnormal foetuses (two-headed babies, etc.) that were born in his vast realm. A very large number of these were still preserved in large glass jars filled with alcohol—not a sight for weak stomachs I can assure you. However, they seemed to fascinate René.

The other hobby was the amassing of a huge collection of what is now called primitive art—artifacts made by primitive societies in Russia's possession, including Alaska. The art of installation was not understood by the good Tsar and his successors so these objects—some of them of surpassing beauty— were like those rarities in the great ethnographic museum in Berlin, and even our own National History Museum in New York, stuffed haphazardly into glass cases of weird design, inadequately lighted and very hard to see. Unfortunately I had not yet been educated to the beauties of primitive art and was somewhat amazed at the ecstasies of joy which René showed as he looked at them.

From our scrutiny in Moscow and Leningrad we compiled a list of some hundred topnotch Russian pictures which we hoped to borrow. However, in our last days when we began negotiating with the higher levels in the Russian government—the Ministry of Culture in Moscow—we ran into a stonewall. This superior body was adamant against sending a major exhibition of modern Russian art to the United States *unless it included* a liberal proportion of Russian propaganda art: the death of Hitler, blond maidens gleaning wheat, workers performing miracles in factories.

After our return from Leningrad, Ambassador Bohlen gave us a farewell luncheon at his residence, Spaso House—an elaborate and not unattractive mansion built by a wealthy industrialist during Tsarist times—attended by the Minister of Culture and the important members of his staff and other lay ministers in a final attempt to put the project across, but like other last minute efforts it failed despite his ability and good intentions.

The American Embassy in Moscow was divided into the elegant residence, Spaso House, and a large Chancery where the business of the Embassy was done and where the families of the large staff lived in a sort of "compound." Whoever was responsible for building the Chancery did a miserable job.

Although all information about sophisticated electronic "bugging" devices was available to the State Department from the Department of Defense, State apparently never even asked for advice about making the new Chancery—very expensive by the way—even reasonably secure. The whole building was built by Russian contractors apparently without any adequate supervision by the United States as far as security was concerned. The Russian contractors honeycombed the whole Chancery building, including the Ambassador's office, with the most sophisticated receiving and transmitting devices so effective that a Russian car across the street from our Chancery or a Russian reception a mile away could record everything that was discussed, anything that was said in any important Chancery office including that of the Ambassador.

It greatly amused me that Ambassador Harriman who was American Ambassador to the U.S.S.R. from 1943 to 1946 and who was unwilling to admit that he *ever* made a mistake discovered that the U.S. medallion behind his desk included receiving and transmitting devices so efficient that everything discussed in his office was immediately disclosed to the Russians. How could he have been so stupid! The secret was not disclosed until Henry Cabot Lodge, Ambassador to the United Nations, exhibited the plaque to the Assembly of the U.N. and showed our innocent stupidity (described as Russian spy activity) before the world. Did Harriman never have his office and the rest of the Chancery "swept" electronically? Such sweeps are standard practice nowadays.

The moment when one retrieves one's passport from the hotel concièrge and departs on the bus for the Moscow airport makes one feel like a prisoner who has served a long sentence and is at last released from jail.

But in our case it was not to be so simple. We reached the airport without trouble, passed through the scrutiny of those iron-faced KGB guards, boarded the immaculate DC-6, were greeted by an immaculate Swedish steward and a beautiful Swedish stewardess who plied us with ice cold schnapps and smoked herring.

We took off all right but then we ran into trouble. The Russians were particularly touchy about foreigners peeking at their defense installations from the air so they always required that foreign airlines carry a Russian pilot observer with them to make sure that foreign pilots strictly observed the Russian requirements that foreign airlines fly at a very low altitude along narrow corridors that avoid all defense installations. This was particularly true at the time of our trip for the area of 300 miles around Moscow which was presumably filled solid with highly classified defense installations. We were required to fly at not over 1600 feet over the area.

Normally this is not a dangerous procedure in good weather in daytime *unless* one has an engine failure in a twin-engine airplane. Well, that was exactly what happened to us. About a half hour out of Moscow one of our usually reliable Pratt and Whitney engines gave up the ghost and we limped back to Moscow with our starboard propeller feathered.

We landed safely. For a couple of hours the Swedish mechanics stationed there inspected the engine. (During this period the passengers consumed what was left of the airplane's large supply of aquavit but gradually became more disgruntled and dishevelled.) Finally the Captain appeared to announce the verdict. We could see from his expression that it would be bad. It was.

The engine could not be repaired with the meager stock of spares SAS kept in Moscow. Since there was no spare engine either, SAS would have to fly a replacement in from Stockholm and install it, which meant a delay of at least one day and probably two.

Of course it was two. So we three disgruntled travelers who thought we had been liberated dragged our way back to the ghastly Hotel National where we eked out forty-eight more hours endeavoring, unsuccessfully, to drown our impatience in vodka. During this process I lost a large filling from one of my key teeth but as I would be damned if I would let a Russian dentist touch my teeth I decided to let the matter go.

Two days passed and the next morning we had the happy news from SAS that a new engine had been flown in from Stockholm, installed, flight-tested, and our flight was ready to go. We rushed to the Moscow airport, had a trouble-free flight to Stockholm where an immaculate SAS DC-6 was waiting to receive us and our baggage and transport us to New York—a city which was beginning to look more attractive every minute.

The baggage was transferred and we were preparing to board the aircraft when a SAS official appeared with a long face to inform us that the fuel truck which was refueling our aircraft had collided with one of the wings and seriously damaged it. In all my years of flying, before and after, this is the only time when two such accidents happened to an airplane in which I was about to fly.

The SAS man said it would take *six* hours to prepare a substitute DC-6, transfer the baggage and be ready for takeoff. This was a long time but not long enough to drive back into Stockholm for a pleasant Swedish lunch. So we wandered around the terminal building for a full six hours in a rather low frame of mind. Finally the new aircraft was ready and we *did* take off for New York and arrived there after a trouble-free flight.

CHAPTER XIII

Ambassador to Belgium

EVER since the beginning of my financial research for
Brown Brothers in 1928 I had moved progressively to a
wider understanding of air power. As the vice-president of the
Defense Supplies Corporation in 1941 I was instrumental in
ejecting the German and Italian airlines from South America
and replacing them with American planes and pilots. Then as
the Assistant Secretary of Air for the Department of Commerce
I was responsible for the inspection and elementary training of
thousands of our military pilots during hostilities and, in the
aftermath, for the postwar regulations of our domestic and intercontinental flights. In my testimony before Congress I successfully opposed Juan Trippe's demand to be "the chosen instrument" overseas, thereby incurring his undying hatred. In
1949 I was president of a private organization, the Institute of
the Aeronautical Sciences in New York, which became custo-
dian of my by-then enormous file on aviation, before it went to
the Smithsonian Institution. Then for two years I was absorbed
in Research and Development under Secretary of the Air Force
Finletter and together with my assistant, Garrison Norton, witnessed the tests of the hydrogen bomb at Eniwetok.

The work I had done in fund raising created a temporary
diversion. Secretary of State John Foster Dulles offered me the
desk of Assistant Secretary of State for Latin America and I

impulsively accepted. Thanks to the family's properties in South America I had acquired an intimate knowledge of several countries, particularly Peru, Ecuador, and Brazil, yet when Peggy and I discussed it we were not really enthusiastic: for one thing I did not speak Portuguese—so essential in Brazil—and for another we were both worried over the health of our son Hamilton. So I requested that my name be withdrawn.

But the possibility left me wondering what post I should most prefer if another opportunity were offered. For me, as for my grandmother and Aunt Ruth, France was my "other country." They both spoke French fluently, they depended on French maids, and almost every stitch they wore was of French make. Donon catered to their taste for the French cuisine, and the Ritz had become their Parisian town house. Peggy and I had covered almost all of that glorious country by motor; the Exhibition of French artists at the Orangerie in Paris had given us an entrée we had never enjoyed before and the French government, in appreciation, had made me an Officer of the Legion of Honor. To be honest what I most wanted was to be Ambassador to France. But I lacked the confidence to say so.

Lunching in Washington with my father's friend and mine, Ambassador Grew, I told him of my talk with Secretary Dulles and he asked, "Bill, what would you really prefer?" "Our Embassy in Brussels," I replied (which was as much as I thought I could hope for). "Well, I don't see why you shouldn't have it." was his comment.

One of the nice things Douglas Dillon did for me while he was Ambassador to France was to have me invited to one of President Eisenhower's famous "stag" dinners at the White House. I was staying in Hobe Sound at the time but hastily flew up to Washington and on the afternoon of the party I stopped by to get the advice of Mrs. Mildred Bliss.

"Bill," she said, "this is the best opportunity you'll have. Ask for a good embassy—Paris would be perfect for you both. Doug Dillon will be leaving by the end of Eisenhower's first term."

I knew that the President liked me—Sherman Adams had told me so at the Republican Convention at San Francisco, when Ike was renominated—and I believed I'd have Christian Herter's approval, as we'd been friends for years. But I was embarrassed when I found myself sitting next to the President. What checked my tongue was the knowledge that Eisenhower particularly objected to anyone *pushing* himself to appointive office.

In the spring of 1957, before the news was public, I had a handwritten note from Douglas Dillon saying, "I am leaving Paris and I feel that you and Peggy should replace us. Get in touch with all your political friends and push your candidacy as hard as you can. . . ." This was obviously the moment to make my bid, to seek the help of Ambassador Grew, Sherman Adams, and Senator Vandenberg, but I held back.

The Paris appointment went to Amory Houghton, president of Corning Glass, a man of ability and utmost charm. His father had been our Ambassador to Germany in 1922–1925, and then for three years to the United Kingdom. Ike was fond of Amory, but "Am," whom I much admired, was still recuperating from prolonged and successful operation for cancer of the tongue and he pled with the President to be excused. But Ike wanted him to cope with de Gaulle and Houghton rose to the challenge, aided by his resourceful wife Laura, and my friend Cecil Lyon, his Deputy, who shared some of the burden.

As Ambassador Grew had predicted, I was offered our Embassy in Belgium, and, being still in the mood of renunciation, I sincerely declined it. I thought at the time, it was France or nothing. The Museum of Modern Art was more demanding than I had anticipated; my family company was thriving in the "good Eisenhower years," my mind was preoccupied by the imperatives of air power.

It was a coincidence that while I was attempting to dismiss Paris from my thoughts, the Council of French-American Societies, an affiliation of all the Francophile groups in New York, elected me their chairman. I was to succeed Amory Houghton. General de Gaulle had returned to power and with characteristic self-confidence was disarming the French generals who were rebelling against his colonial policy. I felt it would be appreciative for the Societies to give a formal banquet in his honor at the Waldorf and I was confident that as many as two thousand guests would attend in full dress to hear him speak. The General was pleased at the prospect of coming to the United States and a date was set.

*   *   *

It was at this time that we were invited to join David and Peggy Rockefeller, and Jack and Mari Watts on a flying trip to South Africa, Belgian Congo, and Rhodesia, sponsored by the Council on Foreign Relations which felt that Americans should be better informed about these sensitive areas. We were to travel on a very tight schedule—only one day in Leopoldville —and what impressed us most were the sharp contrasts between the European colonial and the African native, as these notes, written by Peggy, will show.

Johannesburg, the center of the gold mining territory, is situated on the southern slopes of the Witwatersrand range, on one of the most elevated spots in the Transvaal. In 1886 they had a real gold rush like our own, in fact the city still looks much like an overgrown mining town in our West, with wooden frame buildings and huge mounds of "tailings" around the outskirts. We were taken to see a modern "Township" built by the government outside the city for its African workers. No Africans are allowed to stay in the city at night, but must commute to the townships by train, showing their passbooks or identity cards each day. They particularly resent this. There were row upon row of identical cinder block houses, Bantu schools, and a YWCA, where the girls were taught cooking, typing, etc.

Dinner given by Mr. and Mrs. Fred Bamford that evening. They have a lovely house and rose garden in a suburb. The women guests were beautifully dressed and well groomed—rather better than their equivalents in England. They live in terror of native attacks and show you double locks, sirens and the flood lights outside are left on all night. They have huge dogs—police dogs or boxers. Although they give lip service to improving race relations, they feel at heart that the natives are really savages and, as they put it, "not ready to sit down and have tea with." All the servants, who wear white uniforms with scarlet sashes, come from native tribes, and still go to witch doctors and once in a while a member of the tribe is killed so that some of his organs can be used for rituals against the evil spirits.

The following evening we dined at "Court House" owned by Charles Engelhard and Gordon Richdale and decorated by "Sister" Parrish. Very grand house with large swimming pool; English furniture and some good pictures. There we met Sir Ernest Oppenheimer, who invited us to fly down to his gold mine empire at Welkomin, in the Orange Free State.

At the entrance to the refinery, native miners did a tribal dance for us, dressed in skins and feathers. They seemed to enjoy this hugely, stamping about and imitating crocodiles and monkeys, and would have gone on for hours. We saw the molten gold being poured into bricks—so hot that you had to wear a shield and heat-proof aprons. Most impressive was the Oppenheimer Hospital—staffed by a Belgian nursing order of nuns with scrubbed, happy looking faces. This hospital had remarkably modern equipment. The cases were sixty percent mining accidents and forty percent infectious diseases.

The miners are brought in from the country and generally stay two years, in which time they earn enough to buy a wife. They have to give the father-in-law enough money for two or three cows. If the marriage breaks up this is returned—a very stabilizing influence on the marriages! For the most part the miners are single, living in huge hostels (three or four thousand men in each) which are locked at night. We saw the enormous vats of beer and the meali-meali (corn) which is the staple food. These hostels all have tribal dance arenas, providing space for the favorite exercise which the men do for two to three hours a day.

We then flew on to Kruger Park with Fritz and Olga Fuerst, the manager of Engelhard Timber. They drove us through the Park with an English guide and a ranger. We saw several giraffes, tall and prehistoric looking; herds of zebra and wildebeest; little gray monkeys with black faces taking their families for an outing; and many different kinds of buck—literally hundreds of impala. One hungry and sick looking hyena came right up to the car looking for a handout. We stayed at the Engelhards' guest house at Sabi, and next day drove through magnificent rolling timber country, thickly planted with pines—then back across the endless veldt to "Joburg."

On to Salisbury, where we had cocktails with the Governor-General of Southern Rhodesia Sir William Pawlett. They had beautiful crested cranes strolling over the lawn and marvelous blue and white agapanthus. Met H. E. Lord Dalhousie who founded the university of that name in Nova Scotia. Salisbury boasts the first Museum of Modern Art in Africa, a beautiful building without, as yet, many outstanding pictures.

We had dinner with Kay and Walter Hochschild and next day Bill went to the copper mines, and I went to the Ruins of Zimbabwe, which lie between the Zambezi and Limpopo rivers, built by an unknown civilization probably 1000–1500 B.C. The ruins are surrounded by an elliptical wall, 34 feet high and 830 feet around, surrounding a high conical tower, probably a phallic symbol, and many inner walls and corridors, all built without cement or mortar.

Zimbabwe is supposed to be the Ophir of Solomon's time, and the Queen of Sheba lived there. Here Solomon got gold, ivory and peacocks. It is a majestic monument to pre-European man. Granite boulders, some like spines, some like domes, rise out of rich vegetation fantastic in their forms.

There were successive migrations by sea to East Africa. The Persians settled at Zanzibar. Then came Chinese, Indians, Arabians and Phoenicians and Egyptians from the Nile Valley. They all employed slave labor and all mined gold.

> "The broom of Time has scattered the writings
> on these walls of silence . . . ."
> "Into the darkness whence they came
> They passed; their country knoweth none
> They and their gods without a name

Partake the same oblivion
Their work they did, their work is done
Whose gold, it may be, shone like fire
Above the brows of Solomon
And in the house of God's desire."

Capetown. We stayed at the Mt. Nelson Hotel, huge and
barrack-like, and filled with retired British seeking a warm
climate. At the Africaner Museum we saw colorful Bush-
man engravings and paintings on stone. They are much
like the Lascaux paintings except for the men, who are
attenuated and wear animal heads when they go hunting.
They made them on open rocks or boulders, from the Late
Stone Age—10,000 B.C. to the 19th century. Bushmen are
the last race which plants nothing, but just hunts and
gathers food. They can be traced back to the Middle Stone
Age (50,000 to 10,000 B.C.). Their paintings are rock panels, scattered leaves of a vast chapter of the human history.

The Cape has 16,000 varieties of wild flowers. We saw
many of them at the Botanical Garden in Stellenbosch.
There were tree ferns, the oldest form of plant life, estimated at 3,000 years old. Also papyrus, blue and white
agapanthus, and small succulents that look like pebbles.
Suddenly they crack open and a small yellow flower comes
out.

Battswood Training College. We had a letter from Harold
Hochschild to Professor van der Ross, the head of the college and a Ph.D. He was very bitter about the fact that he
had six white assistants under him, all of whom get paid
twice what he does. He himself was what they called "colored"—not African, not white, but partly East Indian,
dark skinned but not negroid. He said they were starved for

books. The Carnegie Corporation has sent over a library of books on American history and many biographies. He showed where girls are trained in home economics, cooking, sewing and baby care. He also showed us the Art School and the pathetically bare science laboratory.

The Professor took us back to his house, which was in a mixed colored and white neighborhood. He said that new laws would force them to leave that section and move to an entirely colored one. There were three generations at his house. The grandfather looked distinctly Chinese, the grandmother East Indian. The latter was particularly bitter, and said: "Every day we have fresh humiliations, and our color is thrown in our faces as if there was something evil about not having a white skin. I hope my children move out of this country, where there is no opportunity for them."

The Professor's wife said that when she visited New York she was asked what she thought of the tall buildings. She replied that she was so astounded at the freedom with which colored people moved in and out of the buses and stores that she had no eyes for anything else. They told us the phrase "trying for white," which means that the light colored ones try to get into white movies, etc.

Stellenbosch. Mr. Anton Ruppert, millionaire head of Rembrandt Tobacco Co., received us in his air-conditioned office. He is reputed to have done more for South Africa than any other individual. He showed us around the university and the town, which is in a beautiful valley between towering mountains. It is completely a university town, on the order of Williamsburg, and has many old buildings which he hopes will be restored. We visited an aquarium and a fish hatchery. We also saw Groot Constanzia, the first great homestead built in 1685, a manor house of one of the first Dutch settlers. It had vineyards and big barrels of wine in the cellar.

Hermanns. We took a spectacular drive around False Bay —a huge bay surrounded by towering mountains, which the early settlers mistook for Capetown. Hermanns is a small seaside resort on the Indian Ocean. A very cold stream comes up here from the South Pole, but, undaunted, Peggy R plunged in. On coming out she simply shook her hair and it fell into natural curls—what luck!

Beautiful wild flowers all along the way.

Dinner at Bill Maddox, our Chargé d'Affaires. I sat next to Dr. Kiedericks, Minister of Foreign Affairs. He said I should go into the country and see how the natives were living happily in huts, just as in the Stone Age. Bill Maddox said the central problem of the Union was how two races could live in harmony when the dominant one needs the labor of the other, but is outnumbered 10 to 1.

Praetoria, the seat of government is like a Dutch town with bright flowers everywhere lighting up the government buildings. It is famous for its jacaranda trees, which line the avenues; they bloom with huge mauve flowers in October and November at which time the city has a jacaranda festival.

Four miles from Praetoria is the huge granite Vortrekker Monument, a memorial to the Boers who fought their way across the continent against the Bantus and the British in the Great Trek of 1834–1838. They traveled in covered wagons much like our early American ones only they used oxen instead of horses. At night they made a circle of the covered wagons for safety and this monument is a circular one in memory of them, with wagons carved in stone on the exterior. The central figure at the entrance is a Voortrekker woman shielding her two children from the dangers of barbarism. . . .

*   *   *

We returned to New York in early March wondering which of those countries would be the first to break away from the traditional bondage. Belgian Congo or Rhodesia? A far-reaching adjustment in South Africa would not, I thought, come soon. Over the years Peggy and I had become inveterate travelers and this spring which seemed particularly lovely it was a relief to relax after so much flying and enjoy the weekends with our sons and friends at Mt. Kisco.

But it was not for long. I was staying with Shirley at Beverly Hills, sitting by the pool after a Lockheed meeting when there was a telephone call from Douglas Dillon, the Under Secretary of State, to say that Clifford Folger had resigned as Ambassador to Belgium, and would Peggy and I take on the job? It is not often that one is offered the same post twice in government. I spoke to Peggy and this time she agreed without hesitation; Hamilton, as it turned out, in our absence was happy to be "the man of the house."

On my flight home I began to list the essentials to brighten our stay in Brussels. I knew the Belgians were gourmets and it was a stroke of luck that before my appointment David Bruce, who was withdrawing as our Ambassador to West Germany, had written to ask if I would like his superb cellar of Bordeaux wines, including fifty cases of irreplaceable Château Blanc, 1947. I gladly accepted, and the two truckloads that were delivered from Bonn, together with the wines I brought over from New York, *made* my reputation. We also took with us some of our favorite paintings and our Cadillac on which, as usual, I had ordered all the chrome work to be painted over. I was sure that Folger on his return would give me some useful pointers about the Embassy staff which numbered about 135.

Cliff Folger, who had been chairman of the Republican Finance Committee for Eisenhower's reelection, was competent, likable and American as apple pie. He had been rewarded with the Belgium Embassy (after I had declined) and gave me a very amusing account of his ambassadorial experience. The Brussels World's Fair was the major attraction during his two years abroad; he basked in its limelight and entertained the prominent visitors, especially the many Congressmen who came over to see it. And he endeared himself to the Royal Family by his careful arrangement for open heart surgery of young Prince Alexandre. This had been carried out successfully at the Massachusetts General Hospital in Boston and former King Leopold and his beautiful wife Liliane felt deeply grateful.

On the other hand neither Cliff nor his wife Kay spoke French and although they were only a short distance away from some of the best restaurants in Europe they shared the American prejudice against "foreign food" with the result that Cliff habitually ate lunch in the dismal Embassy cafeteria, "the only place in Brussels where you can get a decent sandwich." I am sure Cliff handled substantive matters with authority and, incidentally, he taught King Baudouin how to mix a good martini, for which future diplomats will be thankful.

After a perfunctory confirmation by the Foreign Relations Committee I was sworn in by Secretary of State Herter, a family affair with Peggy, Bill, his wife and Ordway present. Moms was her usual loving self although privately she thought I was taking a menial post in a small country when I should have been going to Paris.

Once these formalities were completed I was given a sketchy

briefing by the Benelux "desk officer," William C. Sherman, a nice intelligent young man over whose desk all messages from Belgium, Holland and Luxemburg must pass. The principles which guide such officers are two: first, things are not as bad as they seem, and, secondly, if you leave a problem alone, it will cure itself. As it happened, I was the last Ambassador both to Belgium *and* to the Belgian Congo; I was informed that the Congo would soon be granted independence, perhaps with some friction but nothing really to worry about. Thereafter there would be a separate ambassador to the Congo and the ball would be in his court.

No one warned me that if there was a real explosion in the Congo it would be followed by instant repercussions in the United Nations and that Cabot Lodge would be busy placating other African nationals. Of course I should have talked with him before the fat was in the fire; whether or not the Department so suggested.

Instead, come what may, I intended that our embassy would be as inviting (and stylish) as I could make it. I knew that the Residence in Brussels had a small dining room holding twenty at most, and as the Belgians love food I thought we'd surprise them with something different from the Folgers' steak dinners. We brought with us an excellent French chef, Joseph Carbone one of the best butlers I ever had, Pierre Chevalier, together with some of our finest paintings. We spent a few days at the Ritz in Paris where for the first time I heard myself addressed as "Your Excellency." Then we took a Sabena plane to Brussels. We were welcomed by Anthony Freeman, my DCM (Deputy Chief of Mission) and thirty-five members of the Embassy staff; their cordiality made up for my disappointing impression of the "Residence" which was no larger than a middle size house in uptown New York. True, there was a capacious living room, a fine sweeping staircase, and our private quarters above with its intimate dining room and sitting room were attractive. But there was not a single bookcase for the scores of reference books I had brought along, so I had them built. In moderate size legations, such as ours, a Chancery is often a part of the Residence which facilitates a constant interruption of the Ambassador. What was worse, when the crises loomed up in the Congo the people in Washington would hold a crash meeting in the evening and haul me out of bed at 3 a.m. *my time* for an accurate analysis of the situation. This happened with increasing frequency.

My Deputy, "Tony" Freeman, had served under eight "political" Ambassadors, including Claire Boothe Luce in Rome, and was one of the best in Foreign Service, a linguist—he was fluent in four languages including Mandarin Chinese—who easily adapted himself to the idiosyncracies of each "political appointee." A few of mine momentarily troubled him: I insisted that we address each other formally as "Mr. Ambassador" and "Mr. Counsellor." Again, when he told me that I was supposed to call on every other ambassador in Brussels—there were one hundred and thirty-five—I balked and we compromised on thirty-one.

We had arrived in early October at the beginning of the hunting season and for our first weekend were guests of our old friends, Baron René and Thilda Boel, at their palatial Château du Chenoy where a genial party was preparing to shoot. But neither Peggy nor I liked the sport and she rebelled (inwardly) at being photographed on the steps of the Château with the morning's massacre spread out below, surrounded by proud gamekeepers, "the guns," and their ladies. "What a glorious sight—400 hare!" as someone remarked. I believed I could get the information I wanted without gunning for it, but we had to submit to several such ordeals until the word spread that we preferred to eat game rather than kill it.

After a fortnight things were running smoothly thanks to our clever maître d'hôtel, Adolphe, who was proud of our chef and pleased to have an ambassador who knew as much, if not a little more, about wine than he did. Our official driver, Benoit, was amused by the comments on our car of one tone, without any glitter of chrome. The word passed that it was an armored car to which Benoit, with a sober face, remarked, "The Ambassador would not have it otherwise," leaving the questioner to wonder.

Brussels is remembered for its rainy, foggy nights, such as Sherlock Holmes liked to prowl in and it was a very wet evening when we gave our first formal dinner for John McCone, then Chairman of the Atomic Energy Commission. To meet him we invited a number of Belgian officials and industrialists, including the head of the public utilities company. The instant we sat down *all* the lights went out, including those in the kitchen and, in fact, throughout Brussels. Our resourceful Adolphe produced hundreds of candles—apparently this was not unusual—but the public utilities magnate in his evening clothes, armed with a flashlight, dashed out in the dark, reached the nearest generating station and the lights in the Residence were blazing before he returned.

I recalled how the same thing had happened when I was visiting the Cerro de Pasco Mine in Peru. Instantaneously we lost all electrical power in the village and in the mine where the pumps ceased to operate and the water began to rise. The chief engineer of the mine was a huge Russian who said simply, "I fix." He seized a giant sledgehammer, raised it on high and struck the generator with tremendous force. Immediately electric current was produced, the lights and pumps started up again—it was just like a grandfather hitting the electric train he'd given the grandchildren for Christmas and smiling as it came to life.

On the day I presented my credentials I was escorted to the

Palace by a regiment of cavalry in full dress. King Baudouin, who was in his thirtieth year, was a modest, pleasant, intelligent man and we got along well on my first appearance at Court. Our mutual interests were sports cars, science and aerospace. He complimented me on my French (better than Folger's, if not as fluent as the King said), and it pleased him that I wore my decorations, which in addition to the Legion of Honor, included the Order of El Sol de Peru, Commander, Cruzeiro do Sul, Brazil, Commander of the Order of Merit, Federal Republic of Germany. The diplomatic corps were present with their wives and I frankly enjoyed the brief, colorful ceremony.

Belgium was unique in supporting two monarchs within its modest frontiers. The deposed king, Leopold III, resided in the Palace of Lacken with his second wife Liliane. He lost favor in 1935 when Queen Astrid, who was very popular, died following an automobile accident with the King driving. He lost his nation's respect at the time of the invasion of 1940 when he capitulated to Hitler, preventing the extermination of Belgian troops but without sufficient warning to his French and British allies. He declined to follow Premier Pierlot and his famous Minister of Foreign Affairs Spaak, who established a government in exile in London. After the invasion of June, 1944, the Germans removed the King and his family to the Austrian village of Strobb near Salzburg where he enjoyed the skiing and he was eventually released by the Americans under General Patch. The Government in Exile on its return refused to make public apology to the King for their accusations and Leopold was subsequently relegated to a comfortable, if private life.

*   *   *

I was fortunate to have such a close friend in René Boel, a man of marked capability and joie de vivre. His first marriage to the daughter of the founder of "Solvay" had led to his taking control of that great enterprise and after her death he married the lovely and younger Thilda. I had seen him frequently in New York, in Brazil, and in London, where he joined other Belgians in exile during the war. Thilda, to avoid the Nazis, had brought their children to Washington, and we loved her. René was there on and off.

Fond as we were of René and Thilda, the winter weekends in their château—or any other—were something of a hardship as their immensely thick stone walls absorbed the cold, and there was no central heating. The morning coffee when it arrived in our bedroom was always lukewarm. As we spent many weekends with the Boels, we decided to buy six Hermes thermoses to assure us of hot coffee while we dressed. Thilda, who rarely thought of creature comfort, said, "Thank you for the lovely coffee pots. We're going to use them in our town house." I was defeated, as I was again later when I accompanied her on a shopping trip in Brussels. She finished her chores at 1 p.m.— lunch time in any language. I was famished and as we drove through town we passed the "Filet de Sole," a well-known restaurant where I mildly suggested we stop for lunch. "Oh, no," she replied, "it will be much quicker to just eat a banana in the car on the way back." Later I described the situation from my point of view, and it became a standing joke, which she tells, too.

During the Christmas festivity it was René who warned me of the trouble beneath the surface. The Belgians did not look forward to the emancipation of the Congo; the Congolese they felt were not ready for it. But ready or not the spirit of independence was contagious throughout Africa. The tribal leaders had attended the Brussels World's Fair in 1958 and for the first time they met together and listened to each others' aspirations. Now on January 20th, 1960, they returned for a Round Table discussion. The meetings went on for a month. While they were in progress I met Patrice Lumumba, leader of the Congolese National Movement, a tall, intense spellbinder, and Joseph Kasavubu, his most serious rival for the presidency of the emerging state.

At the conclusion of these talks King Baudouin set June 30, 1960, as the date for the declaration of Congo's independence. In the interim, elections would be held in mid-May for the Provincial assemblies and a National Parliament. The Parliament would then elect a Chief of State and a Premier to head what would obviously have to be a coalition ministry. But hardly had the procedures been announced than the physical struggle began for who should be top dog. The riots were sporadic but they increased in violence.

The Ministry of Foreign Affairs was of course the branch of the Belgian government with which I was most concerned. It was headed by Pierre Wigny, a professor at the University of Louvain before he entered politics, who had worked for several years in the Brussels branch of the Guarantee Trust Company without learning English or gaining even a vague comprehension of it. As the Congo crisis developed I had innumerable interviews with the Foreign Minister. Wigny preferred that our talks be conducted in French and without an interpreter. At the outset I had the uneasy feeling that he had not understood what I was struggling to say in French and that I may not have fully comprehended his views when I attempted to restate them for Freeman. Our diplomatic exchange was further complicated by Wigny's irritating habit of outlining his case in the academic manner as if he were lecturing. Almost every conversation began with: Point un. Then Point deux, and by the time he reached Point *dix* I had lost the thread.

I had, however, been working on my French with an excellent teacher, Guy Toebosch, three one-hour lessons a week, without

Swearing-in ceremony as Ambassador to Belgium; Leslie, Bill, Peggy and myself; Secretary of State, Christian Herter; Ordway

Escort of Belgian Cavalry on First Visit to Palace

fail, and these became a gradual help. But I had to find some channel of communication with the Belgian Ministry which would bypass Wigny and with "Tony's" help found it in Jean (now Baron) Van den Bosch, the no. 2 in the Ministry, highly intelligent, very pro-American and bilingual, a permanent official. He realized the obtuseness of his political "boss" and at some risk to his career he enlightened me. He and his charming wife Hélène became our good friends, and he went on to be the popular, highly effective Ambassador to the United Kingdom. I depended on the clandestine meetings with Van den Bosch to get my points across. With his diplomacy and as my French improved, an adequate communication with Wigny was established.

The wealth of the Belgian royal family had been acquired by Leopold II. At the Congress of Berlin in 1884 he skillfully persuaded the great powers to recognize his personal Association du Congo as the valid government of almost a million square miles of African territory. Belgian Congo, as it came to be, was eighty times as large as Belgium, and after the discovery of copper it was known to have immense mineral resources, especially in Katanga Province. The humanitarian movement slowly moderated Leopold's ruthless slave labor; the missionaries slowly spread elementary education and by the time of my mission the more powerful tribal leaders were expecting liberation and vying with each other for control.

In March Peggy and I set out on my first and intensive inspection of five of the six provinces of the Congo. Their size is indicative of their importance:

Province	Capital	Popular Names	Population	Number of Europeans	Elevation
Leopold-ville	Leopold-ville	Leo	366,790	16,790	1,007 ft.
Kasai	Luluaburg		61,202	3,202	2,077 "
Katanga	Elisabeth-ville	E-ville	170,344	13,344	4,035 "
Kivu	Bukavu		34,696	4,696	4,790 "
Oriente	Stanley-ville	Stan	71,040	5,040	1,404 "
Equateur	Coquilhat-ville (not visited)	Coq	31,400	1,400	1,214 "

We were accompanied by Stanley Cleveland, the senior economic officer in the Embassy, an extremely intelligent man of about thirty-seven who spoke perfect French and who, during his stay in Brussels, had gotten to know all the Congolese leaders that had come to Brussels as well as the principal Belgian officials. We also had my assistant, Steve Petschek, a classmate of Bill's, and his delightful wife Sue along with us to help on reporting the trip.

We flew first to Leopoldville, the capital, a modern city with a population of 366,790, almost as hot as Washington in summer but more depressing because of the very high humidity and the growing apprehension of riots. Order was maintained by the "Force Publique," a military police made up entirely of Africans through the rank of noncoms and commanded by Belgian officers. It had proved efficient but numbered only 25,000 to cover the entire country. They had been able to put down the small riots thus far but the violence between the various tribes was rising.

One of the conspicuous institutions in Leopoldville was the

University of Lovanium, the Catholic university organized in cooperation with the University of Louvain in Belgium. The rector, Monsigneur Gillon, was very energetic, more of a fund raiser than a scholar, a type which one finds at home. He succeeded in raising government and private funds for the construction of a really monumental university, well situated on a hill about twenty miles outside of Leopoldville. But pathetically, there were only 248 African and 117 non-African students in residence. The first graduating class of *five students* received their degrees in July of 1958, which was indicative of the grave shortage of university graduates at this critical period.

Actually, there was a shortage of Congolese who had been to secondary schools, to say nothing of universities. The Belgians provided more primary school education than in any other colony in Africa, for some 1,200,000 children, which was not bad out of the total population of thirteen million. Yet only three or four thousand had gone on to the secondary schools. This was a deliberate policy on the part of the Belgians, who thought that if they did not provide higher education to the Congolese, the natives would not develop political ambitions. They developed their political ambitions anyway in keeping with the political movements throughout Africa, and the immediate problem for the emerging Congolese government was to elect 400 members to the new Chamber of Deputies and the Senate, which meant that 400 of the educated Congolese would be transferred either from government or business life to the world of politics.

At the Department of Education I heard the belated plans to expand secondary school education. There were government and missionary schools, both Catholic and Protestant, some run by American missionaries. However, they all taught a curriculum modelled on that in Belgium. The church schools spent a great deal of time on theology, which the Africans consider unproductive. Far too much time was devoted to the history of Belgium, and too much emphasis on Latin and Greek than is justified for an emerging state needing as *many* people as possible *reasonably* well educated.

At the time all instruction was in French but the Congolese naturally were anxious to have it done in native languages, with French taught only in the upper grades. Until 1958 the teaching of English was discouraged. French, of course, was compulsory and Flemish (hardly a very useful language for the Congolese) was the only second language. When English became available, approximately eighty percent of the Congolese who wished a second language chose English. I sat in on several English classes, but a Flemish-speaking Belgian teaching English in French could hardly produce satisfactory results. The Congolese were very anxious to get as many English teachers to the Congo as possible and I hoped to be able to help them.

On March 12 we flew from Leopoldville to Luluaburg. Luluaburg is the capital of Kasai Province and had been in the press recently because of the serious rioting which took place between the Lulua and Baluba tribes. We had on our plane Albert Kalonji, the leader of the Mouvement National Congolais (M.N.C.) party. It was expected there would be a large political demonstration in his honor and the Provincial Governor took no chances on our getting involved in it. When we landed we found a Sikorsky helicopter with the rotor idling right alongside, in which we were flown to the Governor's residence over the line of the parade in honor of Kalonji, some fifteen or twenty thousand natives lining the streets. We were impressed with the Governor's description of the rioting between the tribes. He thought it will take years before this antagonism can be subdued.

Unfortunately I was laid up for a couple of days in Luluaburg with the usual "African complaint," so I was unable to accompany Peggy and the rest on their visit to the King of the Bakubas. She had stood up well under the heavy schedule and the heat but she now decided to return to Brussels and then to New York to be with our boys during their Easter vacation. On the flight she wrote these notes of what she had seen.

"The purpose of our trip was for Bill to talk to as many Congolese leaders and Belgian officials as possible, to learn from them what their most pressing needs are, and how the U.S. in cooperation with Belgium, can best help them. Everywhere the question was asked: 'What is the U.S. going to do for us?' and 'When can my children come to America on a scholarship?' There are stacks of applications for scholarships on the desk of every leader with the pathetic hope that America will take care of them all.

"My first impression is one of turbulence—riots breaking out everywhere and martial law operating in the cities. A hundred and fifty people were killed in Elisabethville the weekend before we arrived, and there were soldiers in battle uniform at strategic street corners, barriers shutting off one section from another, and a curfew at night. Paratroopers had been dispatched from Kamina Air Base to deal with emergencies.

"In Leopoldville, in sharp contrast to the Union of South Africa, the African officials are beginning to be received by the Europeans at home, and we met nearly all the new leaders and their wives at a reception at our consulate and at other functions. The men all dress in European clothes, speak French, and would be perfectly at home anywhere. Their wives are literally hundreds of years behind them in evolution. I made a special point of asking to meet the leaders' wives in every city, as I was particularly interested in finding out how they were reacting to the new experience of mingling with the Europeans.

"At a very formal dinner at the Governor General's, the wives came in native dress (which is printed cotton, tied around them, and a turban), and every one of them had a baby strapped on her back. The babies were the best behaved I have ever seen. They didn't make a sound and nothing seemed to surprise them. When dinner was announced the Governor's wife asked the number 1 boy to take the babies into the kitchen and give them some milk. This was probably the first time they had been separated from their mothers during her waking hours, as they carry them on their backs until they can walk. But they did not cry.

"Belgians say that the Congolese are utterly unreliable about keeping appointments, and this was certainly proved at this dinner. Two or three who were expected did not turn up, and one came who had been invited for the previous week. This presents quite a problem for the aide who has to juggle the place cards around at the last moment, and he was tearing his hair out in despair.

"The women tend to stand or sit in *monumental* silence, and are pretty heavy sledding conversationally, partly due to knowing little French, and partly because the girls are just beginning to go to school. It was rather hard to find topics of conversation within the framework of their experience, but children, schools and clothes elicited some slight response. They have great natural dignity and I think handle these new situations remarkably well, considering that at home they serve their husbands' meals separately and sit on the floor in the background, eating with their fingers out of a communal bowl. The use of a knife and fork is something utterly new for them.

"The women marry at fourteen or fifteen and are apt to have a baby every year. They begin to look heavy in their twenties, although they have a magnificent carriage, and can swing along with the most incredible amounts of groceries and household goods on their heads.

"Eight tenths of the Congolese live in rural areas, and when I say *rural* I mean it! The women do all the hard work. They may start the day by having to walk a mile or so with a jug on their heads to get water, although some villages have a common watering trough where they can take their washing. (The African version of the Laundromat!) Then they must gather the manioc, which is their main staple, and pound it, standing up for this and using a pounder 8 or 9 feet long. They then cook dinner outside the grass huts and work in the fields the rest of the day, while the husbands offer helpful criticisms from a reclining position!

"In the towns and mining centers, the Belgians have replaced the grass huts with frame or cement block houses, consisting of two rooms, one for sleeping and one for everything else. The most valued possession next to a bicycle is a radio, which is the only thing that they will save money to buy. This is why we heard on all sides: 'The country that gives the Congo television will have the most spectacular influence on it.' The Russians have installed a network in Nigeria, and no doubt have their eyes on the Congo as well. The Russian-controlled Cairo broadcasts are continually blaring in African languages: 'The white man has everything—you have nothing. He lives in a fine house—you live in a shack. Rise up against him and claim your rights.'

"The missions are doing an extraordinary work both educationally and medically. The outstanding missionary that we met was a Texan, Dr. Poole, the 'flying surgeon,' who has established three clinics in the middle of the bush, to which he flies in his little plane from the main Mission hospital base. He treats between two and three hundred sick natives every day, and operates for everything from cataracts to appendixes!

"Dr. Poole invited us to visit these outposts and we flew in his single engine Piper Cub to what seemed to be the middle of nowhere, until we saw a little conglomeration of grass huts and a tiny air strip. This air strip had been made for him by grateful patients—the women stamping down the earth by doing tribal dances on it!

"The plane was immediately surrounded by tribal chiefs. I felt that I had stepped back into prehistoric times, as the local dignitaries with plumed headdresses, spears, and monkey fur skirts, with red powder on their hair and tatooings on their faces, swarmed around us, evidently finding us just as bizarre-looking as we found them. Some of the women were pygmies, unhampered by any clothing above the waist, with their heads either closely shaved or their hair knotted in dozens of three inch pigtails.

"Dr. Poole carries his stethoscope very obviously in front of him, and kept gesturing with it as a sign of medical authority. They all seemed to regard him with a certain awe, and believe me we stuck very closely to him, as we had heard that if they did not like some gesture or expression of a stranger, they pulled out their knives quickly.

"At the clinic (which was just a shed in the middle of the grass huts), he found a very ill woman on the floor who had had one twin three days before and was unable to have the

language. One of the missionary wives said to me plaintively: 'We get them all dressed up in white shirt and tie for Sunday School, and then on Monday they're back at the witch doctor's.' "

After Peggy's departure we inspected the mines beginning in Kolwezi, where the Union Minière has its great open-pit copper mine and refinery. Unfortunately the weather was extremely bad for this flight, and even more unfortunately, we were flown by a colonel who had not had very much flying time. When we got over the airport at Kolwezi and broke out under the hundred foot ceiling he was half way down the runway and at about a forty-five degree angle to it. After a couple of bounces he pulled up the wheels and started around again. This was hair-raising as he kept under the ceiling and one wing tip was practically dragging the ground. On his second attempt he was still about a third of the way down the runway when his wheels touched and was barely able to brake to a stop at the end of the runway. This was the most dangerous landing I had had in an airplane for a good many years.

At last on terra firma in Kolwezi we saw some magnificent open-pit copper mines and the very large new electrolytic copper refinery which will come into production in that June, and which represents an investment of some twenty million dollars. This was said to be the most highly automatized refinery in the world. The general attitude of Union Minière, which owns these giant mines, was that over the long run things will work out all right and that they will continue to show confidence in the new country by continuing to make investments and modernizing their properties. This has proved to be so.

Of all the provinces I visited Katanga was by far the richest in the Congo, as it contains very large copper mines, very rich uranium deposits and important diamond mines. A higher proportion of Belgian "colons" (or settlers) dwell in Katanga than anywhere alse. They are particularly annoyed at their own Belgian Government for having granted independence so rapidly to the Congo and a number of them have been agitating for a separatist movement, which would either make the Katanga an independent republic or join it to Northern Rhodesia, which is right next door. They feel that Katanga, being the richest province, would have to pay an unduly large part of the cost of maintaining the rest of the Congo. This argument, of course, always comes up in all federations and even in our own United States, where the population of rich states, like New York, are always objecting because their taxes pay a large part of the cost of federal sponsored highways in such states as Utah.

All in all, the Belgian settlers in Katanga have very much the same point of view towards the Congolese state that extreme right-wing Republicans had towards President Roosevelt when he came into office. They can see nothing good in the present situation and object to everything that is happening, although they don't have many ideas as to an alternative.

It seemed unlikely to me that Katanga would split off as a separate state, at least in the early stages of the new Congolese Republic. The Africans themselves do not like the idea and do not wish to join with Northern Rhodesia, where they would be under British domination. At Elisabethville, the capital, we stayed at the very comfortable Union Minière guest house and had many interesting meetings with the Governor, the heads of the Protestant University which is established there, and the African leaders.

Elisabethville, very cool and pleasant is at an altitude of 4,035 feet. There had been quite serious rioting the weekend before we got there. Patrice Lumumba, one of the leading African politicians, had just visited the town and a few days afterwards representatives of the rival party, the Conakat (which is backed by white settlers and which has been advocating an independent Katanga) staged an attack on his supporters. At least fifteen people were killed and a hundred or more seriously injured. But the riot was finally brought under control by the Force Publique, with the Conakat coming off a very bad second. The authorities feared there might be a further riot the weekend we were there. Fortunately, this did not take place.

On my return to Brussels I summarized what the United States was trying to accomplish in the Congo.

> 1. First, in the immediate future we hoped to establish prompt and effective diplomatic relations with the new Republic by sending down a good Ambassador and an American delegation to represent us at the Independence Day ceremonies on June 30. I would probably accompany them.

> 2. We must avoid leaving a vacuum which might be filled by Communist influences, as happened in the case of Guinea, where the French pulled out rapidly because of a feeling of "pique." Fortunately the Belgians will not do this; many of their civil servants want to remain.

> 3. The Congolese have a very warm feeling towards the United States and I think will welcome closer relations with us. We hope to be able to extend a modest amount of technical aid, in education, agriculture and communications. It will be necessary to send an American survey team down promptly to find what practical projects can be carried out within our rather limited financial appropriation.

The Congo is probably going to need very substantial financial assistance from the West over the years. This will have to come principally from Belgium, but it will probably be necessary for other countries, including our own, to join in. It will be one of my principal jobs to explore this and make recommendations.

The economy of the Congo is sound for the long term. It has more raw material resources, mineral and vegetable, than most of the countries of Africa. Naturally, it is suffering from severe financial difficulties at the moment. Government and private building has practically ceased in the last eight months (the government stopped building in order to balance the budget and private interests stopped building because of uncertainty about the political future). As a result, there is a great deal of unemployment. A further problem is that the population of the Congo, like most countries in the world, is increasing extremely rapidly.

I want to pay a tribute here to our American missionaries in the Congo. We visited several little missions in the bush and found them invariably selfless, dedicated, and fearless people, with very little to work with and a most unstable and unrewarding flock. One missionary's wife told me that one of her Sunday school pupils failed to appear in class, so she asked his classmates where he was. "Oh, my village had a special celebration yesterday and Joe had to be sacrificed," she was told.

In spite of giving medical care, clothes and teaching, the missionaries are in constant danger, and are aware that they would be the first to have their throats cut if there were any anti-white uprisings.

The first thing to remember about the Congo is that it is *tribal* in structure. There are seventy major tribes with four hundred different dialects, religions and customs, each hostile to the other. They are accustomed to the fierce authority of the tribal chief, and are reluctant to obey any central head of government if he comes from another tribe.

Ever since Leopold II bought this area (as large as the United States east of the Mississippi) as his private game preserve, the Belgians, and now the United Nations, have treated these six loosely federated provinces as one colony. This enforced political togetherness has nothing to do with reality, but seems a myth imposed on reality.

CHAPTER XIV

Brussels and the Congo

I RETURNED from those three weeks of nonstop inspection and assimilation realizing that the Congo, even in its partially developed state, was by far the richest of all the colonial empires, and that in its emancipation it might break up into quarrelsome tribal states or stumble into a gradually cohesive statehood. It could go either way and I suspected that the Soviet Union would be happy to see it dismembered. The outcome would depend on the loyalty of the "colons," the Belgian technicians responsible for the development of the resources— would they continue at their posts under black rule? Even more would depend on the ability of the relatively few educated Congolese leaders. I had been given a ringside seat in a struggle destined to be decided in a few months and, as in the days before Waterloo, diplomacy might be interrupted at any moment by bloodshed.

In early April my son Bill and his wife Leslie came to us for a short visit and on the evening of my fifty-fourth birthday, April eighth, we gave a dance in their honor at the Embassy. Bill was now working for the *Washington Post* and it was refreshing to get his view of the capital. Later in the month, after their departure, Peggy and I made an overnight flight to New York to attend the Council of French-American Societies' banquet for General de Gaulle. The flight over gave me a momentary breathing spell to piece together my impressions of Belgium.

At first sight Brussels appears a sober—Voltaire called it "torpid" and pragmatic, capital. Another Frenchman, when asked how he would compare Brussels to Paris remarked, "It's like going out with the sister of the woman you love." But in six months I had come to appreciate the charm, the judgment and the spirit which have prevailed through so many centuries of rough usage.

Belgium lies athwart the principal route from the Rhine to the English Channel and along that path have come conquerors, Gauls, Franks, Romans, the Spaniards, Napoleon, the Kaiser, and Hitler. Julius Caesar rated the Belgians the most courageous of all the Gauls. The country has lived under Roman, Frankish, Burgundian, Spanish (one of the best small hotels in Brussels, "L'Amigo," is on the site of the old Spanish jail), Austrian, French, and Dutch rule until 1830 without losing its character. Belgium is profoundly Catholic and the Court the last surviving Catholic Court in Europe.

It has been said that the Belgians are the most Germanic of the Latin peoples and the most Latin of the German people. The country is cut straight across into two divisions on a line as clearly marked as by a saw cutting through a plank: Flanders to the North, populated by Flamands who speak Flemish (and who imposed the teaching of Flemish on the Congolese), and Walloons in the South who speak French (and were equally insistent that the Congolese learn French). There are political as well as linguistic differences yet perhaps the skill with which Belgium composes these differences make Brussels the ideal meeting place for the Common Market and the like movements seeking European solidarity. From the year of its independence the country, out of respect for its two halves, has named its monarch, King of the *Belgians*.

Finally, there are those stalwart, small cities whose names are like battle flags: Antwerp, Bruges, Ghent, Ostend and Ypres in Flanders, Liège, Namur, Mons, Charleroi and Bastogne in Wallonia—and the famous University town, Louvain in Flemish Brabant, near Brussels. From earliest times, these city-states were known for their stubborn free will.

What immediately attracted me to the Belgians per se was their intense enjoyment of life. To them eating and drinking is a serious business and it is not coincidence that three or four of the ten best restaurants in all Europe are in Belgium. The aristocracy and middle class (thanks to the shrewd investment in the Congo) have the means to indulge their taste, and they do. Although one can motor the length of the country in a day, there are a number of old châteaux with large game preserves. The surplus of the shooting is sold to the markets, and one can dine on roebuck, a small deer with delicious flesh, wild boar, hare, pheasant and other wildfowl with delectable sauces— better cooked and far more plentiful than in New York. At dinner parties it is "de rigueur" to serve every dish *twice*—no wonder one may be at table for two hours.

Inevitably my thoughts returned to the Congo. Should the rioting become so widespread as to require the intervention of Belgian troops, the government, as I saw, had a powerful installation in the Kamina Air Base. It is very large and well manned, with 11,000 foot runways and elaborate facilities for training parachute troops and a substantial number of C-119s and C-47s. They were also running a jet training course, using French jet trainers, for military pilots in both the Belgian and Dutch Air Forces. The weather is so bad in Holland and Belgium that it is much more practical to do their air force training in the Congo.

One of the activities at the air base was a severe "survival course" which all parachute troops must take so as to prepare them in case they should be forced down in the jungle. They were required to cover 160 kilometers in the bush with no food except what they can either shoot or trap themselves. They each carried emergency rations, but if the emergency rations are opened the soldier flunked the course and could no longer stay in the parachutists. The troops were accompanied by one man who had complete rations. During the first half of the trip he cooked his meals at a distance away from the trainees so that they would not be disturbed, but in the last half he subjected them to psychological stress by cooking pleasantly aromatic (onions and garlic) and very flavorsome food in full sight of the starving troops. Approximately eighty percent of the "paras" passed this course successfully. In one case (we saw photographs of this) they succeeded in killing a thirty-foot python which had just swallowed a live antelope. They thereupon cooked the antelope and atc it. I spent two nights at Kamina and was impressed by the readiness for trouble.

It was good to be back in New York, if only for forty-eight hours. At the banquet, which was fully subscribed, Peggy, looking her loveliest on the receiving line, was flanked by myself and the tall, impressive de Gaulle. I introduced the General (in English), his French was eloquent and he concluded with an allusion to our long-standing alliance so crucial *in three wars,* that brought us to our feet. The following morning I went to Washington to report to Secretary of State Christian Herter who questioned me about the Congo and whether there were likely to be uprisings in the provinces once they became independent. I told him the Belgian government was confident the transition would be under control but that the rioting had made me dubious. Then we flew back to Brussels.

*   *   *

Three Congolese leaders emerged in the mid-May elections: President Joseph Kasavubu, who favored a loose federal rule and the retention of close ties with Belgium; his foremost opponent, Premier Patrice Lumumba, the radical, eloquent leader of a strong national party demanding total unity, and Moise Tshombe, the Premier of Katanga Province, one of the first to threaten secession. While the jockeying for political power went on in the Congo, the government calmly prepared the steps for the transfer of authority, assuming everyone would sit tight.

One of the most interesting personages we admired in Belgium was the dowager Queen Elizabeth, the Duchess of Bavaria, who had married King Albert I in Munich in 1900. When the German troops invaded Belgium in 1914 she and Albert courageously remained in an unconquered sector and she renounced her German heritage, saying in words now famous, that the Kaiser had erected "an iron curtain" between her native country and herself. She and Albert were adored and she lived on long after his death in a mountain-climbing accident in 1934. At our first meeting she questioned me about the Museum of Modern Art (proof that royalty does its homework), and smiled as I told her of our abortive effort to import a selection of Russian paintings from the Soviet Union. She was highly intellectual, interested in everything, and Peggy and I met her privately several times in her little château, Château du Stuyvenberg in Laeken. She was especially devoted to music, and had established a three-year revolving competition for young musicians, the first for pianist, the second for the violin, and the third for composition. The prize for the pianists in 1960 was won by an American, Malcolm Frager, and so it fell to us to give a bang-up luncheon for the Queen and the winner, and as many distinguished music lovers as we could seat, not in the dining room but in the more spacious living room of the Embassy. I really took pains over the menu (to be honest I knew more about appetizing food than about good music) and had my reward when I overheard René Boel say to his daughter Jacqueline, "You see, my dear, this is how a Queen should be entertained. Only the Burdens could do it."

There is an annual meeting of the United States ambassadors to Western Europe which is always well attended, if for no other reason than the pleasure of being in Paris in May. But this year the meeting had a special importance as it coincided with the preparations for the proposed "Summit Conference" between Eisenhower and Khrushchev, also to be held in Paris. Unhappily the Summit was never reached as Khrushchev angrily reprimanded the President for the Soviets' detection and shooting down of our U-2 reconnaissance plane near Sverdlovsk in Central Russia. The U-2 program had been conceived by Allen Dulles, after Edwin Land had perfected the high-altitude camera, and it might have been more discreet had the flights been suspended temporarily. As it was, the shooting down of Gary Powers put an end to détente for the time being and President Eisenhower cancelled his plans to visit the Soviet Union.

This was a temporary embarrassment for American diplomats, but we put aside our dismay at a spectacular dinner given by Baron and Baroness Philippe de Rothschild for the departing British Ambassador to Paris, Gladwyn Jebb. I remember the affair chiefly because we were served the finest Bordeaux I have ever drunk, not for anything witty Ambassador Jebb had to tell us in his farewell remarks.

Belgians are among the finest gardeners in the world. Perhaps it was their vile climate which prompted Leopold II to build the enormous Royal Greenhouses, with kilometer-long corridors, close to the Palace at Laeken. They cost him several million pounds and are permanently endowed to the tune of

£200,000. As a result the Royal Palaces are always decorated with a profusion of superb flowers. It is touching that when he knew he had only a few days to live, King Leopold had his bed made up in his favorite, the Palm House and there, before he died, he married his mistress, Baroness de Vaughan. Afternoon receptions are held in the Royal Greenhouses; the one we attended for the Shah of Iran was a lovely, fragrant affair.

King Baudouin's proclamation of Congo's independence on June 30th was the calm before the storm. On July 5–6 a unit of the *Force Publique* in Thysville mutinied against their Belgian officers; the mutiny quickly spread to Leopoldville and then to the other provinces, accompanied by pillage, looting and attacks on Belgian civilians, thousands of whom fled across the Congo River to safety in Brazzaville, capital of the French Republic of Congo just as others in Katanga found refuge across the border in Northern Rhodesia. Belgian troops—there were only 3,000 —immediately went into action and civil war hung in the balance. A fortnight after independence Lumumba showed his true colors by appealing to the Soviet Union for military assistance against "imperialistic aggression." He also appealed to the United Nations Security Council and in mid-July the first contingent of a peace-keeping United Nations force arrived at Leopoldville. This was according to the American policy although strongly criticized by the Belgian government.

I was on the telephone constantly with the Department, reporting Belgium's determination that they could cope *without the U.N.*, and more disturbing, that planes, trucks and personnel from the Soviet Union were being flown in. I was told that Herter and Dillon would be talking to Lumumba after he arrived in New York for a conference with Secretary General Hammarskjöld. Both meetings proved to be futile: evidently no one could persuade Lumumba to put his trust in the United

Nations rather than the Soviet Union. Allen Dulles flew to Brussels for a quick survey; he briefed me on the recent decisions of the National Security Council and he believed that the leader we could depend on in a showdown with Lumumba was young Colonel Joseph Mobutu, second in command of the Congolese army. It was at this juncture that I had a tip from Larry Norstad, an old friend from Air Force days who was then Supreme Commander of SHAPE, who told me that André de Staercke, the Belgian Ambassador to NATO, was a wise diplomat whom I must be sure to consult in Brussels or Paris. I did so, and found him as helpful as Baron Van den Bosch.

Dulles was right but it was Hammarskjöld who courageously broke the impasse: he led the U.N. troops (over 15,000) units mainly from Morocco, Ghana, Ethiopia, Guinea, Tunisia, into Leopoldville where they relieved the Belgian troops. Additional units from Sweden, Iceland and Canada arrived to replace the Belgians and when Hammarskjöld sequestered the airports for U.N. forces only he shut off further mischief from Russia. Flaming speeches by Lumumba incited the beating of eight Canadians in Leopoldville and a like number of airmen in Stanleyville, and at this President Kasavubu proclaimed the ouster of Lumumba and called on the United Nations to take over the responsibility for law and order. Results proved that the Belgian government could not extinguish the hatred of Colonialism as effectively as the U.N. Peace came slowly as Lumumba's power dwindled; finally a coup by Kasavubu and Colonel Mobutu brought about a consolidation and when Lumumba was murdered by his Congolese enemies, the sky began to clear. As I look back it seems unbelievable that civil war and the secession of the rich provinces were averted in less than a year and *by the intervention of a neutral force*. Today under President Mobutu Zaire is one of the most secure of the new nations in Africa.

The resistance was dragged out as long as there was any hope by the Soviets and their African allies, Ghana, Guinea and Mali. The Soviet Ambassador, a tough, implacable Communist bureaucrat, looked sullenly at me the few times our paths crossed. Probably, his intelligence having reported Allen Dulles's arrival, he suspected that the two of us framed Lumumba, which was not so.

However, there was a lull in September when King Baudouin announced his engagement to Dona Fabiola de Mora y Aragon, daughter of an old aristocratic Spanish family. Their courtship had been a well-kept secret, the King was popular and the preparation for the wedding in December dispelled the anxiety which had been hovering over Brussels for so many weeks. I had been dutifully on the alert, with many a night of broken sleep as late calls came through from Washington, and when Amory and Laura Houghton invited us to spend a weekend at the American Embassy in Paris we accepted with alacrity. During those very delightful days, Amory told me that if Nixon were elected they would urge him to appoint us as their replacement when they resigned in December. But I thought less of our chances after our return when we sat up to watch the Kennedy-Nixon debate on television. Kennedy was so much quicker and to the point in his responses that I felt Nixon was doomed, as was proved in the November election.

The atmosphere in Brussels as the date of the Royal Wedding on December 15 drew near was one of joy and optimism. Most of "the crowned heads of Europe" (the few that were left) were there except for the British who instead of being represented by Queen Elizabeth and Prince Philip sent Princess Margaret and her dismal Cockney consort, Lord Snowden. The sovereign who caught my eye was the redoubtable Queen Juliana of the Netherlands, possibly the richest woman in the world, and cer-

Peggy and the future Diplomatic Corps of the Congo

Luncheon for Queen Elizabeth of the Belgians

Before the Royal Ball, Brussels. Mrs. Wiley Buchanan, Mrs. Christian
Herter, myself, Secretary of State Christian Herter, Peggy
and Wiley Buchanan

tainly her jewels surpassed those of any other present. Her consort, Prince Bernhard, I had known slightly before, and we had a pleasant exchange about sports cars and airplanes.

The United States was represented by our very tall, aristocratic Secretary of State Christian Herter and his equally tall and distinguished wife, Mary Carey ("Mac" to her friends). They were accompanied by Wiley Buchanan, Chief of Protocol for the State Department and his wife, and as often happens in such affairs there was a shortage of tiaras for the ladies. "Mac" Herter had a beauty, but I had arranged to borrow a rather modest tiara from the New York jeweler Harry Winston on the rather vague "come on" that if Peggy liked it we might keep it. It amused me to discover that Wiley Buchanan had also borrowed one from the same source for his pretty wife.

The marriage was performed in the State church, the majestic Cathedral of Saints Michael and Gudule. It was built in 1215 and two superb towers were added in the fifteenth century. But the builders made no concession for those who, centuries later, and lightly dressed, must stand and kneel for three hours in the dead of winter. Peggy and I had never heard of thermal underwear; she in evening dress and I in white tie and tails, plus decorations, shivered. We particularly envied the heavy, handsome uniforms of the Knights of Malta, a Catholic order, warmly clad in gorgeous wool tunics, and thigh length black patent leather boots.

What revived us was the wedding reception at the Royal Palace after the ceremony. The enormous rooms of the large building were jammed with two to three thousand guests—the visiting delegations, the diplomatic corps, and hundreds of Belgian industrialists, officials and politicians. The food and wine were magnificent and the Belgians dove into both with the enthusiasm which has characterized the Flemish race since the

Middle Ages, and been so truly depicted by Brueghel. There were dozens of buffet tables before which they would line up, two or three deep, those in the first row holding their places until they had consumed at least two helpings *standing up*, then backing off until appetite compelled an attack on a different table with its fresh assortment.

The dinner dance at the Palace the night before the wedding was, of course, more elegant and restrained, and it was there that we had a most agreeable meeting with Bishop Sheen whose broadcasts had become so popular at home. We were waiting for our car when he appeared in his purple cape and robe. Peggy recognized him, and asked if he wouldn't like to see our Embassy. He accepted and we had a delightful talk. Yet the Royal Buffet, so like a British "rugby scrum"—except everyone was in full dress—was the sight I still remember.

We were to remain in residence until President Kennedy's appointee arrived in early March and in some ways those intervening months were most pleasurable. There was no longer the daily strain of uncertainty about the Congo. The collaboration between President Tshombe and Colonel Mobutu remained steadfast, and, after a second attempted secession of "a mining state," led by Albert Kalonji in Kasai Province, was put down, the tribal feuds began to subside. Many of the executive "colons" returned to their work. To the relief of Brussels, Zaire seemed to be a going concern.

An Ambassador's life is a combination of ceremonial—sometimes boring—functions, of personal, often very pleasant encounters from which he occasionally picks up valuable information, and of the most serious consultation with our policy makers in Washington. Because of the crisis which was shaping before I arrived, I was precipitated into the approaching liberation of the Congo, wondering if there were resourceful leaders with the power to prevent it from flying apart.

My Brussels diary reminds me of the flow of events, some trivial, some grave, which occupied us in the last half of 1960. For instance, a week after our ambitious luncheon for Queen Elizabeth in mid-June the Garry Nortons came for a visit and we took them to see the Grand Prix de Belgique at Spa, a blue-ribbon race on the fastest track in Europe. It was won by the Germans in their souped-up Mercedes, averaging 150 m.p.h. and although there were no fatal accidents, the danger of the track at that speed was so apparent that the authorities said never again.

On June 27 Edgar Sengier, who had been decorated by our government for having shipped invaluable uranium to the United States on his own responsibility before the war, called on me to return his Medal of Merit (the first bestowed on a foreigner) because he so resented the American criticism of Belgium in the Congo crisis. I persuaded him to give up the idea.

On July 1 my son Ordway, Shirley's son Carter, and their friends, Ralph Valentine and Bob Hale returned from Moscow and regaled us with their impressions of life under the Soviets.

On July 10 the Congo crisis was so threatening that I recalled "Tony" Freeman from his holiday on Elba and a few days later we flew to Geneva for talks with Ambassador Wadsworth and Undersecretary of State Dillon, our aim being to moderate the attacks on Belgium in the American press. The next two months leading up to Lumumba's death were a turning point.

Clare Booth Luce is always good company. In mid-September she flew in for a visit and we planned a special dinner for her. She waited until all our guests, some twenty, had arrived, then she swept down our long staircase in a spectacular dress, trailing a scarlet handkerchief gracefully in one lovely hand. She was greeted with the "Ohs" and "Ahs" she had expected and accepted the adulation with her cocktail.

During her ambassadorship in Italy she had suffered from a

mysterious ailment caused by arsenic impregnated dust which had been falling on her dressing table from the ceiling of her bedroom in Rome. An American physician had discovered the cause of her poisoning (whence the witticism, "Arsenic and old Luce"), now she was herself again and in high spirits. She reminisced with "Tony" Freeman who had been her DCM, and she made us laugh as she described the reticence with which Henry Luce, when in Italy, had accepted the part of her "Prince Consort." When they were entertaining she as the Ambassadress sat at the head of the table and she joined the men to talk after dinner as the ladies withdrew. When they were driven to formal functions she sat alone in the official limousine, Henry following after in a second car.

Clare is a good writer and after her resignation in 1956 she published in *Foreign Affairs* an article entitled "The Ambassadorial Issue: Professionals or Amateurs?" which is an objective analysis of the relative merits of career ambassadors and the so-called "political ambassadors." In any such comparison it is usually forgotten that *all* cabinet officers, undersecretaries, and assistant secretaries are "political appointees." The point is that those who represent us in the capitals of the countries with which we have the closest ties must be persons in whom the President has confidence—which would not necessarily be the case were they trained diplomats in order of promotion. Clare and I were in complete agreement on the second point that ambassadors to those posts where linguistic knowledge is imperative, as for instance, the Soviet Union, may be better served by an expert in our Foreign Service such as "Chip" Bohlen.

In 1959 President Eisenhower appointed Clare Ambassadress to Brazil and she was confirmed after strenuous opposition from Senator Wayne Morse of Oregon. To which Clare remarked that Senator Morse had never made any sense since he had been kicked in the head by a horse (the kick was actually true). But her tart words did not sit well with the Senate and she sensibly withdrew.

Clare told me that she spent $30,000 a year of her own funds on matters connected with her official duties. I said it had cost me more than that in Brussels and that I imagined Am Houghton in Paris and Jock Whitney in London had spent substantially more.

Later that autumn Peggy and I attended a very touching ceremony in Notre Dame de Laeken marking the twenty-fifth anniversary of the death of Queen Astrid. I flew to Washington to attend the luncheon at the White House for the Prince of Liège; reported the turn of events to Secretary Herter, and made reservations for the John Mason Browns to stay with us. (The talk he gave to our embassy staff was sparkling.) And the big meeting I had with Dillon on future plans for the Congo, principally financial, resulted in advantages to both sides— thanks to the confidences I had received from André de Staercke and Baron Van den Bosch. Gaining the trust of "the insiders" is the touchstone of diplomacy.

There are a number of good indoor tennis courts in Brussels and I tried to play there at least three times a week to offset the miserable weather and to work up a thirst. We saw a good deal of the Boels in these closing days. René had preserved a splendid wine cellar despite the German occupation. He told me that the instant he heard of their break-through he had all the bottles of his old wine buried beneath the many flower beds surrounding the château with the flowers in bloom carefully restored. As in all the great houses he bought his red Bordeaux and Burgundy in huge tuns, each holding the equivalent of 228 bottles. The year was stenciled on the tun and the wine remained in the wood for twelve to fifteen years before it was bottled and served.

This aging was ideal for the red burgundy but fatal for the white which turned brownish ("Maderisé") and lost its fine taste. I objected that this was nonsense, and proved it at my dinners by serving white burgundies that were in their prime of five and six years which is the French standard. I also served young Rhine, Saar and Moselle wines which I suppose they resisted in principle because they came from their traditional enemy, Germany. But they became converted very rapidly.

There is another custom that struck me as odd: the red wines are served in filled glasses on a tray, not poured from the bottle individually as we do. But whatever the differences the Belgians love wine and in Brussels are a number of small clubs which exist for the pleasure of good talk and good dinners. I was happy to become a member of "Club des 33" and shortly before our departure I gave a "diner de dégustation" for my gourmet friends and members of the club, of seven courses and twenty wines. The president of "33" raised his glass with this toast: "I cannot believe that anyone not a Belgian could have offered such a superb dinner with such superlative wines. My congratulations to Ambassador Burden."

Two great men, Jean Monnet of France and Paul Henri Spaak, are responsible for the creation of the European Economic Community. This was the first step in the eventual merger of Coal, Steel, "Euraton," and the Common Market in the "European Community" and Brussels has become its capital, with over 300 foreign representatives, many of whom are of ambassadorial rank. I applaud this consolidation and it is appropriate that Brussels which has weathered such turmoil and bloodshed should become the capital of "Eurocrats." I doubt if its hospitality is any more delightful than it was in my day.

Truly it is Peggy who deserves the praise for our mission. On our trip to the Congo she repeatedly sought out the native wom-

CAVIAR

BOLLINGER 1952 magnum

DOM PERIGNON 1952 magnum

BERNCASTELER DOCTOR 1949
Wachstum Wwe Dr H. Thanisch

CONSOMME DE CANARD SAUVAGE

SCHARZHOFBERGER AUSLESE 1957
Von Egon Muller zu Scharzhof

TURBOT SAUCE RICHE
POMMES DE TERRE NOUVELLES

CHATEAU LAFITE 1945 magnum
CHATEAU LAFITE 1947 magnum
CHATEAU CHEVAL BLANC 1947

SELLE D'AGNEAU BOUQUETIERE
TRUFFES

RICHEBOURG 1945 magnum
Grivelet
CORTON GRANCEY 1945
Louis Latour

MOUSSE DE BECASSINE
SALADE MIMOSA

MONTROSE 1928
COS D'ESTOURNEL 1928

FROMAGES

NIERSTEINER PETTENTHAL 1953
Trockenbeerenauslese
Iermanshof Weingut–Franz Karl-Nierstein am Rhein

SORBET DE MANDARINES

SCHLOSS VOLLRADS 1953
Trockenbeerenauslese
Graf Matuschka Greiffenclausche

FRAISES

FINE CHAMPAGNE 1900–caves de l'Hôtel Ritz
GRANDE FINE CHAMPAGNE–Réserve no 6-Régnaud
GRAND BAS-ARMAGNAC 1918–J. Beyrie
EAU DE VIE DE MARC 1935–Marquis d'Angerville
VIEILLE FRAMBOISE–Broussault
CHARTREUSE JAUNE–Pré-Expulsion
GRAND MARNIER–50 ans d'âge.

February 26, 1961

en and her sympathy and understanding penetrated the barrier of language. Wherever we went she was accepted not as an alien but as an ally. In Brussels she was recognized as the perfect hostess and within the Embassy her solicitude for the members of the staff won their hearts. I remember her attention to Queen Elizabeth, her praise of the American pianist, her happiness in being with Thilda Boel, and her admiration for John McCloy. At our last gathering in March, 1961, the American Embassy wives composed their affection for her in some verses:

To Mrs. Burden
with affection and warm appreciation
from the American Embassy wives
Brussels, Belgium
1961

Farewell to Peggy,
Not of our choice
Parting's a sorrow
We had no choice.

Over the ocean,
Though she departs
With her she'll take
Part of our hearts.

Happy our memories
May hers be too
Pleasures we shared
Now seem too few.

Blessings in plenty,
All of the way
Joy through the years
Godspeed, we pray.

CHAPTER XV

IDA and the Smithsonian

AFTER her trip to Paris when Aunt Ruth was dying, my mother resolved never to go abroad again which explains why she did not desire to visit us in Brussels. She was approaching her eightieth birthday and lived quietly in her apartment below ours at 820 Fifth Avenue. I had built a staircase connecting the two and on our return in 1961 the light in her eyes showed how happy she was to have us once more within easy reach. Both Peggy and I had been subject to a rather tight schedule in Belgium and in 1961 we resumed our relaxed weekends at Mt. Kisco, and began to catch up with our sons and grandchildren.

Because of our years in Washington the four boys had all attended St. Alban's School which we thought one of the finest in the country. Bill, the eldest, had gone on to Milton Academy and to Harvard where he and Leslie Hamilton had been married before his graduation. He made a good start in journalism, first on the West Coast under Tom Braden, then conducting a column on the Washington *Post* and recently had shifted to research at the Johns Hopkins School for International Studies. He and Leslie lived in Georgetown with their children, Will, and Wendy. Edward came later.

Bob, our second, who graduated from Groton and from Harvard in 1955, was a born teacher. In Cambridge he had fallen deeply in love with Tenley Albright, the Olympic skating champion in 1952, but she was not to be diverted from her career in medicine. After serving a two-year hitch in the Army Bob was invited to teach at the Thomas Jefferson School in St. Louis. He accepted with alacrity; his subjects were physics and Greek; the boys responded to him and as he was very good at tennis he became the tennis coach as well. He had found his life's work and was much beloved.

Our third son, Hamilton, was very ill at birth and it was not until his years at St. Albans that he began to find himself. Writing was on his mind and early in his freshman year he sought the encouragement of Edward Weeks, editor of the *Atlantic*. But Harvard was not the right place for him and he left mid-year, came home and tutored with Dr. Reinhold Paul Becker, professor of German at New York University, on Nazi politics and the mass mesmerization at the party rallies. His book *The Nuremberg Party Rallies, 1923–1939*, with a foreword by Adolf Berle, is a standard, and was later translated into German, and was used as a textbook in certain German schools.

If Hamilton is our writer, Ordway, the youngest, is our expert on law enforcement. Harvard was the place for him, both the College and the Business School. He was one of the undergraduates who tried to preserve order during the Harvard Square demonstrations of the 1960s. He became a Deputy to Massachusetts Sheriff, John Buckley, and while at the Business School, as an auxiliary policeman he came down to New York every Wednesday to patrol Central Park on horseback until midnight with five other volunteers, returning by the late train to Cambridge. He said that the hardest part was getting the horse out of the stable. He is today founder and head of the Law Enforcement Assistance Foundation (LEAF) which has its headquarters in New York City, and a regular contributor to the *Law Enforcement News* with his bi-monthly article, "Burden's Beat."

From this it will be clear that I have rarely interfered; the boys have followed their own bent.

For going on twenty years Robert Stewart—"Mac," that big, self-confident Canadian who had first joined my staff in Washington in 1942—had served the Burden interests with loyalty. His judgments about the family's companies, the South American Mines, Union Sulphur, Cerro de Pasco, Austral Oil and Willian A. M. Burden and Co. had been far-sighted and sound. He once said to me casually that "a man should be aware of his own talents" and the remark revealed why he was so difficult to work with: he was so confident that he was always right that he had become overbearing, even brutal to his associates. Now that I was regularly in the office I concluded it was time he retired. There were those in the market who said I had dealt too generously with him but on the contrary I remember how much he had accomplished during my absence in Washington and abroad and I felt that the five million he took with him was well earned.

A much younger man, Robert Barker, a Harvard graduate, even-tempered and very able had joined me in the same year as Stewart. "Bob" was far-sighted; he had virtually been fired by the Guarantee Trust Company for stating that travel by air would shortly make our railroads obsolete. Like "Mac" he continued to work for me after his service in the Navy. He had kept his temper and won his spurs and he rightfully moved up to be the new head of the Burden partnership.

* * *

One of the things which used to discourage me as an uninformed youth was the family feeling that any member of the

Vanderbilt clan who entered politics or attempted to do something uncommonly serious was beyond the pale. Never seek publicity. There was nothing improper in protecting or even increasing one's inheritance, or in writing a reference book on Auction Bridge and defending the America's Cup, as Mike Vanderbilt did, but when George Vanderbilt "squandered" much of his fortune building "Biltmore" in North Carolina and investing time and thought on forest conservation, or when his nephew William Vanderbilt served one term as Governor of Rhode Island, they were regarded with suspicion and laughter.

I really think that my mother's idea of the kind of life I should lead—and this despite her integrity and her great love for me—was to be a sort of English gentleman type, taking care of my substantial fortune by clipping coupons, not working too hard and *certainly* not venturing into the hurly-burly of government or competitive business. That I did both was due to the stout-hearted encouragement of my wonderful wife Peggy. World War II gave me the opportunity; Peggy gave me the push. Now as I returned to civilian life I had a far wider choice of activities than either of us could have imagined twenty years earlier.

Before I accepted my ambassadorship in Belgium I had been given in 1957 a totally unexpected appointment as "a public trustee" of the Institute for Defense Analyses. It became one of the top priorities of my life and it came about through my friendship with Dr. James R. Killian, Jr., the president of the Massachusetts Institute of Technology. In 1956 President Eisenhower's first Secretary of Defense, Charles E. Wilson, wished to strengthen the scientific and technical work of the Weapons System Evaluation Group, then the principal analytical agency reporting to the Secretary and the Joint Chiefs of Staff.

With its combined staff of military officers and civil servants WSEG was unable to cope with the complex, technical, and often contentious problems in the missile-electronic era. Wilson asked Killian if M.I.T. would assume the responsibility of providing such in-depth scientific studies. Wisely, Killian, as an alternative, proposed that the scientific consultants be drawn from a consortium of universities, operating as a non-profit corporation, known as the Institute for Defense Analyses and funded by the Defense Department. He brought together the first five institutions: The California Institute of Technology, Case Institute, Stanford, Tulane, and M.I.T. Each was represented on the board of trustees—often by its president—and there were two "public trustees," Laurance Rockefeller and I. When Killian became Eisenhower's Scientific Advisor he resigned from IDA and I, as a "neutral," was elected chairman in May, 1959.

In the evolution of IDA even before I went to Brussels the analyses were shifting to a "stable deterrent" concept and away from the earlier emphasis on "arms superiority." The atmosphere of urgency that followed Sputnik in 1957 and the need to communicate—by satellite or otherwise—with one's friends, without interception by one's enemies, produced the Advanced Research Projects Division, with Herbert York in charge. Mathematicians were in demand when IDA founded the Communications Research Division (under contract to NASA) with separate facilities located in Princeton. IDA provided a temporary home for a new Institute for Naval Studies. In time, seven more universities were added to the consortium: Princeton, as I have explained, the University of Michigan, Penn State, and Columbia in 1960, the University of Chicago in 1961, the University of Illinois in 1962, and the University of California in 1964, bringing the total to twelve.

The small organization of less than a hundred staff members which I had joined in its second year had grown to nearly five times that size, with its quarters in Washington and Princeton, carrying out a wide range of studies and analyses, mainly for Defense, occasionally for non-defense sponsors. Once IDA was well underway the university trustees decided that the chairman should continue to be a "neutral" trustee, not directly connected with any participating institution and he should have final authority. Presumably my involvement in the development of air power qualified me for my short term as chairman in 1959, and I was very pleased to be re-elected chairman in March, 1961. I must have preserved my "neutrality" and exercised judgment as I remained in the chair for twenty years.

Happily, Garrison Norton and I were brought together again in IDA of which he had been appointed president in 1958. During his final year I observed how skillfully he had established a climate in which creative scientists like to work, despite their aversion to highly classified projects. His finest achievement was to persuade Charles H. Townes to leave the Physics Department at Columbia to accept the vice-presidency of IDA. The presence of this great scientist, about to become a Nobel Laureate, put IDA on a new footing with the scientific community, as evidenced by the expansion of IDA's University membership from five to twelve. The creation of the JASON Division under Charlie and the caliber of the work it performed was the high point during Norton's tenure.

There were bound to be problems, other than scientific. IDA was caught in the crossfire of Pentagon battles between Secretary McNamara's people and the military. Then in 1963 Congress began taking a closer look at governmental not-for-profit research centers and we had to defend ourselves. Inevitably, the defense research and the seminars on campus aroused student agitation as the situation in Vietnam worsened and the demonstrations rubbed off on IDA and sometimes me personally.

In 1964 IDA centered its activities, formerly scattered

throughout Washington, in a building of its own and I chaired my first Board meeting there that October. There followed a reorganization over a six-month period arranged by Maxwell Taylor, the new president of IDA, involving all the leading officials of Defense, McNamara, Vance, Wheeler and Foster. There were questions as to what IDA customers wanted that IDA was *not* providing and there was a regrouping of the divisions the better to utilize our entire talent. New divisions were placed on a functional basis, essentially as they are today, and the Weapons System Evaluation Group had served its purpose and was dissolved. Finally, a statement of Principles of Operation was approved by the Trustees in October, 1967, and they are still the "ten commandments" which govern IDA.

One of the unfortunate side-effects of the student protest movement against the Vietnam War was that IDA itself became a target for anti-war protests (as many of the defense laboratories and other private "think tanks"), and its member universities were subjected to faculty and student pressures to cancel their ties. IDA finally terminated the formal institutional membership of its twelve sponsoring universities and reorganized as a private corporation of individual members, drawn from both the academic community and the public at large. To ensure strength and continuity during the transition, the university representatives then on the board were prevailed upon to continue as individual members, demonstrating continued support by the academic community as a whole. The student agitation eventually subsided and IDA continued on under its own banner as sound and sturdy as before.

One of my closest friends, John Nicholas Brown, had been a member of the Smithsonian Board of Regents since 1957. On my return he suggested that I might enjoy becoming a Regent. The then Secretary, Leonard Carmichael, on behalf of the Board of Regents, inquired about my interest in becoming a member of the Board of Regents. There were only six (now nine) so-called "citizen regents" and there cannot be two from the same state. Luckily, there was no one from New York and they were glad to accept me. The Smithsonian Board of Regents is a combination of government officials and private citizens. The Chief Justice of the United States presides at all meetings and the Vice-President is also ex officio a member of the Board. Three Regents are appointed by the President of the Senate and three by the Speaker of the House of Representatives. By and large, this has produced a versatile Board.

The history of the Smithsonian is fascinating. It was established by James Smithson, an illegitimate wealthy son of the Duke of Northumberland. He had never been to America but he foresaw that an institution dedicated to the increase and diffusion of knowledge might have a part to play in the new world, and in his will he left $500,000 in gold (equivalent to about seven million in 1980 dollars) for its foundation. The gift was accepted in 1836 and duly forwarded to the Treasury Department in 1838. Congress debated its use off and on until 1846 when legislation was enacted creating the Smithsonian Institution. John Quincy Adams was perhaps the most influential in securing the acceptance of the bequest and in creating a high ideal for its administration. Smithson's will was very broad but he clearly intended the gift to come to the United States. (An interesting sidelight is that my wife's father, the famous sculptor William Ordway Partridge, did a bas-relief of James Smithson, which is displayed inside the entrance to the "Castle.")

The new Secretary, S. Dillon Ripley, who came in 1964, has fulfilled everything that had been said about him. He is imaginative, courageous, and influential with the Senators and Congressmen. Things began to happen pronto. The Hirshhorn Museum was created by a private gift. Meanwhile, the Washington Zoo, over which the Smithsonian has control, took on

Hamilton

Title Page of Hamilton's book

Adolf Hitler, Robert Ley, and Rudolf Hess at the 1936 Party Day

The Nuremberg Party Rallies: 1923–39

HAMILTON T. BURDEN

Foreword by Adolf A. Berle

PRAEGER PUBLISHERS
New York • Washington • London

Ordway, serving as a Special Game Protector of the Division of Law
Enforcement of the New York State Department of Environmental
Conservation

R. McLean Stewart

Robert R. Barker

Board of Regents, The Smithsonian Institution

Mike Collins, a leading Astronaut, first
Director of the Aeronautics and Space Museum

Mrs. John D. Rockefeller III who suceeded me as President
of the Museum of Modern Art
(Credit: Larry C. Morris, *The New York Times*)

Chief Justice Warren E. Burger and Secretary of the Smithsonian,
S. Dillon Ripley

Dr. John Rattaliata and I being sworn in by Frank Sanderson
(with President Eisenhower looking on) as members of the National
Aeronautics and Space Council

President Pompidou, President Nixon and I at the Council of
French-American Societies' dinner for President Pompidou,
March 2nd, 1970

Dr. Dillon Ripley (Secretary of the Smithsonian) and Mrs. Ripley
congratulating me on receiving the Joseph Henry Medal of Smithsonian

new life. Then the *Smithsonian* magazine, for which I was the principal protagonist, was launched and soon became a tremendous success.

The story of the Air and Space Museum is typical. The original bill providing for the Air and Space Museum was passed in 1946 and the site authorized in 1958 but no funds were specified. Many national difficulties during the following years delayed the project. One objection from the Congress was that the Vietnam War was draining the national economy, and no museum should be built until military expenditures were reduced.

I counted both Eisenhower and Nixon as friends. As the Bicentennial celebration was approaching I persuaded President Nixon that it would be a glorious thing if the Air and Space Museum were built to be opened on the 200th Anniversary of the United States. "Bill," he said, "it's high time." Redesign funds were approved in 1972, and finally, for 1973, the President's budget included construction funds in the amount of thirty-eight million dollars which was approved by the Congress.

The Chief Justice of the United States, Warren E. Burger, had decided views about architecture (he was otherwise a most agreeable man, but everybody considers himself a judge of architecture). He viewed the preliminary model of the Air and Space Museum with profound disgust. It had been designed by a brilliant Japanese architect. He said, "It doesn't have any columns." (Everything else in Washington, particularly the Supreme Court building, has masses of columns.) I finally convinced him that columns were not appropriate for an Air and Space Museum. Then he was gungho about the nude men with rearing horses which adorn the Arlington Bridge, and he said we should have a sculptor copy them.

The Museum was opened on the day of the Bicentennial and the traditional ribbon was cut by a new device, a laser beam from Mars. It was a sunny warm day. The new President Gerald Ford, members of the Supreme Court, and the Regents and friends of the Smithsonian, as well as Astronauts Mike Collins, Neil Armstrong, and Buzz Aldrin, all of us were seated out on the terrace on the Jefferson Drive side of the building. The President stood in front of the entrance with a back-up man behind him with a pair of shears in case the laser beam was off target. A voice came over a loud speaker saying, "This is NASA in Pasadena—the beam will arrive at the Space Museum in thirteen seconds." Everyone held his breath as the seconds ticked off, and sure enough, the ribbon across the door was severed by an unseen ray.

Earlier, I had persuaded Michael Collins, one of the most articulate astronauts, to take charge of the Museum and he did so with enthusiasm for a decade. Currently, it is visited by about ten million people a year, substantially more than either the Metropolitan or the Louvre.

This new museum was a natural repository for my enormous collection of books, periodicals and clippings, beginning with the commercial development of air power which I began far back in 1928, and, in addition, I donated my ballooning memorabilia, most of which is now exhibited in the Balloon and Airship Gallery. This includes eighteenth-century furniture inlaid with balloons, antique porcelain, Louis XVI chairs, prints, miniatures—even a commode celebrating the balloon—as well as books and plaques of the period. To the Natural History collections I also contributed some twenty-five archaeological specimens from Greece, Egypt, Italy and Palestine.

Beforehand, as members of a Regents sub-committee, John Nicholas Brown and myself (the only members of the Regents who liked modern design) were responsible for recommending a sculpture for the Mall entrance to the Museum of American History. We chose Jose de Rivera who produced a turning model of the solar system representing the harmonious movement of the planets. But we were not at all sure that it would pass the entire Board; luckily, at one of the regular meetings all of the Regents were invited to the White House. John Nicholas Brown and I did not attend; instead we held a meeting of our sub-committee and unanimously recommended the sculpture. When Rivera proposed a twenty-two-foot turning sculpture, the only comment that the Regents had (it was the era when the hippies were dominant) was that they feared happy hippies would hang on the sculpture and that some of them might be injured or killed and the Smithsonian would be liable. So we had an engineering report which stated that twelve hippies could ride peacefully on one side of the sculpture and, of course, twelve on the other side, to keep it in balance. So, this is how a marvelous Rivera sculpture came to adorn the National Museum of American History—and at this writing no one has been injured.

Since my appointment on July 2, 1962, I have been reappointed by the Joint Resolution of Congress for three additional terms. In addition to my continuous pressure for construction of the National Air and Space Museum, I have taken ever since 1970 a leading part in the handling of the Institution's investment funds, first on a committee of three with Crawford H. Greenewalt and James E. Webb, and later as the continuing chairman of the Investment Policy Committee.

On May 3, 1981, at a dinner of the Board of Regents the Chancellor, Chief Justice Warren E. Burger, presented me with the Joseph Henry Medal, "for outstanding service to the Institution over the course of (my) four terms as a Regent." Two days later the theatre in the National Air and Space Museum was dedicated to the memory of Samuel Pierpont Langley, the third Secretary of the Smithsonian Institution. Speaking at the ceremony Senator Barry Goldwater said:

". . . These two gentlemen (William A. M. Burden and James E. Webb) are the quintessence of what is best about Washington, where even great ambitions like the National Air and Space Museum need experienced guidance to reach fruition.

"William Burden was one of the most supremely qualified to aid in this process. Deeply versed in the intricacies of commercial aviation finance, Mr. Burden had a distinguished career serving aviation in government as well, as Assistant Secretary of Commerce for Air. Over his long career his advice was sought by leading aeronautic and space personalities on countless occasions. And as advisor to Presidents, when he championed the cause of the National Air and Space Museum, he was listened to. His close personal ties with leaders of every facet of aviation provided a lens which brought the new museum into focus, with the amazing results we have seen and enjoyed with 45,000,000 other Americans for the last five years."

*   *   *

I am always interested in important developments of technology and was fascinated by the way that radio set the stage for television. Of the individuals responsible for this none has been more of a perfectionist than William S. Paley. His father had a profitable cigar factory in Philadelphia and when Bill as a young man put on a radio show advertising his father's cigars —and the sales jumped considerably—the old gentleman was delighted. Bill had some money as the result of his father's company being listed on the N.Y. Stock Exchange. Bill used the money to purchase the Columbia Radio Network and became an innovator and taste-maker. He first heard "Amos 'n Andy" at a vaudeville show in Chicago, went backstage to their dressing room and said, "I don't care what you're getting here. Come with me." He heard a record by Bing Crosby and said to one of his scouts, "Whatever his figure, get him!" His was the first network to put on the New York Philharmonic, Toscanini conducting on Sunday afternoon. He offered a very special program to the Firestones for Sunday afternoon. "Nobody will be listening," said the family representative, "they'll all be playing polo."

As the war approached Bill made swift preparations for the need to cover it if it happened. Ed Murrow was in London as CBS's European representative whose main job was to find interesting speakers in Europe who would broadcast back to the States. As the war neared, Bill asked Murrow to start to build a news organization. He signed up such people as Bill Shirer who was sent to Berlin, Eric Sevareid, Charles Collingwood, Howard K. Smith and Winston Burdett. Murrow covered London beautifully and became the most important voice from Europe to America.

Bill and I lived in the same apartment house and our friendship began when he followed me as President and later, Chairman of the Museum of Modern Art. We were both fond of Impressionist paintings, motor cars and good food. He introduced me to Zabar's Delicatessen and every time we went there he insisted I try at least three of their specialties. His weight would shoot up to 190 pounds, then he'd go on a diet until he was down to 175—and the process would begin all over.

Everything at CBS is luxurious. Bill and Frank Stanton had the new CBS building designed by Eero Saarinen and it is one of the most beautiful in New York. The offices were furnished with modern paintings (whether the occupants liked them or not), and in its initial phase Stanton even forbade family photographs to be on the office walls. This provoked a palace revolution and the order was promptly rescinded.

Bill Paley had a high opinion of my ability, and we were the best of friends, but it never occurred to me that he would want me to be one of his Directors; however, he did, in 1964, and I have been a Director and member of the Executive Committee for fifteen years. The Board Room was paneled by Janssen of Paris. Bill has a dining room which seats twelve and is served by a Swedish cook who is a master. The walls carry some very high quality pictures—Picassos, Roualt, Ben Nicholson, Franz Kline, Derain, Andy Warhol, Soulages and Hans Hoffman, among others.

Bill has about seven provocative ideas a week: some impractical and some brilliant in the extreme. His indispensable consultant was Frank Stanton, a former psychologist. It was a new experience to me to hear about the problems of working with a bunch of actors. They are the most temperamental creatures on earth; their feelings are very sensitive and they are constantly threatening to resign over what they regard as the slightest snub. Their salaries have skyrocketed. Barbra Streisand on one album, recently pressed, got a ten million dollar royalty.

The Annual Stockholders' Meeting in April is held in a different city every year.

One year it was held in Nashville, the home of country music. The CBS Directors were put up in the hotel which was built by the stars of country music, when Elvis Presley was the guiding spirit. It was quite a hotel, fourteen floors, each floor the property of a star. Each had a large sitting room, three large bedrooms, of course a bar, and a complete kitchen. There was no dining room but a French chef was available for meals in the room. Country music has become a money machine in the United States. The stars have erected a museum of country music where their costumes, instruments, and their motor cars are reverently preserved.

We had a typical Nashville dinner and washed it down with perfectly delicious moonshine which was distilled only a couple of days before the dinner. The country music stars are, of course, not exclusively from the hill country; some of them come from Chicago, Indiana, and Texas, but they all adhere to the same bizarre costumes and of course the same training in Nashville.

Paley is an interesting man. He was President Truman's Chairman of the Materials Policy Commission, which has proved extraordinarily accurate. He is now Chairman of the Museum of Modern Art and takes a passionate interest in its future. He was married to Barbara, the most beautiful of the daughters of Harvey Cushing, the famous Boston brain surgeon. Her sisters married Jock Whitney and Vincent Astor, a fine trio of multimillionaires.

During my second term as President of the Museum of Modern Art Peggy and I were better prepared for what was expected of us. The administrative chores were not slight nor the sociabilities. I had asked Emily Stone, a lifetime friend, to be in charge of membership and entertainments; she is a powerhouse and her cocktail parties at the Museum and ours at home became an attraction, however demanding. We, of course, looked forward to the opening of each important exhibition: "Chagall —The Jerusalem Windows" was a novelty, and "Bonnard and His Environment" in October, 1964, brought in 187,000 viewers. I was beginning to wish that our galleries were wider; even more when half a million came to see Cézanne. Usually the opening would be followed by a dinner for the artist at our apartment. As our dining room only holds sixteen the invitations were limited to friends of the artist, those who had lent important canvasses (and might be induced to give them in time), members of the Museum staff, and a promising donor or candidate for the Board of Trustees. Peggy's charm as she presided was beyond price. Privately we were loaning pictures which would eventually be acquisitions and I had pledged the Museum one million, in installments.

A surprising pleasure for us both was the invitation from Mauricio Nabuco, the Foreign Minister of Brazil, to fly down to Rio to open their new Museum of Modern Art, the first I believe in South America. Nabuco, like his father before him had been the Brazilian Ambassador in Washington and he spoke perfect English; as Master of Ceremonies he was full of humor and not at all pompous. The building, handsome and modern, was beautifully situated at the outer tip of Rio Harbor with a superb view of the curving beaches and the mountains in the background. Of the painters the work of Portinari seemed to me the most striking and I admired the sculpture of Oscar Niemeyer.

The latter invited us to his studio where he showed us the design for Brazilia, which was to be the new ultramodern capital of Brazil. The houses of the Chamber of Deputies and the Senate were shaped like two bowls; the Chamber of Deputies like an up-turned bowl, and the Senate like a bowl turned down. This was rather a shock to the more conservative Brazilians.

There was a law in the Constitution that the capital had to be in the very center of the country, equidistant from Rio and São Paulo, and 1600 miles from Manaus. But the building of it had been postponed for seventy years, until President Kubichek decided to have it done. The solitary site was a large plain, railroads and roads had to be constructed to bring in all supplies and the workers, a huge undertaking needing two or three years to complete. The Brazilia which emerged was somewhat like a frontier town in our West and the dress and swagger of some of the workers reminded me of our cowboys.

But it *was* the capital, and every foreign ambassador had to move his embassy out there, which they were naturally quite reluctant to do, as Rio is such a gay and exciting city.

The irreplaceable loss to the Museum in my administration was René d'Harnoncourt. Albert Barr had taught him to be an avid bird watcher and while observing the spring migration in the country, René, intent on what he observed through his binoculars, was run down and killed by an intoxicated woman driver. At the memorial service Nelson Rockefeller expressed the deep grief of us all. Albert was inconsolable. My thoughts went back to those many hours in Moscow and Leningrad when the three of us had searched for an important exhibition of nineteenth-century Russian painting only to be stymied by Soviet propaganda.

The Council of French-American Societies in New York, exuberant at the success of the banquet for General de Gaulle, was eager to continue our celebration of leading figures in our two democracies and the man we honored in 1962 was my old friend, Charles E. Bohlen, former Ambassador to the Soviet Union and then to France, now Special Assistant to Secretary of State Dean Rusk. "Chip," who had begun to write his memoirs, was in fine form, and his reminiscence of his years in Paris was particularly delightful. With such encouragement we planned for the year following, not one but three dinners, the first for General Lauris Norstad, recently Supreme Commander for NATO, the second for Consul General Michel Legendre, and the last, a man I was keen to hear, Gaston Palewski, French Minister of State in charge of Research, Atomic and Space Affairs.

Thereafter the Council entertained at dinner such distinguished guests as Edgar Faure, former Prime Minister of France, Valery Giscard D'Estaing and Alfred Max, editor-in-chief of *Réalités*; and from our side, Cyrus L. Sulzberger of the *New York Times*, Eugene Rostow, and General Georges F. Doriot, President of American Research and Development Corporation.

Before leaving Brussels I had been "promoted" to Commander of the Legion of Honor and decorated by Belgium, with the Grand Cordon of the Order of Leopold. I was proud of these medals and wore them in miniature on the lapel of my full dress. As the time approached for our banquet for President Georges Pompidou of France I was informed in advance that I was to be made "Grand Officer, Legion of Honor," which is very rarely conferred. But when His Excellency arrived he discovered that he had left the medal, a very handsome affair which is worn at the throat, back in Paris. The French Embassy did not possess one. But in the nick of time I remembered the scarlet medallion which hung about the neck of the statue of General John Pershing in the Smithsonian. Dillon Ripley said "Yes," I might borrow it for one night, a messenger flew to Washington and raced back to the Waldorf in time for President Pompidou to conduct the ceremony, followed by kisses on both cheeks, in the hotel elevator that was carrying us to the banquet hall. The General had his medallion restored the next day, and mine came by airmail.

Reverie

HARVARD, like most universities, keeps a watchful eye on the graduates who are doing anything unusual and seeks to keep them affiliated. In 1942 I was appointed Chairman of the Advisory Committee for Aviation Research at the Harvard Business School and later, Honorary Curator of Aviation Literature at the Baker Library. For twenty-seven years I was a member of the Visiting Committee to the Harvard University Library and for a shorter term on the Committee considering the University Resources. I took more than casual interest in these concerns and observed that the Business School, under Dean David and again under Dean Baker, was one of the best run and most productive graduate schools in the country.

Early in my research on aviation I acquired a collection of inlaid furniture and decorative china which mirrored the French mania for ballooning in Europe during the nineteenth century. They had originally belonged to Gaston Tissandier, a famous aeronaut, 1843–1899, and they formed what we called our Balloon Room at 10 Gracie Square. This led me to begin a library on ballooning.

In my only meeting with Winston Churchill, which took place prewar at Bernard Baruch's plantation in Georgia, he dismissed the airship as being too slow and too large a target for modern warfare but my curiosity continued and in time I acquired over six hundred books and manuscripts ranging from 1493 to the log of the transatlantic flight of His Majesty's Airship R34 in 1919, and including the imaginative works of Montgolfier, Wilkins, Cyrano de Bergerac, Lorent Cavallo, Genet and others. There were many pamphlets and five exquisite little French almanacs in "balloon" bindings. These I presented in 1954 to the Houghton Library at Harvard of which our friend Philip Hofer was curator.

Later I decided to make Harvard a more substantial gift. I recall the opposition I encountered from Moms and Shirley whom I expected to share the cost of what I had in mind. What I planned was a large auditorium, to be named Burden Hall, in memory of my father, a building more capacious than any then available. Moms shied away. Shirley protested that Harvard had "new buildings running out of its ears—and why me?" I pointed out that Harvard's only half-decent meeting place was the obsolete Saunders Theater with no parking such as would be available at the Business School. My persistence won and eventually they agreed to share the cost of approximately two million dollars. A site was chosen at the Business School, and plans drawn for an auditorium seating 1000. At the dedication in 1968 Moms stood beside me as President Pusey read the wording of the plaque, commemorating my father and, also, my son Bill.

Burden Hall

1971

Built in memory of

William A. M. Burden
A.B., 1900
A.M., 1901

William A. M. Burden III
A.B., 1953
M.B.A., 1955

The gift of

Florence V. Burden

William A. M. Burden II
A.B., 1927

Shirley C. Burden

Life has its ups and downs. In Peggy's and my case our devotion to each other has been a lifelong "up." But few couples can be continuously happy and we were fortunate that not until the 1960s were we overtaken by tragedy and sorrow. The sudden death of our eldest son Bill was a grievous shock; we asked ourselves could anything have been done to prevent it? Young Bill, so high strung and at times morose, had given us cause for worry. Bob, with his sunny disposition, had found complete happiness in teaching and it seemed a cruel stroke of fate when on June 18, 1974, as he was driving to see a friend, his small car collided with a truck and he was killed instantly. I think one best remembers one's children in the sunlight of youth and we have found consolation in our nearness to Hamilton and Ordway and in our grandchildren. Will is a stone carver who finds his inspiration in Maine, his sister Wendy, who graduated from Cornell, is a commercial artist whose studio is in Greenwich Village, and Edward, the youngest, a student, who loves New York as we do and is often in our apartment.

To celebrate Moms's seventy-fifth birthday Shirley and I arranged a dinner party at the River Club, December 20th, 1956. Each of us rose to express our love and I teased her when I said she had "achieved slim and eternal youth on a diet consisting almost exclusively of potatoes and ice cream, salad rigidly excluded," which made her laugh.

In her eighties—she lived to the end of her eighty-eighth year—Moms was very much alone: she sat in her chair near the living room window of her apartment for long hours, physically passive but mentally alert; she passed her time knitting sweaters for the grandchildren and listening to the radio. She loved cards and when she was in California with Shirley she played countless games of Canasta; when we were in New York in our apartment I would run down the stairs and her eyes would brighten as we compared notes about the family affairs which meant so much more to her than my business. In her loneliness she must often have recalled her girlhood at "Florham" before her brother Hamilton was drowned. She worshipped my father and with her unshaken Christian faith she looked forward to rejoining him in Heaven when her time came.

In November, 1969, Peggy, Shirley and I went to Hobe Sound, Florida, for a short stay in the lovely house Moms had just given me. She was happy to see us go as she always took pleasure in the joy of others. But as I kissed her I noticed how frail she was.

A few days later on November 17 the phone rang. Moms had died suddenly of a heart attack, we were told, instantaneously and without pain. Beside her chair lay her knitting needles, broken. In my grief I remember her saying to me, after so many of her friends were gone, "You know, Bill, it's not much fun waiting around to die." Every mother has her collection of keepsakes. When Shirley and I opened Moms's locked chest, containing her much thumbed Bible, family photographs, one of father in his prime, and many letters thanking her for her donations, we wept.

I realized what a single-minded and courageous woman she

was. Love was the guiding principle in her long life: love of her family and love of our wonderful father. When he died of leukemia after their brief marriage, darkened by his illness, she declared, "I have had the best," and she turned to devote herself to the sons he had never really known. She had been brought up surrounded by great wealth but she never took money so seriously as to let it warp her life. In the early happy years of her marriage my father insisted that they live on his income and she willingly economized. Here in the chest were a few hundred dollars in new bills to be given to the doormen and servants, and those letters thanking her for her generous gifts, in recent years to Columbia University, St. Peter's School, The Salvation Army, which was always one of her great interests, the Episcopal Mission Society, Harvard, The Women of St. Thomas, The Metropolitan Museum, the Dominican Nursing Sisters, Fairleigh Dickinson University (which bought "Florham") and the Community Service Society.

Moms's gifts to me were for life. The first, beginning in early boyhood I have never lost: I mean my love for books. To me and Shirley she read aloud, not now and then but *every night*, cutting our teeth on juveniles but passing soon to the great English novels of the nineteenth century whose narratives and heroes held me spellbound long before I appreciated the necessity of the love story. *Ivanhoe*, *The Cricket on the Hearth*, "Mr. Pickwick" and *David Copperfield* lived on in my imagination and at Harvard I got an "A" in the course on the novel without having to re-read my favorites.

I went through the various stages of book infatuation, buying them in expensive, leather-bound sets, to fill the shelves at Mt. Kisco, then beginning to concentrate on my subject—aviation; in Washington reading the war books, those on foreign policy and memoirs of the leaders, until the shelves at Georgetown,

Mt. Kisco, and our apartment in New York, held a library of about 30,000. I still read voraciously at midnight, on planes, before dinner, less fiction now but more biography, history, and everything authoritative about our national defense.

Moms's second gift was less tangible. She had been brought up without a trace of ostentation and she took more pleasure giving money to others than spending it on herself. I had a preposterous allowance at college and frittered most of it away but, in retrospect, what I spent on cars and my acquired knowledge of powerful motors was the stepping stone to my knowledge of aviation.

*   *   *

All men brood over things they wished they might have achieved. In my affiliations with Harvard I served on many committees, the duties were not demanding and I took them in stride. But the opportunity I should have most enjoyed was to be a member of the Board of Overseers; I was nominated for the six-year term but did not receive sufficient votes from the alumni; the fate of many New Yorkers.

In diplomacy I was eager to succeed Amory Houghton as our Ambassador to France. I loved the country second only to my own; I have driven all over it and have made some eighty visits to Paris. I had entrée in artistic circles and was respected as an authority on national defense. After my term in Belgium, where I was wisely advised, and my French greatly improved, I believe I was qualified. What told against me was my political "neutrality" during the early years in Washington and my shyness in pressing my candidacy when Eisenhower was President, and Herter, Secretary of State.

I have never ceased to wonder how I would have developed

The Grandchildren: Wendy, Will and Edward at Mt. Kisco, 1966

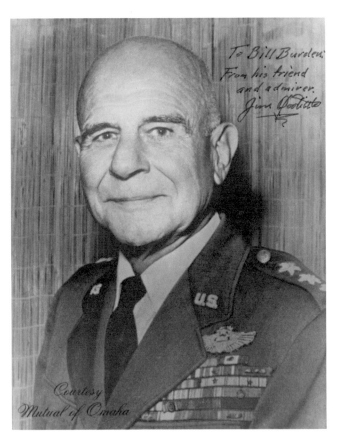

General James H. Doolittle

had my father lived. He was a prize boy in school, a natural leader in college and a devout Christian. I would surely have disappointed him in athletics and in religion, too, unless his influence caused me to be less of a Doubting Thomas. It is useless to speculate. What is true is that Shirley and I were each "slow starters" in our quite different pursuits, that we both had the whole-hearted backing of our mother, and that our loyalty to each other has never wavered.

In my eight years of service in our Government I came to know many able and dedicated men and for four of them, Will Clayton, General Jimmy Doolittle, General Maxwell Taylor and General Quesada I hold deep affection. When I came to "Mr. Will" in the Department of Commerce I had expertise in my field but was green in my knowledge of Washington and all its works. In a very personal way he instructed and encouraged me, chose me for a post he believed I could handle, and would have pushed me further but for the bitter opposition of Juan Trippe.

I am not normally a hero worshipper but of the military men I have known Doolittle with whom I had a close friendship, "Pete" Quesada and General Marshall, whom I admired at a distance, are my heroes.

Never did a man inherit a more inappropriate surname than James H. Doolittle, born in Alameda, California, in 1896. He has performed magnificently in aviation and done so with surpassing energy and efficiency and with zest and humor. He is one of the few great pilots to hold degrees in aeronautic engineering, a Master of Science in 1924 and Doctor of Science, 1925, at the Massachusetts Institute of Technology. For a period, while working for various oil companies he concentrated on setting new world speed records: the Schneider Trophy for Seaplanes in 1925, the Thompson Trophy for landplanes in 1932 at 258.68 m.p.h., the Mackay and the Harmon Trophies—and carried out pioneer work in blind landing.

Jimmy's splendid physique (despite his small size) and his irresistible personality made him the ideal choice to lead the mission to Tokyo. One hundred and forty airmen volunteered of which the crews of sixteen bombers were assigned to the small carrier *Hornet*. The original plan was to approach undetected to within 400 miles of the mainland, launch the planes, fly over the Japanese cities, bomb in the dark and continue through the remainder of the night, landing after dawn in China. When the *Hornet* was 800 miles from Tokyo she was sighted by a Japanese boat which was sunk in three minutes but the Americans could not be sure the signal had not been given by radio and the bombers were launched immediately, knowing they would have to bomb in daylight and fly on to unknown terrain in the dark. Fifteen of the sixteen did so, all cracking up in landing. A year after the raid fifty-five of the eighty airmen were back in service or in the United States. All were decorated, Doolittle with the Congressional Medal of Honor. It was a bold exploit which lifted American morale at a critical period.

Doolittle was promoted to Lieutenant General in command of the 12th Air Force in North Africa (where he did not get on well with the British), and, in 1945, Commander of the 8th Air Force in Okinawa. My turn to work with him came years later when he was special assistant for Research and Development to Chief of Staff Hoyt S. Vandenberg and I with a similar assignment under Secretary of the Air Force Finletter. It was a period of evolution in which the central problem was to *leapfrog* from the manned airplane (the B-52 plus the KC-135 tanker) to the guided ballistic missile with an atomic bomb (warhead), traveling as far as five thousand miles from the launching point in the United States. Jimmy and I were struck by the slow and not very expensive manner in which the Air Force approached this, one step at a time. They had been warned by the AEC that more powerful atomic bombs would be bulky and had to be delivered by large refueled airplanes. Meanwhile the Soviets leapfrogged over a series of intermediate systems to the desired result.

Jimmy and I were in close collaboration; I found him inspiring, ingenious, highly intelligent—and unsparing. On one lengthy trip of three weeks we inspected *all* the principal R&D establishments and projects. At every Air Force base he was greeted as a hero, and throughout we lived by the Doolittle rule that "wheels up" should be at dawn every day—often at 5 a.m., which meant rising at 4. It never seemed illogical to Jimmy that we were often through our work at 3 p.m.!

Occasionally the unexpected occurred. At Wright Field where we spent two days we were accorded a particularly formal and splendid reception and so too at our takeoff when at least twenty officers of General rank, headed by Lieutenant General Ben Chidlaw, lined up to salute us on departure. As we began the slow, climbing turn from the field I noticed that gasoline (this was before the days of jet engines) was streaming over the top of both wings. The flight mechanics had forgotten to screw on the caps to the fuel tanks and there were red faces when we returned to have this done.

I am completely convinced that the significant developments in our Research and Development must be shielded. Our enemies must be kept guessing. I see nothing in the recent history of Soviet foreign policy to indicate that if the USSR achieves parity or convincing superiority over the United States they will exchange their policy of world-wide penetration and imperialism for a policy of permanent peace. I totally reject the naive notion that the basic conflict between the free world and communism can be resolved by the unilateral disarmament of the United States.

On the other hand I am elated by our enormous investment of scientific skill in our space program. I agree with Dr. Harold Urey when he says that "The space program is not only scientific in purpose but also is an expression of man's insistent determination to do the nearly impossible—to explore the unknown even at great risk. Therefore the proper attitude of a scientist should be to try to participate in the program so that scientific objectives can be attained along with the thrills of exploration."

It is this conviction and my long and dear friendship with Dr. James R. Killian, Jr. which prompted me to endow the Massachusetts Institute of Technology, of which he was formerly President, with a fund of one million dollars to support a new professorship in Astrophysics.

Shirley's production of training films for the Navy, Army and the U.S. Office of Education was completed before the end of the war and Tradefilms, Inc., then went out of existence. In 1946 he opened his still studio in Beverly Hills and his commercial work began to appear in *House and Garden, The Architectural Forum, Arts and Architecture*, and *McCall's*. Then, like Edward Steichen and Ansel Adams, he was absorbed in the artistic possibilities of the camera: his pictures were exhibited in the Tokyo Museum in 1953, in a series of seven shows at the Museum of Modern Art, such as "Family of Man" (1955), "Diogenes With Camera IV" (1956), "70 Photographers Look at New York" (1958); in exhibitions in Detroit, Eastman House in Rochester, Boston, at several museums in California, and in the Annual World Exhibition of Photography, Hamburg, West Germany. When Steichen resigned as Curator of Photographs at the "Modern," he wanted Shirley to be his successor but my brother would not leave California. To Moms's quiet satisfaction Shirley (who had become a Catholic) went on to publish three books of his photographs, *God Is My Life* (1960), *I Wonder Why* (1963), also in a German edition, and *Behold Thy Mother* (1965).

When Shirley's wife "Flobe" died suddenly of a heart attack on January 7, 1969, he was inconsolable. He told me they had not spent a night apart in the thirty-five years of marriage. It was his youthful admirer Julie Valverde, now a widow, who drew him from his grief and they were married in January 1971. His two latest books, *Presence* and *The Vanderbilts in my Life* were both published in 1981, proof that a boy who never liked to read can produce artistic books in his maturity.

In 1979 Peggy in her book entitled, *Borrowed Insights*, brought together the truths, the quotations, which had given her strength and delight down the years and there are two of them with which I wish to close this memoir.

The first is what James Michener wrote in *The Fires of Spring*. It bespeaks my joy and gratitude when I "surrendered" my "inner life" to Peggy in 1931.

> "For this is the journey that men make: to find themselves. If they fail in this, it doesn't matter much what else they find. Money, position, fame, many loves, revenge are all of little consequence, and when the tickets are collected at the end of the ride they are tossed into a bin marked FAILURE. But if a man happened to find himself—if he knows what he can be depended upon to do, the limits of his courage, the position from which he will no longer retreat, the degree to which he can surrender his inner life to some woman, the secret reservoirs of his determination, the extent of his dedication, the depth of his feeling for beauty, his honest and unpostured goals—then he has found a mansion which he can inhabit with dignity all the days of his life."

The second is by that eloquent Rabbi, Joshua Liebman:

> "We will become psychologically mature in our idea of
> God as we come to recognize that we human beings should
> never expect final knowledge about Divinity. Our minds
> are fragmentary beams of light, like the flashes of glow-
> worms in a summer's night. The fleeting illumination they
> provide enables us to see in the midst of the darkness many
> wonderful summits of social achievement still attainable
> by the restless feet of this youthful race of men. Divinity is
> here both on the earth that provides the possibility of life,
> order, intelligence and also in the *insatiable moral hunger of*
> *man—man never quite ready to accept tyranny as natural, defeat as*
> *inevitable, society as irremediable.* Religion can help us to re-
> tain the faith that, in the cosmic night, that Great Western
> Star, God, and the lesser stars, men, will not be extinguished
> to all eternity."

The italics are Peggy's. Although I regard myself as an
agnostic, to that I say "Amen."

Peggy and I
(Portrait copyright © by Arnold Newman)

PRINTED AND BOUND BY
THE STINEHOUR PRESS OF LUNENBURG, VERMONT,
WITH REPRODUCTIONS BY
THE MERIDEN GRAVURE COMPANY
OF MERIDEN, CONNECTICUT.